Local Space Astrology

Although it is not as well-known, Local Space Astrology is the natural counterpart of predictive astrology, the astrology of time. In this comprehensive book Steve Cozzi not only describes in easy-to-understand terms the nature of the Local Space system of horoscope interpretation, but he also offers detailed delineations, something not found previously in print. Author Cozzi brings to this important branch of astrology some genuinely pioneering ideas and concepts which link modern astrology with the astrology of the ancients, an astrology in which space and direction were emphasized.

But there is more here than just Local Space. As the book progresses, the author tackles other aspects of spatial astrology, including what has come to be known as astro-mapping or astro-cartography. Beyond this are intelligent discussions of various astrological and non-astrological theories regarding possible grid patterns which overlay the earth—and from which useful information about one's locality may be obtained.

Perhaps it is inevitable that a work on Local Space Astrology should end up being a work which also examines the magical properties of space. Cozzi, who is well versed in a number of esoteric traditions from around the world, offers the reader insights into Feng Shui, Geomancy and other bodies of knowledge that recognize and attempt to explain the mysterious forces which surround and influence our lives. This is an important book for practical and experimental astrologers as well as dowsers, geomancers and occultists.

—**Bruce Scofield**
Electional Astrology

ABOUT THE AUTHOR

Steve Cozzi began his study of astrology in 1968. He began teaching astrology in 1970. He has lectured at the AFA '84 and '86 conventions, and at the UAC 1986 convention. Steve is a member of all the major astrological groups in the United States and abroad. As the co-chairperson for programs of the Colorado Fellowship of Astrologers, he has brought in many of the best astrologers to speak to that organization.

He has been active in the area of Locality Astrology since 1979. His research into the practical methods of Local Space astrology and his invention of the first geomantic compass in the West qualify him as one of a handful of practicing geomancers.

Steve has been a sincere student of Yoga for many years, and has a wide-ranging interest in the field of metaphysics. Along with his writing and teaching activities, he also works in the areas of business management and the travel industry. He lives in Lakewood, Colorado with his wife, Janet, and their two children, Anthony and Nicholas.

TO WRITE TO THE AUTHOR

We cannot guarantee that every letter written to the author can be answered, but all will be forwarded to him. Both the author and the publisher appreciate hearing from readers, learning of your enjoyment and benefit from this book. Llewellyn also publishes a bi-monthly news magazine of New Age esoteric studies, and some readers' questions and comments may be answered through the *New Times'* columns if permission to do so is included in your original letter. The author participates in seminars and workshops, and dates and places may be announced in *The Llewellyn New Times*. For further information on Local Space, to write to the author or to secure a few sample copies of the *New Times* write to:

Steve Cozzi
c/o THE LLEWELLYN NEW TIMES
P.O. Box 64383-Dept. 098, St. Paul, MN 55164-0383, U.S.A.

Please enclose a self-addressed, stamped envelope for reply, or $1.00 to cover expenses.

THE LLEWELLYN MODERN ASTROLOGY LIBRARY

Books for the *Leading Edge* of practical and applied astrology as we move toward the culmination of the 20th century.

This is not speculative astrology, nor astrology so esoteric as to have little practical application in meeting the needs of people in these critical times. Yet, these books go far beyond the meaning of "practicality" as seen prior to the 1980's. Our needs are spiritual as well as mundane, planetary as well as particular, evolutionary as well as progressive. Astrology grows with the times, and our times make heavy demands upon Intelligence and Wisdom.

The authors are all professional astrologers drawing from their own practice and knowledge of historical persons and events, demonstrating proof of their conclusions with the horoscopes of real people in real situations.

Modern Astrology relates the individual person in the Universe in which he/she lives, not as a passive victim of alien forces, but as an active participant in an environment expanded to the breadth *and depth* of the Cosmos. We are not alone, and our responsibilities are infinite.

The horoscope is both a measure and a guide to personal movement—seeing every act undertaken, every decision made, every event, as *time dynamic*, with effects that move through the many dimensions of space and levels of consciousness in fulfillment of Will and Purpose. Every act becomes an act of Will, for we extend our awareness to consequences reaching to the ends of time and space.

This is astrology supremely important to this unique period in human history, when Pluto transits through Scorpio, and Neptune through Capricorn. The books in this series are intended to provide insight into the critical needs and the critical decisions that must be made.

These books, too, are "active agents," bringing to the reader knowledge which will liberate the higher forces inside each person to the end that we may fulfill that for which we were intended.

—Carl Llewellyn Weschcke

Other Books by Steve Cozzi

Generations and Outer Planet Cycles, AFA, Tempe AZ, 1986

Forthcoming Books and Concepts

A New Look at Mundane Astrology—The Art of Predicting World Events

The Local Space Charts of Cities and Countries

The Astrological Quatrains of Nostradamus

PLANETS
in
LOCALITY

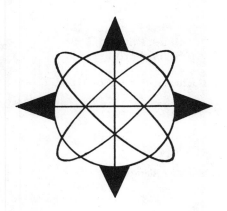

Steve Cozzi

Distributed by:
W. FOULSHAM & CO. LTD.,
YEOVIL ROAD, SLOUGH, SL1 4JH ENGLAND

International Standard Book Number: 0-87542-098-2
Library of Congress Catalog Number: 88-45190

First Edition, 1988
First Printing, 1988
Second Printing, 1988

Library of Congress Cataloging-in-Publication Data

Cozzi, Steve.

Planets in Locality
(Llewellyn Modern Astrology Library)
Bibliography: p.
1. Astrology. 2. Planets—Miscellanea
I. Title. II. Series.
BF1708.1.C697 1988   133.5'3   88-45190
ISBN 0-87542-098-2

Cover Painting: David Egge
Book Design: Tom Streissguth
Illustrations: Charles T. Smith
Production Staff: Brooke Luteyn, Terry Buske, Norman Stanley

Produced by Llewellyn Publications
Typography and Art property of Chester-Kent, Inc.

Published by
LLEWELLYN PUBLICATIONS
A Division of Chester-Kent, Inc.
P.O. Box 64383
St. Paul, MN 55164-0383, U.S.A.

Printed in the United States of America

DEDICATION

Dedicated to my beloved spiritual grandfather (Parum-Guru), who has shown me that time and space are variables.

ACKNOWLEDGEMENTS

Special thanks to Michael Erlewine, whose research, encouragement and assistance helped make this book become a reality. A deep appreciation to Sue Osterhaudt for her editing of part of the manuscript, to Joan McEvers and Tom Streissguth for their complete editing and excellent suggestions, to my wife Janet for her art work, and to Carl Weschcke and Julie Lockhart.

CREDITS

Figure 1 (facing page 1)—Copyright ©1976 by Robert Kyle Grenville Temple. Reprinted by permission of Harold Ober Associates.

Figure 3 (page 9), *Figure 4* (page 10)—from *Living the Sky* by Ray W. Williamson. Copyright ©1984 by Ray W. Williamson. Line illustrations copyright ©1984 by Snowden Hodges. Reprinted by permission of Houghton Mifflin Company.

Figures 5 and 6 (pages 12-13)—From *New View Over Atlantis* by John Michell. Copyright ©1983 Harper & Row.

Figure 11E (page 40)—From the International Association of Geomagnetism and Aeronomy (IAGA) Bulletin No. 52. By D.R. Barraclough and D. J. Kerridge.

Figures 14 A—C (pages 65-67)—Matrix Software ©1982 by Michael and Margaret Erlewine.

Figures 16, 17, 18, 19 (pages 136, 138-141)—From *Astrophysical Directions*, ©1978 by Michael and Margaret Erlewine.

Figure 21 (pages 150-151)—Astro*Carto*Graphy® copyright ©1981 by Jim Lewis.

Figure 22 (page 153)—From Astro Computing Services. Reprinted by permission of Neil Michaelson.

Figure 27 (page 186)—Copyright ©1983 by Becker and Hagens. Reprinted by permission.

Figures 28, 29, 31, 32, 33, 34, 35 (pages 188, 189, 191, 196, 197, 198, 200, 201)—From *Pursuit*, Second Quarter 1984, by Becker and Hagens. Reprinted by permission.

Figures 36 A and B (pages 204-205)—From *Bridge to Infinity* by Bruce Cathie. Reprinted by permission.

Figures 37 and 38 (pages 206-207), *Table 21* (pages 208-209)— From *The Sirius Mystery.* Copyright ©1976 by Robert Kyle Grenville Temple. Reprinted by permission of Harold Ober Associates.

Figures 39 A and B, Figure 40 (pages 210 and 212)—From *Mysteries of the Mexican Pyramids.* Copyright ©1976 by Peter Tompkins. Drawings by Hugh Harleston Jr. Reprinted by permission of Hugh Harleston Jr. and Harper & Row.

Figures A, B, C, D, Appendix A (pages 242, 243, 245 and 256-257)— From *Astrophysical Directions.* Copyright ©1978 by Michael and Margaret Erlewine.

CONTENTS

FIGURES

TABLES

INTRODUCTION

*I*t has been some 15 years since I developed Local Space astrology as I have come to understand it. Now, thanks to Steve Cozzi, we have a book on this fascinating subject.

We live in a world that is a tangle of signs and signals, a veritable web of reference and meaning that seems to point or lead us this way and that. It is up to us to sort it all out. The space around us is filled with indicators of all kinds. As we learn to read these signs and directions, they always seem to lead or refer us within. They point the way to inner knowledge, to our getting to know ourselves.

Our inner world too is filled with pointers and references, the majority of which appear in the form of "meanings." *What do things mean or portend? Where do they lead or point to?* All this directionality, and by that I mean *all references* and *all meaning*, cannot help but point or lead us to the selfsame end: the experience of ourselves.

This is a book of directionality—a study of signs and directions in space (the external world). The real message of Local Space (or any of the directional techniques described in this book) is that all directionality, whether measured in the outer world of compass directions, etc. or as measured within ourselves in the form of meaning and other forms of reference, leads to the same conclusion: action or experience. They can but direct us to an experience. In the last analysis, directions always refer us to an action. . . to the very brink of an experience. All thought. . . all reference. . . all direction ends in action or points to action.

Yet, it is up to us to take the plunge. I might add that the experience or action referred to is always our own, the simple experience of ourselves, the "Be Here Now" that we are told about. The primary purpose of astrology is not to predict. Astrology is, above all, a way to know ourselves—a way of knowledge.

It is ancient wisdom that we must know ourselves. Yet, little has been mentioned of the importance of being known—that there be someone to be known. It is hoped that techniques such as Local Space will lead us to the very edge of action and experience itself, for they point right at it. Having arrived at the edge by means of all the pointers, signals and directions that there are, we should have no further hesitation, but, recognizing an opportunity when we see it and a duty, plunge in and be known.

Michael Erlewine
September 1987
Big Rapids, Michigan

The universal geometric forms are created because the geographical biosphere merges with the geocentric-great circles in the atmosphere—all is geodetically aligned and geomantically interpreted. The sacred geometry, a crystal network of form and number defining time and space.

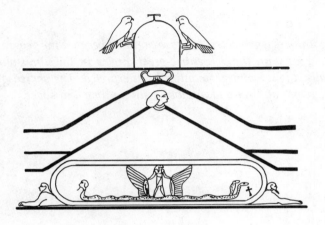

Fig. 1

Egyptian papyrus depicting Sokar, the god of orientation. The gadget on top of the **omphalos** *is a standard Egyptian measuring ruler (and also the symbol for the sky). The two pigeons facing each other are the standard glyph for the laying out of parallels and meridians.*

CHAPTER 1

THE HORIZON SYSTEM

Before any practical techniques are discussed, it is important
to cover some basic historical and technical information. With an
understanding of where this unique system came from and how it was
developed, we will be better able to grasp its subtle importance as well
as its practical qualities.

Although the Horizon System may be new to you, it is actually an
ancient system widely used throughout the world. Why it became
dormant in modern times is difficult to explain. Perhaps astrologers
became obsessed with the Ecliptic System commonly used in Western cultures. Unfortunately, converting the Ecliptic to the Horizon
System before the advent of computers presented most astrologers
with a real challenge in mathematical calculations.

What exactly is the Local Space/Horizon System and how does it
work? Well, first of all, it is not a strange system that was just dreamed
up. All the evidence points to it being at the very heart and soul of astrology. In fact, the calculations necessary for a natal chart can't be
done without taking into consideration the coordinates used in the
Horizon System.*

---

*The explanation of the three major coordinate systems in astrology is very important, because
in the process we need to see the functional beauty of how all three systems work as one. The
information contained in Chapter 6 is not just for the technically oriented student of astrology. It
contains a deeper conceptual message that works on the inner levels of our awareness to somehow spark a visual and functional insight on the rotational and orbital movements corresponding to Earth and the solar system.

In my own life and in the lives of others, Local Space Astrology has proven itself again and again. It has helped many people live more productive, satisfying and happy lives. The following is a list of how Local Space and the whole of locality astrology can help those using its methods:

It can put you in touch with your personal planetary patterns, acting as an aid to discovering your *own* personal myth. It depicts a journey through all your strengths and weaknesses. This journey is plotted in the heavens, but it can literally take you across the planet in search of those special places that can add meaning and vitality to your life.

It can help uncover how these planetary energies manifest in your daily life. It shows how to perceive and interact in a new "art of living." The improvements that follow will certainly make your home life more comfortable and enjoyable. It can systematically describe the many influences in your community or natural surroundings that may affect you for good or ill.

Basically it offers you the freedom of choice in determining not only how you want to live but where you should relocate or travel to. Locality astrology can tell you what influences are at work anywhere you may be on Earth. You'll find out how each direction you travel, or the location you live in, affects your psychological and physical health.

It can answer questions like: Where is the best place to add on to the home? Where is the proper place for the pets to stay or the musical instruments to be stored; which is the right wall for the bookshelves or china closet? In what part of town will I find a suitable partner? What is my strongest and weakest element, i.e. psychological tendency? Where in my house is the best place to meditate? Why do I almost instantly like people from some parts of the country and have an aversion to others from different locations? Where is the best location for my career in the United States, New Zealand, or elsewhere?

The solid knowledge that Local Space Astrology offers will allow you *greater* freedom of choice, based on *real* knowledge of the factors involved, with the results to be anticipated. The Local Space technique is a system whereby the intangible becomes tangible, where abstract qualities become concrete, and where intuitive feelings are confirmed in an orderly and realistic fashion.

This Local Space/Horizon System is really just one of the four "great circles" used in navigation, astronomy and astrology. The *horizon, ecliptic, equator* and *prime vertical* are the great circles and coordinate systems whereby mankind can measure Earth's position/relationship with the solar system and beyond. Each of these great circles represents a different view, yet each one is mathematically related to the other three.

What is the Local Space/Horizon System? Picture yourself in the middle of a large transparent dome located in a wide open field. You could be facing in any direction: north, south, east or west. At night all the stars and planets are there for you to observe. As you turn completely around in a circle, you will have covered 360 degrees on the horizon. These 360 degrees are called *azimuth*. This visible horizon around you is a local piece of the Earth's surface and a localized view of space: a "local space." The horizon that is seen in this local space perspective is *not* the same view as the standard zodiac which is the ecliptic, i.e. the path of the Sun (more on this later). In any place you may be on the planet, you'll have these 360 degrees of azimuth surrounding you. It is a circle on the Earth's surface acting as a compass to guide us in any one of the 16 directions.

Throughout the day the planets and stars will continually change position due to the Earth's rotation. Different stellar bodies will be seen at different heights above the horizon. These heights are expressed as *altitude*. When above the horizon, height is expressed as +0° to +90° altitude; when below the horizon it is expressed as -0° to -90° altitude.

Local Space is very much a person-centered astrology, for the observer and the observed. We *are* the center, with the *zenith* directly above us and the *nadir* directly below. So in review, we have 360 degrees of azimuth around us, +0° to +90° of altitude to the zenith, and -0° to -90° of altitude to the nadir below.

You may be wondering what the other three systems of measurement are. They are based on the ecliptic, prime vertical, and the equator. The ecliptic is the most commonly used. It is the Earth's path around the Sun, and commonly called the zodiac (the Earth rotates on an axis with a 23.5° tilt).

The prime vertical is a circle running directly east and west overhead and below. It is drawn through the zenith and nadir. The Equatorial System is mostly geographical in nature, dividing the Earth into latitudes and longitudes. All four systems are based on circles of 360 degrees. (More on these systems in Chapter 6.)

If you have a computer-generated standard chart for your pres-

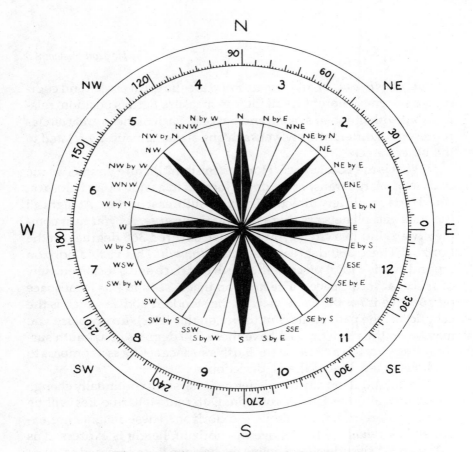

Fig. 2—*The Horizon and the Houses*
A Local Space or Azimuth chart reverses house positions and places planets on the horizon.

ent location or birth location it most likely has the *Vertex* (VT) position listed. The Vertex is due west and the opposite point, the *Anti-Vertex*, is due east. The Tenth House cusp is always due south and the Fourth House cusp is due north, in the Northern Hemisphere. (As you can see in Figure 2, this reverses the customary position of the houses.) You can determine if any of your planets are within a few degrees of the cardinal directions. (See Chapters 2, 3 and 4.)

The altitude of the planets can't be given because this is *not* a true Local Space chart, but a standard chart, and therefore the planets are on the ecliptic. What you need is the planets on the horizon measured in azimuth. In some computer programs, you can ask for a Local Space or azimuth chart; usually it is displayed on an open wheel or "Aries" chart. (See Appendix E for computer programs and steps to take.)

Another thing to remember is that a standard or Local Space chart must be for your present location; i.e., the date and time (*true* local time) stays the same but the Midheaven/10th, and Vertex, are (including Ascendant) determined by the latitude and longitude of your present location.

If you place yourself back inside the dome you see that the planets are at a certain altitude. By drawing a line straight down from each planet to the horizon you would find that it is in a certain compass direction. Each planet has its own direction. If you walked in that direction within or outside of the dome you would be walking on that *planetary line*. Venus could be south, Saturn southwest, while Jupiter might be pointing north, etc.

This planetary line will be different in every place to which you travel or relocate, because it is calculated for a specific latitude and longitude. Your birth time and date cannot be changed. Time remains frozen but space/place *can* change. This is the primary truth underlying the whole field of locality astrology.

In other words, the aspects between the planets will always be constant but the cusps or angles—Ascendant, Midheaven (Medium Coeli or MC), Vertex, etc.—will vary from one location to the next. So even though the planetary aspects among themselves remain the same, the aspects to the angles are different in *every* location.

Your Sun trine Jupiter or Venus conjunct Mars would not change. Their house positions would change, and they will make *new* aspects to the angles or compass directions on the chart. So you can see that every new location presents us with a new set of influences. Thus the obstacles and opportunities, fiascos and fortunes, and the whole complex assortment of favorable and unfavorable influences can be known *before* you go to a certain place, or for that matter have dealings with people who live there! Preplanning takes on a whole new meaning with locality astrology.

Although there are a number of favorable locations to move to, it's not likely that most people will do so. National, cultural and economic boundaries may cause you to stay within a familiar region. However, you can still choose the best possible location within limited geographical areas.

The grass always seems greener just over the fence; the truth is that in many ways it *is* greener. We all need change—variety is the spice of life. Relocating may not be the answer for everyone, but traveling is an option that can be undertaken by many. It seems to be human nature to get into ruts; we are often enslaved by the boring, monotonous, humdrum routines of daily living. Travel knocks you out of your ruts temporarily, and sometimes permanently, and can be incredible fun. It can be frustrating and tiresome, but it is always stimulating, because you are subjecting yourself to different and unaccustomed planetary influences.

These influences are more than just people and places on a superficial level. Each of us has different reactions to warmth and cold and to the four elements. If cold planets dominate in your chart you may be attracted to warm climates. If heat-producing planets are strong, the pull is to cool areas.

The Planets

Sun	*warm*
Moon	*cool*
Mercury	*neutral*
Venus	*warm*
Mars	*hot*
Jupiter	*warm*
Saturn	*cold*
Uranus	*cold*
Neptune	*warm*
Pluto	*hot or cold*
Transpluto	*warm*

As for the elements: Earth/practicality, Water/feeling, Fire/energy, Air/communication. You are drawn toward your weakest element, so that its physical presence can trigger new understanding in that area of your life.

What if your lifestyle limits your travel, and your chances of relocating are not very high? Local Space Astrology still offers a great deal of information. There is the home and community where you spend most of your life. That transparent dome referred to earlier could very well be your home—a home with the planetary lines running through it and beyond it into the community and/or neighborhood.

The bottom line is that you are (as sociology suggests) partly a product of your environment. So if you change the environment, you will effect the product, thus causing changes in health, thinking and inner life.

So whether the journey is short or long, the Local Space Horizon acts as a magic circle, a circle offering many paths. Each path is a choice that pulls you onward to greater discovery, challenge and fulfillment.

History of the Horizon System

The exact origins of this fantastic system are hidden in the early centuries of recorded history, perhaps as far back as 6000 BC. The convenience of this system is an important reason for its early development, since naked-eye observations formed the earliest basis for locating the directions of the planets. If we can trust astrological history, it wasn't until 300 BC that the Greeks introduced their version of the Ecliptic System, which later became the standard astrological operating procedure. In China the Ecliptic System wasn't widely used until the 1800's. The Chinese (along with Middle-Eastern civilizations) seemed to favor the equatorial and horizon coordinates.

The Horizon System used in geomantic practices seems to have its deepest roots in four areas: Italy, western Africa, what is now called Iraq/Iran, and China. In West Africa and Nigeria there are some surviving methods, yet they are not always clearly definable as horizon-based systems, and there are many unknowns and confusing points about systems used in the Middle East and elsewhere.

Some confusion with this subject has arisen because the words geomancy, astrology and divination are mistakenly lumped together. Both major systems of geomancy in the East and West used astrology; however most schools of astrology do not take geomantic principles into consideration. Although geomancy can be used for divination, it was used exclusively for that purpose only in the West.

Geomancy in a strict sense implies the usage of the Horizon System. "Geo" means that which pertains to the Earth, and because the Horizon System is based on seeing the planets in relation to the cardinal directions on the Earth's surface, it must be considered to be the prime astrological system used in geomancy.

Geomancy in northern Europe is really a 15th-century divination system.[1] This form of geomancy has a strong astrological basis, using the common system of twelve signs and the seven ancient planets. The seven planets are each given a helpful and a harmful quality (thus giving fourteen factors); when the Nodes are added to the dual natures of the seven planets we have a sixteen-factor system. Questions are formulated and dots are chosen randomly. The order of these dots places the planets in various houses. Interpreting their positions answers any number of possible questions.

The most comprehensive locational system to come down to us is the Chinese system of geomancy called "Feng Shui" (pronounced *fung shway*). It means literally "wind and water," and is such a vast system that to attempt to explain and describe it in a few pages would be a definite injustice. It should be known, however, that the system involves ecology, biology, zoology, geology, geography, cartography, topography, navigation, electromagnetism, architectural design, landscaping, interior decorating, ceremonial magic and, of course, astrology.

It's quite a comprehensive system, and although certain important practical parts of this sytem will be explained in Chapters 2 and 4, it is beyond the scope of this book to cover the many areas that Feng Shui can encompass. However, in specific areas I sincerely feel that this book will advance this ancient art and science of geomancy past its present boundaries.

There has been much speculation about the exact origins of geomancy. From the evidence available, and considering the nature of the subject, it is best to assume that it had many points of origin, unless you talk in terms of occult history and say that almost all the sciences came from the "lost" island of Atlantis.

The geomantic systems in Europe were practiced by a variety of schools, cults and individual authors. Henry Cornelius Agrippa wrote a famous book on geomancy in 1655, as the fourth in a series of volumes on occult philosophy. Other geomancers, including Christopher Cotton, Aleister Crowley, Robert Fludd, and Raphael (Robert Cross Smith), helped salvage and restore Western geomantic systems. Some authorities claim that the European systems of geomancy had their origins in Babylon and that the knowledge traveled to Europe through Egypt, later being influenced by Greek theories.

There are, in fact, a number of geomantic-type systems practiced in Africa today. One stems from the voodoo gods of Petra and Rada Loa on Africa's west coast; the Ifa divination is used in Nigeria, and the "khatt ar-raml" is based in northern Africa. These and others still employ the same sixteen-factor system originally used in Europe.

The use of the Horizon/Azimuth System as a geomantic science was also practiced in the Americas. Although most of the oral tradition behind it is still kept secret, or is lost, anthropologists and archaeologists are discovering an increasing amount of information. Significant discoveries have been instrumental in developing the spe-

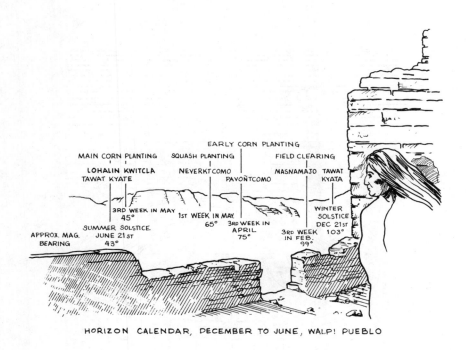

MAIN CORN PLANTING EARLY CORN PLANTING
SQUASH PLANTING FIELD CLEARING

LOHALIN KWITCLA NEVERKTCOMO MASNAMAJO TAWAT
TAWAT KYATE PAVOÑTCOMO KYATA

3RD WEEK IN MAY WINTER
45° 1ST WEEK IN MAY. 3RD WEEK IN SOLSTICE
65° APRIL DEC 21ST
SUMMER SOLSTICE 75° 103°
APPROX. MAG. JUNE 21ST 3RD WEEK 99°
BEARING 43° IN FEB.

HORIZON CALENDAR, DECEMBER TO JUNE, WALPI PUEBLO

Fig. 3—*Sunrise Horizon Planting Calendar*
from the Hopi pueblo of Walpi

cial field of archaeoastronomy in the last two decades. Recordings in
rock buildings and kivas date back to at least 1100 A.D. It is a fascinating
fact that over 700 years ago horizontal methods were used by the
ancient ones—the Anasazi. Because of the dry climate and rocky
terrain in the Four Corners area of the southwestern United States,
many important observational techniques remain preserved in rock.
The ancient ones and their ancestors watched the horizon very care-

9

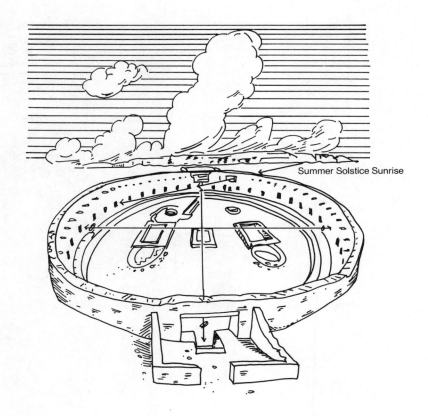

Summer Solstice Sunrise

Fig. 4—*Astronomical Alignments*
at Casa Rinconanda, Chaco Canyon N.H.P.

fully to be able to prepare themselves for the seasonal variations of rain and sun, the necessary ingredients for growing crops. Ray Williamson and others have shown that near-exact solstice and equinox measurements were in use; and that the risings, settings and culminations of planets were observed (see Figures 3 and 4). In addition, the cardinal directions were pinpointed and used with a high degree of accuracy.[2]

10

This practice is not just confined to the American southwest. Evidence shows that the Horizon System was used in varying degrees everywhere across America, including South and Central America. In Central America, the Aztecs, Toltecs and Mayans developed the most intricate system, not only in the Americas, but in the entire world. Their system consists of a complex series of cycles within a 260-day solar calendar. 20-day periods, each with its own sign, repeated 13 times in any 260-day period. The result was that in 52 years, or 18,980 days, no two days were repeated in any of the 260-day cycles.[3] This illustrates the fact that astronomy and astrology were in a highly developed stage in the Americas, and that the horizon/azimuth observations were used as foundational and core techniques.

From the hidden pyramids in the Andes, to the lines of the Nazca plains, across Central America to the ancient Mayan and Toltec structures, farther north to the great kivas and medicine wheels, the Horizon System was the astronomical and astrological standard.

The observation and use of the Horizon System is in fact a worldwide phenomenon. In England the Horizon System reached amazing levels of sophistication. In John Michell's work *The New View Over Atlantis*, many remarkable discoveries are explained.[4]

The whole system in England is centered around what are called the "ley" lines. A ley is an actual path that is marked across the surface of the Earth by shallow trenches, lines of rocks, or mounds of various sizes, all of which are aligned in straight paths. Quite often these ley lines are not visible on the surface but are exactly aligned by a variety of stone monoliths and/or water wells. The sites which are used in alignments are in fact a network of interconnected ancient ceremonial sites, which in our present day are usually occupied by a church or some other important building (see Figures 5 and 6).

Researchers have found that most of the lines and sites are on the azimuth of the Sun, Moon or certain stars.[5] A number of investigators found that different sites had different characteristics based on the azimuth of the celestial bodies they measured.[6] These lines run for hundreds of miles in most cases, and a straight line on a map can be drawn from site to site without error. The long-forgotten builders of the ley lines connected the hills, valleys, streams and overall landscape with the planetary movements, thus creating a pure geomantic tapestry, mirroring the above and the below. Mitchell describes it as "a fusion of the terrestrial current with the influences emanating from the heavenly bodies."[7]

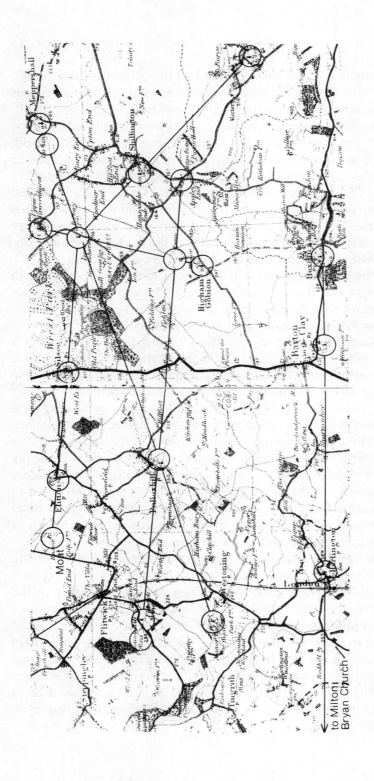

Fig. 5

Leys, two of them running parallel, on the Bedfordship-Hertfordshire border, formed by alignments of churches on ancient sites, earthworks and stretches of tracks which often lead up to churches. The reader may find more alignments than those marked here.

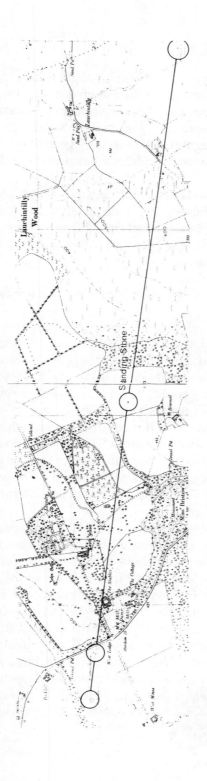

Fig. 6

A line of four standing stones, one of them in the stone circle at Castle Fraser, Aberdeenshire. This pattern of megalithic alignments from stone circles is repeated throughout the country and provides the primary evidence of the ley system.

The sacred geometry and geomantic engineering that was used to construct countless sites across the planet is becoming less a mystery all the time. Amid speculation on their purposes, some things are known. Certainly they were used for many types of ceremonies, and because of the electromagnetic currents they generated, it is conceivable that they served as a worldwide communication and transportation system.

The discovery of past scientific and ritualistic techniques is important and exciting, but we can't realistically wait for all the pieces to slowly come together. Now is the time when the recent discoveries in this area can blend with the past to produce a hybrid system with substantial practical value.

Local Space Astrology: The New Geomantic Science

The concept of space/place in astrology during this century has until recently taken a back seat to other astrological specialties. Until the 1970's very little had been done in this general area. A minority has always known about locality chart methods, but fewer still have used them, or knew how to use them. The average astrologer and client alike were not quite ready to accept the relevancy of changes in space/place on the birth chart. It was common knowledge that you changed your Ascendant and Medium Coeli when you moved from your birthplace. It was also common knowledge that the planets were thus shifted into different Houses and formed new aspects to the Ascendant and Medium Coeli, and this was about the extent to which movements in space were used.

There were a few notable exceptions. L. Edward Johndro was the astrologer who in theory and practice kept the concepts of coordinate systems alive. It is still hard to believe that his two major works were written and published around 1930.[8] Johndro had a sort of "living systems" approach to coordinate systems. In other words, he attempted to expose the inner workings (systems) of the astrological clock, instead of continually focusing only on the hour, minute and second hands, as had been done for centuries. His theories deal with a multi-system planetary approach. He viewed astrology as a dynamic interplanetary gestalt where various forms of gravity and electromagnetism constantly played upon each other, producing effects on organic life, thus triggering events. (In Chapter 6, Johndro's theories will be explained in more detail.)

Charles Jayne is another astrologer in this area whose many articles have demonstrated his research and technical skills.[9] There are others who have contributed directly or indirectly to coordinate systems, such as James Neely, David B. Black, Mark Pottenger, Zipporah Dobyns, Steve Blake, Axel Harvey, Gary Duncan, Jim Lewis, Theodor Landscheidt, Ken Gillman, Bruce Scofield, Angel Thompson, John McCormick, Seiggruen, Lt. Com. David Williams and M. Kahila. All of these astrologers as well as many others have played various roles in the overall development of time/space coordinate systems.

However, it wasn't until Michael Erlewine (founder of Matrix Software and the Heart Center) and his wife, Margaret, began their research that the practical significance of the Horizon/Azimuth System was realized. Once the tedious mathematics were worked out in converting the ecliptic/zodiac planetary positions to their azimuth and altitude, then a new and extraordinary revelation took place.*

At an early stage in their research the Erlewines realized that "The visible horizon being much like a magic circle [meant that] here is a map, in space, of an event from a topocentric perspective, or local center; and thus, an astrology of Local Space."[10] A chart or graph in Local Space is really the clearest representation of the planets in space in any locality from the point of the observer. In the Horizon/Azimuth System it is often the case that "what you see" is exactly "what you get."

Michael Erlewine has stated that: "Coordinate systems are great Languages or Orderings of our total reality, and each one raises to our attention its characteristic Gestalt or whole dimension of life."[11] The beauty of Local Space is that it automatically links you with the immediate natural surroundings: the general landscape and its inhabitants, the animals. Whether in your home, filled with its various objects, or out in nature, it "gives a sort of flat Earth perspective, as it were, the visible horizon being much like a Magical Circle."[12]

The Local Space chart is truly a magical circle, as Michael says, and more so than most would care to realize. I believe Erlewine says it

---

*It should be remembered that one of the major obstacles in the development of Local Space charts was the fact that you couldn't just open an ephemeris and find the azimuth of the planets. There were no such books, and there still aren't. Instead the information is stored in navigation manuals and more recently in a few computer programs. Before the time of programmable calculators, who would be willing to sit down for a couple of hours and perform complex calculations to satisfy his curiosity? Another factor is that Local Space charts are based on exact times of birth, and until the last fifty years exact birth times were hard to obtain.

best: "I must confess, a somewhat magical view of our world begins to emerge: one in which every city and friend becomes a radiating center of influence. Here for the first time the long history of Magic, witchcraft and sorcery takes on a practical reality, where local deities and preferred directions become the rule, and we are thrust forever beyond the threshold of the just slightly remarkable. The psychedelic character in Local Space charts is unmistakable and it appears as a kind of grand talisman and vast ritual ground through this perspective. The closest popular image of a similar nature in the modern consciousness is the remarkable world of Don Juan as generated by the author Carlos Castaneda. Here is not a subtle plane, but a personal landscape painted in bold and clear strokes. A world where the modern man is learning to move across the face of the Earth in an endless adjustment and tuning of his radix—of himself. Individuals driven in particular directions on a checkerboard world, unable to resist traveling to a goal that is no particular place on Earth as much as it is a direction within them: the direction of a force, or of a planet: 'There! where Power hovers!,' to use Don Juan's expression."[13]

The Erlewines were the pioneers in the field; they were the first to develop and implement a practical system using the horizon/azimuth, which they more accurately called "Local Space." History has shown us that the Horizon/Azimuth System has been used for many centuries and in a variety of ways, yet it was almost completely abandoned for hundreds of years in the Western world. The average person in past civilizations never had the advantage of having a personal, accurate Local Space chart. The Horizon Systems of the past were of a broad and general nature and were constructed for the use of everyone. Even though those systems revealed many mysteries about people and places, they were *not* geared to the birth moment, and therefore to the specific destiny of the individual. The Horizon/Azimuth Systems of the past were employed for the use of the many, the collective, and for the ceremonial, agricultural, procreational needs of the tribe, city or state. The Erlewines for the first time put the magic circle of directed force contained in the Local Space charts into the hands of the average person.

They noticed early on that planets close to the major directions (i.e., north, south, east, west) played a significant role or had a determining influence on a person in that specific locality. They also discovered that people traveled and relocated along certain planetary lines. These two points were major breakthroughs, because nobody had realized that horizon planetary positions were important in relocation, nor had anyone figured out that a planet's azimuth was actually a line that could be plotted on a map across the Earth's surface, connecting people and places. After many charts had been analyzed by the Erlewines, a unique and valuable system began to take shape.

Their findings were quite an inspiration to me; the possibilities of what this system could do for people multiplied over and over in my mind. I knew that locality astrology had the answers to many questions, questions that were not or could not be answered by conventional astrological methods. The Erlewines have made a major and historic contribution to the astrological community and to the general public, and the writing of this book is a direct result of their research. The fundamental principles contained in their research are expanded upon in the following chapters, and many of the Erlewines' insights directly and indirectly have caused new and meaningful techniques to unfold. (See Appendix A for the complete article.)

Please keep in mind as you study Local Space that it is still a young system (in its new and present form), and even though it has grown in scope and direction, it remains wide open in its possibilities. The sky's the limit!

An Introduction to Feng Shui—Chinese Geomancy

The philosophical and practical qualities of Feng Shui blend so perfectly with the basis of Local Space Astrology that it seems appropriate to elaborate further on this subject. In doing so the correlations between Local Space and geomancy should become clearer.

This is a most complete system; in fact there are many volumes on the subject written in Chinese. Feng Shui is presently used openly by many practitioners (mostly in Hong Kong); it has been rendered into English, so it can be of great value to us.

To learn Feng Shui it would be best to locate an experienced practitioner in the Far East and learn directly from that person. Since extended travel is not possible for most people, written works will have to do.

The most informative books on the subject are: *Feng Shui* by Sarah Rossbach,[14] *The Living Earth Manual of Feng Shui* by Stephen Skinner,[15] and *An Anthropological Analysis of Chinese Geomancy* by Stephen Feauchtwang.[16] The latter is by far the most comprehensive. However, all do a good job of describing the basics of Chinese geomancy.

Feng Shui has been called an "astro-biological mode of thought,"[17] and an "astro-ecology,"[18] by investigators. Skinner correctly states that "Feng Shui was thus the mother of the systemic use of magnetism, navigation and geography, just as astrology was of astronomy, alchemy of chemistry."[19] Another well-taken point of his is that ". . . Feng Shui bridges space and time using the compass to interpret both."[20]

Methods can vary widely among geomancers. This variety stems from the fact that there are so many different areas for them to focus on at any one time. Occasionally this very complexity has been used as a protective smoke screen. Sometimes they found it necessary to exploit the ignorance of others, or to save their hides when they were found in error.

The geomancers use what has been called a "geomantic compass" (see Figure 15). Each ring on the compass contains a new set of information. Depending on the situation any number of these rings can be used separately or together. (See Chapter 4 for the uses of the Western version of the geomantic compass.)

The rings as sources of information are used with one goal in mind: to interpret gross and subtle energy patterns. This all-pervading energy is called *Ch'i*. There is constructive and destructive Ch'i, cosmic and earthly Ch'i, and male and female Ch'i. Flow of Ch'i can mean the flow of spirits, money, friends, health, etc. It is at once the most powerful and wonderful *force* in nature and in the universe.

It has been mentioned that the electromagnetic forces in concert with planetary energies make up what the Chinese call Ch'i. This primeval and vital force manifests in a variety of ways, and it is the task of geomancy to detect, channel and generally make use of this ever-present energy.

The accumulated knowledge about Ch'i comes from the two primary schools of Feng Shui. One is the "form school," whose major proponent was Shuh-Meu. He was an Imperial Feng Shui master from 840 to 888 A.D. The form school didn't use the planets or compass very much; instead, it centered itself around the natural architecture—the contours, structure and shapes found throughout nature. The form school practitioner had the eye of an artist, the feelings of an environmentalist, the quickness of a photographer, along with some of the skills of a geologist. The difficulty with the form school is that each person sees different things in nature, and therefore interprets them in a personal fashion. What is true for one may not be true for the many. It was harder to reach a general consensus, but once it was agreed upon, the natural or man-made object became a useful part of a Feng Shui map.

The other notable school was the "compass school." It was developed in and around 960 A.D. by various teachers in the Sung Dynasty. It uses the compass, I Ching trigrams, stars and planets. The process seems to be straightforward and simplistic. However, it requires practice and intuitive skills to make sense out of a Chinese geomantic compass. (We explore the uses in Chapter 4.) The fact remains that not all natural structures easily lend themselves to practical guidelines.

The Feng Shui geomantic compass is a complex hand-held plate consisting of about 30 concentric rings. All the rings are correlated with the four major and twelve minor directions. Planets, stars, signs, months, days, numbers, elements, seasons, times of day, I Ching trigrams and many other factors are all used. Each bit of information can be used in connection with all or any of the others.

There are basically three types of Ch'i: terrestrial, cosmic, and a combination of both, in humans. This Ch'i naturally has a Yin/female part and the accompanying Yang/male part. The female and male components are both external and internal. The Feng Shui experts tell us that the vital Ch'i is more noticeably present during the period from midnight to noon (Third through Tenth Houses), and that the torpid Ch'i is more prevalent from noon to midnight (Ninth through Fourth Houses). There is an ebb and flow of Ch'i just as there is in the tidal rhythms. It is common knowledge that the tides are strongly influenced by the Moon and to a lesser degree by the Sun. Feng Shui also says that the Ch'i changes its direction and quality every two hours. Astrologers will recognize this as the average time it takes for 30 degrees of a sign to rotate over a given point, such as the Midheaven and/or Ascendant. In the yoga schools it is taught that the prana (the Hindu word for Ch'i) changes every two hours, and that this can be detected in the shifting of breathing from one nostril (nasal passage) over to the other about every two hours.

The Moon's effects on Ch'i are quite strong. It has been proven that the Earth's geomagnetic field has an hourly flux in accordance with the positions of the Sun and Moon. The readings that prove this were taken at Greenwich, England from 1916 to 1957.[21]

In another study quoted by NASA, it was shown that the geomagnetic field is the most calm just before the new and full Moons. Just after the new and/or full Moon there is an immediate disturbance of the geomagnetic field.[22]

Other researchers in this area have found that a lunar-induced modulation of the field occurs only when the Moon is within 4 degrees of the ecliptic plane and between the full Moon and the last quarter, i.e., between the 15th and 23rd days of the lunar cycle. It was also theorized that if the full Moon is near the ecliptic, powerful geomagnetic storms will occur especially around noon, with a quiet period before sunset. The maximum effect would be to have a total solar or lunar eclipse occurring close to either solstice or equinoctal points and to have it at noon or midnight local time.[23]

Tibetan astrologers say that the peak of male Ch'i occurs on the 10th day, i.e., five days before the full Moon, and the peak of female Ch'i is on the 25th day, or five days before the new Moon.[24] The peaks of male and female Ch'i do not fall in either of the disruptive periods mentioned above.

There are many studies that could be quoted to illustrate how the cosmic and terrestrial Ch'i interact; the oldest of these works is by J.H. Nelson. He developed a theory in the mid-1950's while working for RCA. It showed how the planetary angles affect the solar winds; and with this knowledge he was able to predict with great accuracy when solar winds would disrupt television and radio communications, along with significant effects on the weather.[25] In a study by Theodore Landscheidt, accurate predictions of the time and intensity of solar flares which strongly relate to the 11- and 22-year sunspot cycles have been formulated.[26]

Don't lose sight of how living things are directly influenced, because the sensitivity of various life forms can be startling. For example, a very basic organism like the volvox (a single-celled organism), which has been around for millions of years, responds to magnetic fields, and even detects specific lines of force, i.e., directions.[27] Many types of whales have enough metallic particles in their heads to detect magnetic directions. When these magnetic lines are temporarily altered the whales still follow these paths, even when it means beaching themselves! Not only whales but birds, monkeys, cockroaches and pigs exhibit certain atypical behaviors just prior to major earthquakes. It is thought that they somehow pick up on certain geomagnetic waves under the Earth. These waves are called "S" and "P" waves by Russian scientists.[28]

Humans also respond to all sorts of subtle stimuli. For example, the lack of energy experienced just before a New Moon, and the overabundance of it at the Full Moon can, in part, be attributed to the lack of negative ions in the air. These ions with extra electrons are in short supply at the New Moon, but there are generous amounts of electrons at the Full Moon. At this time rain and lightning strikes are more common, which is one way that the biosphere is recharged with more electrons.

There are many advantages and opportunities that come from time-tested techniques and knowledge that was once hidden. We are only now beginning to explore Local Space Astrology, Feng Shui, and the whole fascinating field of locality astrology.

Important Pointers from Feng Shui

The following is a list of important tips. It is practical, detailed, and directly applicable to Local Space charts.

1. The primary concept in Feng Shui is to gather the needed amount of Ch'i (vital energy) without allowing it to stagnate. Moderation, balance and harmony on a practical level form the basis of this system. Good Ch'i, like magnetic lines from the poles, always flows in a curved and rhythmic pattern. Bad Ch'i tends to flow in straight lines and either manifests suddenly or slowly. The damage of bad Ch'i is often unnoticed or undetectable at first.

2. Generally anything man-made or natural that is convex is considered male. Anything concave is female. Any feature or shape, symbolic or actual, that corresponds to Fire and Air elements is male; the Water and Earth elements are female. Therefore valleys and caves are female. Ridges, large rocks and trees are male. Feng Shui indicates that the ideal proportion is a ratio of three male to two female. When these two forces meet with such a ratio it produces the perfect or balanced Ch'i; a valley (female) sheltered on three sides by mountains (male) with the south side open is the classical example.

3. The Ch'i fluctuates more in urban areas, and can change from positive to negative over very short distances.

4. The shapes of houses are important. It is necessary to have equal proportions in the outline of the house. A house can be odd looking and yet still have balanced dimensions. Certain shapes are not conducive to the inflow of good Ch'i. Houses with one or more rooms added on improperly will not allow the Ch'i to circulate fully throughout the house. Good house shapes are circle/dome, square, rectangle, and octagon.

5. A house should have a large entrance (in proportion to the rest of the house) and be free from obstructions, such as large trees, small buildings, and walkways that detour excessively.

6. The plot of land should not be shaped so that its symmetry inhibits the natural landscape. (The actual shape of the plot is less important than house size and shape).

7. A southern exposure about halfway down a hill or mountain is best. The main entrance facing east is the next best, followed by west; north entrances are usually not considered good.

8. If water flows by the home it is more favorable if it bends inward toward the property. If it flows outward it is not as helpful. If the river or stream is very fast or very slow then the Ch'i either flows by too quickly or it becomes stagnant.

9. Remember the flow of Ch'i is not only the flow of energy, but also of friends, information, money and other forms of wealth.

10. You don't want to have your house or business located at the intersection of streets in a "T," or in the apex of a "V." These street intersections can be most harmful. The Mars/Saturn force of the automobiles will cut right into a home or business.

11. If the land is extremely flat the Ch'i will tend to be stagnant. If the land is too steep and/or broken, then the Ch'i will flow by too swiftly or it will become scattered.

12. Locating near the confluence of streams or rivers or close to the ocean or a lake will provide an excellent source of good Ch'i. If the air currents are moderate and the water is relatively unpolluted, it is even more favorable.

13. People are encouraged to plant bushes and trees to the north and west to neutralize bad weather Ch'i as well as adverse thought-forms. Small ponds with or without fish can increase the Ch'i in an area where it is poor. Fountains serve the same purpose. When centrally located they have the added ability of channeling the Ch'i to many areas in the house or yard. Some people sink a long pole (10 to 20 feet) into the ground and put a red light on the top of it, which is said to attract and draw Ch'i up from the Earth, not symbolically but physically.

14. Inside the house fish tanks, plants, musical devices, burning good incense, bells, pictures, mirrors and chimes are ways to disperse bad Ch'i and also to help circulate good Ch'i. So if there is a problem area in the house you have a variety of options to choose from. (For more stringent measures see Appendix C, "Banishing Rituals.")

15. One of the most common tactics used is to set up mirrors. A mirror can reflect the bad Ch'i back to its source, e.g., back to a neighbor's house. Although mirrors can't stop industrial or auto pollution, they are effective in decreasing people pollution. Simply place the mirror in such a way that it faces the source of inharmony. Mirrors (and in some cases pictures) can also be used inside the home to reflect bad Ch'i outward so it can be circulated by chimes, fish tanks or the natural air currents from windows.

16. The locations of businesses should be at regular corners, but not apex or dead-end points. The establishment should have large double doors or revolving doors so that people and money can flow in easily.

17. Interiors are very important, especially in colder cities where many hours are spent indoors. A house is alive just like the people within it. The windows are the eyes, doors become the mouths, vents are ears, heating systems the heart, and ducts, plumbing and wiring are the arteries, veins and nerves. Because there are any number of possibilities that will arise, it must fall upon your own best judgement as to what is or is not balanced.

18. The front door should open to a large room, and afford a maximum view of the interior. Doors should not face each other, nor should they bang into each other when opened. Don't have a bed or office desk close to the door. Your side and/or back will be too close to the door, and this could lead to problems, such as not being able to see those entering the room.

19. Heavy beams in various places can be a problem, especially in bedrooms where a beam over the bed can be oppressive and cutting. Moving the bed and putting chimes on the beam is recommended. (Doors and beams are given considerable attention in Feng Shui, and it seems appropriate since doors and beams are linked to Saturn.)

The Ch'i in rural areas does not fluctuate as dramatically over short distances as does the Ch'i in a city, which can change every 50 feet or so. In the country specific locations are measured in hundreds of yards and sometimes even miles.

The female Ch'i is in rivers, lakes and ponds, etc. Neptune is connected with large bodies of water, salt water, and all very slowly moving water. The Moon is linked with streams, rivers, and lakes and all quickly moving water. Pluto is associated with water underground, hot mineral (healing) springs, and all water at night.

The male Ch'i is concentrated in mountains, hills, and trees of all sizes. If you live in a place which is relatively flat, then all water sources, trees and rocks play an important role. According to my findings, oaks are linked with Saturn, elms with Pluto, pines and cottonwoods with Jupiter, lodgepole and bull pines are related to Mercury, magnolias to Neptune, most fruit trees to Venus, willows to the Moon. Maples, birch and ash seem to be a mixture of Pluto and Venus. The Sun is indirectly related to all the trees because of photosynthesis.

The shapes of mountains reveal their planetary connections (see Figure 7, page 25). Mountains with very high and sharply pointed peaks and/or a series of sawtooth peaks are linked with Pluto. Volcanoes are also Pluto types, but their point is the convex cone within the crater. The average high, pointed peak is a Mars type. High mountains or hills that are somewhat rounded at the top are Jupiter types. Softly rounded or bell-shaped hills and mountains are of the Venus type. When a mountain or hill is mostly flat at the top it is a Saturn type. When the flat plain is broken and fairly uneven then it is a Uranus type; all mesas are therefore Uranus types. Mountains or hills that have a series of small domes at the top or long, rounded, hilly ridges are linked to Mercury.

It becomes obvious that the solar system is a master key in describing how the planetary energies link up with the biosphere—the terrestrial and celestial reflecting each other.

Fig. 7
Physical features reveal planetary connections through their shapes.

Notes

1. Skinner, Stephen, *The Oracle of Geomancy*. New York City: Warner Destiny, 1977.
2. Williamson, Ray, *Living the Sky*. Boston: Houghton Mifflin Co., 1984.
3. Scofield, Bruce, "The Astrology of Ancient Mexico" in *American Federation of Astrologers*, Vol. 46, No. 12, Tempe, AZ.
4. Michell, John, *The New View Over Atlantis*. San Francisco: Harper & Row, 1983.
5. Michell, p. 46.
6. Michell, p. 47.
7. Michell, p. 66.
8A. Johndro, Edward, *The Stars*. New York: Samuel Weiser, reprinted 1970.
8B. Johndro, Edward, *The Earth in the Heavens*. New York: Samuel Weiser, reprinted 1970.
9. Jayne, Charles, *An Introduction to Locality Astrology*. Astrological Bureau, 1978.
10. Erlewine, Michael, *The Astrology of Local Space*. Heart Center, 1977, p. 2.
11. Erlewine, p. 3.
12. Erlewine, p. 3.
13. Erlewine, p. 4.
14. Rossbach, Sarah, *Feng Shui*. New York: E.P. Dutton.
15. Skinner, Stephen, *The Living Earth Manual of Feng Shui*. Boston: Routledge & Kegan Paul, 1982.
16. Feuchtwang, Stephen, *An Anthropological Analysis of Chinese Geomancy*. Vithanga, Southern Materials Center, Republic of China, 1974.
17. Wheatley, Paul, *The Pivot of the Four Quarters*. Chicago: Aldine, 1971.
18. Bennett, Steven J., *Chinese Science*, Vol. 3, pp. 1-26. University of Pennsylvania, 1978.
19. Skinner, p. 73.
20. Skinner, p. 85.
21. Leaton, Malin & Finch, "The Solar and Luni-solar Variation of the Geomagnetic Field at Greenwich and Abinger," *Observatory Bulletin of Great Britain* 53: 273, 1962.

22. Lieber, A.L., *The Lunar Effects*. Garden City, NY: Anchor Press, 1978.
23. O'Dhaniel, Noah, *Earth Mysteries, Considerations*, Vol. 1, No. 2. Mt. Kisco, NY, 1984.
24. Reynolds, John M., "Tibetan Astrology and the Kalachakra," *Geocosmic News*, Vol. 9, Nos. 3 and 4.
25. Nelson, J. H., "Shortwave Radio Propagation Correlation with Planetary Positions," *RCA Review*, December 26, 1951.
26. Landscheidt, Theodore, A paper and lecture at the National Oceanic and Atmospheric Research Conference, Boulder, CO, August, 1983.
27. Palmer, J. D., "Organismic Spatial Orientation in Very Weak Magnetic Fields," *Nature* No. 198, 1963.
28. "Whales and Dolphins Navigate Via Magnetic Grids," *Brain-Mind Bulletin*, Vol. 10, No. 3, December, 1984.

CHAPTER 2

THE LOCAL SPACE CHART IN THE HOME AND COMMUNITY

Most people spend over 85% of their lives in and around their home and workplace. Eight hours a night is spent sleeping, another eight working; travel time, reading, watching television, etc. absorb the balance of our lives. Isn't this environment worthy of more attention? Now you have the Local Space chart as the perfect tool to tune in the wide variety of conditions in your immediate environment.

In the Local Space chart the planets surround you on the horizon circle. Below you is the nadir, and over your head is the zenith. You are the center of all that is around you—the observer and that which is observed. You are truly a intermediary between Mother Earth and Father Sky, standing in a dual role of Earth steward and cosmic citizen.

The planets on the horizon are always around you. You occupy the hub of the wheel, and they radiate in various directions at different elevations. When you change locations, the planets point in different directions. If you stay in one place, the planets stay fixed until you move again. Actually your Local Space chart is good for about fifty miles in any direction from where you live. Once you go beyond that planetary positions will have changed enough to warrant a new chart.*

---

*—People born above the mid-latitudes (above 30 N 00 or below 30 S 00), and who remain living in those latitudes, tend to have their Local Space planets in many directions around the chart. As they travel closer to the equator the planets will begin to bunch up or group along the east/ west directions. Therefore, below 30 N or above 30 S the Prime Vertical Circle chart is used—see Chapters 3 and 6.

Before I describe the uses of the Local Space chart in the home and community, you need to understand something about the underlying basis of this system. There is no better way to do this than to examine again some of the basic principles of Feng Shui.

As you have learned, this ancient Chinese system of geomancy places the greatest emphasis on understanding the flow of Ch'i, the vital life energy. Ch'i pervades all existence, flowing in everything and everyone. There is a cosmic Ch'i coming from the planets and beyond, and an Earth Ch'i which is partly electromagnetic. Both these types merge and flow over the Earth in continuous and rhythmic patterns. Ch'i is carried by water and is also channeled by the winds. The Ch'i is *in*, as well as *on* the Earth at all times. There are four basic kinds of Ch'i: male and female, torpid and vital. The most auspicious location to find the vital Ch'i is where the male and female forces meet.

The biosphere of Earth is alive and pulsating with energy; it is up to each of us to make use of it in the best possible ways. Man, the organic computer composed of electrochemical and electromagnetic substances, responds unceasingly to the flow of Ch'i in all its forms. The vital energy within all living things has to be understood, and the Local Space chart along with the wisdom of Feng Shui can help you understand how to live a more productive and enjoyable life. Landmarks, planets, stars, compass directions, all come together in this new geomantic science of Local Space Astrology.

One of the qualities that contributes to accuracy of a Local Space chart is its basis of a near-exact birth time. Most ancient astrological charts were not constructed to the exact hour and minute of birth. The Feng Shui system is a good example of a method used for the masses. The nearest this system came to an exact birth time was the birth hour; but in most cases only A.M. or P.M. of the day of birth was used. Only royalty and those in other positions of power were given the consideration of an exact recorded birth time (in Chapter 1 some guidelines for Feng Shui were given).

For one reason or another we all have learned to turn off to some degree certain perceptions about our immediate environment. If you ask people to describe the ways in which their jobs influence them, you get conventional answers in the majority of cases. The same is true of the home. There are all kinds of things that affect you on subliminal levels, yet because it is hard to locate and define exactly what they are, you either dismiss or generally attempt to forget these subtle influences. This is how the ancient geomantic knowledge, along with the discoveries in Local Space, can help immensely. The obvious answers are not discounted but are taken into consideration, along with viewing situations in a new way—a way in which many other factors that you've learned to ignore can answer questions and play an important role. For example: Why do the pipes always leak in the west bathroom and not elsewhere? Why do the dogs always knock over the garbage cans on the north side of the house? Why do certain appliances work in one place but not in another?

There are countless questions like these which may have practical answers, but what about the unnoticed or unexplained factors involved? There are any number of occurrences in your home and workplace that are difficult to explain unless you can view your environment in a new way.

Astrology is a cosmic science that helps one discover the real causes behind the apparent ones. Local Space charts can do the same and often in more practical ways. After all, what could be more down-to-earth than relating the planets to rocks, trees, rivers, hills, and buildings (with the objects and fixtures within them)? Granted there are always going to be people who find conditions as well as causes that simply don't exist, but this can happen no matter how clear or foolproof the system.

Everything around you has a symbolic and literal meaning, and through the use of the Local Space chart you can begin to discover the vast interplay of the spiritual and material worlds.

The first step is to get a Local Space chart for your present location. This can be done in a number of ways. The correct procedure to follow with software programs, and information on where to order your Local Space chart, is given in Appendix E.

The important thing to remember is that the planets are no longer in the 360 degrees of the Zodiac/Ecliptic System. In a Local Space chart they are viewed in 360 degrees of azimuth, measured on the circumference of the horizon. There are no signs in this system, and the houses are reversed (see Figures 2 and 8).

Azimuth is simply a way of finding out the directions of the planets. The beginning point of 0 degrees azimuth is usually due north. Some people prefer to start at east. It really doesn't matter where it starts as long as you know that 90 degrees in either direction puts you at another cardinal direction, i.e. north, south, east or west. If due north is 0 degrees azimuth, then 90 degrees clockwise will be due east, 90 degrees counterclockwise will be due west, and 180 degrees is

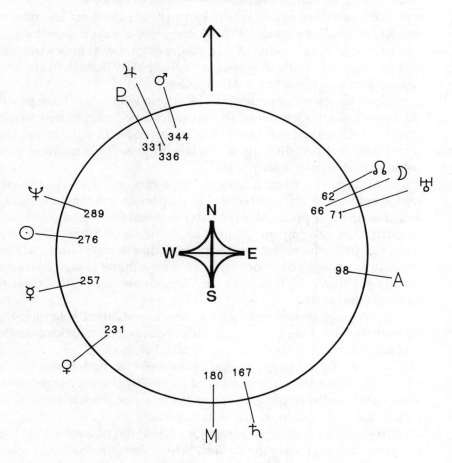

Fig. 8
*On a Local Space chart, planetary positions are indicated in
degrees of azimuth.*

due south. (The international standard is due north=0 degrees of azimuth; then east is 90°, south 180° and west 270°.)

Planetary Lines in the Home

In order to go any further you'll need to have a non-graphic, or round, twelve-house Local Space chart, as described above.

Remember that on a Local Space chart the houses are reversed from the birth chart. In this chart the Seventh House is to your left, *not* right, and the Fourth House is at the top, *not* bottom (more on this later).

Once you have your Local Space chart for your present locality, the next step is to get a floor plan of your home and/or office. Since this is not usually available, I suggest you make one. Draw it on an average 8½" by 11" piece of paper and add as much detail as you think necessary (the more the better). I suggest that you put in all rooms, furniture, windows. The more you include, the easier it will be to see where the planetary lines are going (see Figures 9 and 10).

The next step is to find out where due north is in your home. People living in urban areas built prior to 1960 should not have a problem, because most of the streets were built during this time on a north/south—east/west axis. If you live in a rural area or in the newer suburbs, then it is likely that the standard alignments were not used. The simplest way to find out is to use a local map. If you want accuracy, you can find due north with a compass. Figures 11A-E show the magnetic deviation from true north for your area.[2] Magnetic *declination* is the difference between true north, i.e., astronomical north, and the location of magnetic north. It is measured in azimuth degrees. For most places in the United States, the difference will be somewhere between 23 degrees east of north to 23 degrees west of north. (Magnetic north is 102 W 03 and 77 N 00 as of November, 1984. It moves about 1 degree of latitude northwest every 10 years). Look at Figure 11E to find the most recent magnetic deviation (from the North Pole) for your area. Once you have the degrees, you can find true north by facing in a northerly direction and matching the degrees of deviation on the map to those observed on the compass. If you live in a place where the deviation is 15 degrees east of north, then as you face north move the compass slowly until the needle is on 15 degrees east of true north, i.e., toward the magnetic pole. Whichever way the top of the compass is now facing indicates due north.

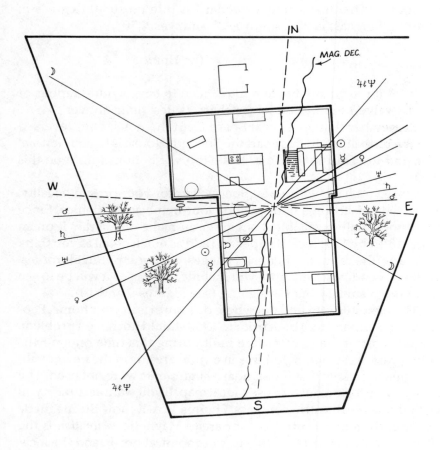

Fig. 9

Floor plan with planetary lines and compass points indicated.

This matter accomplished, the next step is to find the approximate center of your home or job location, keeping in mind the structure's orientation to the compass points (see Figures 9 and 10). If you
move around continuously at work, then you should use the center of
the entire work area, which may be a part or whole floor in a high-rise,

34

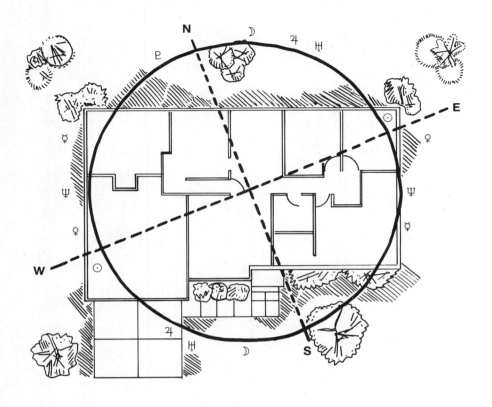

Fig. 10
Floor plan with planets indicated on Local Space horizon.

or in a ground-level office/shop. If you have your own office or work station, then you can find the center of it with very few problems. It isn't critical that you find the center to the inch, but it is necessary that you locate the center within a couple of feet. In some cases the center can be found by standing where you assume it to be and measuring by eye from that point to see if all directions are equal in distance. If there are a number of different rooms and objects in the line of sight, it is more difficult, and you may need to use a tape measure.

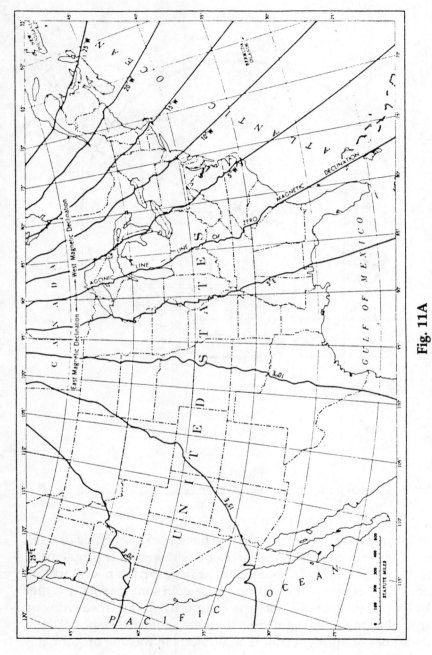

Fig. 11A

Magnetic declination in the United States for 1945.

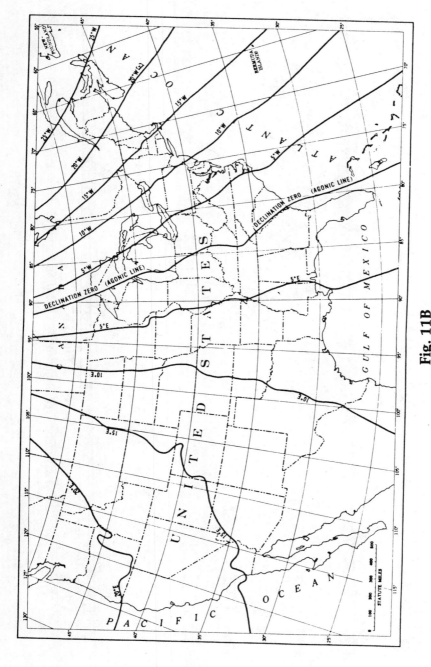

Fig. 11B

Magnetic declination in the United States for 1955.

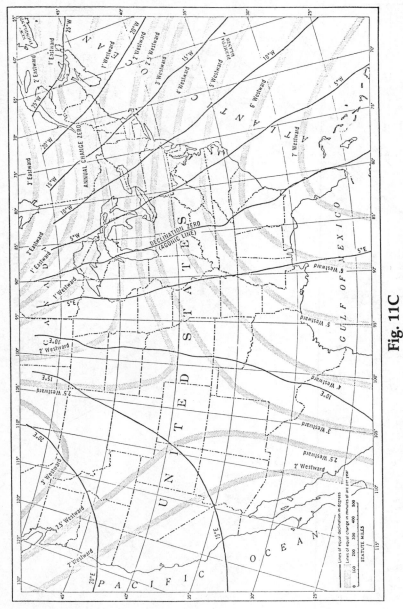

Fig. 11C

Magnetic declination in the United States for 1965.

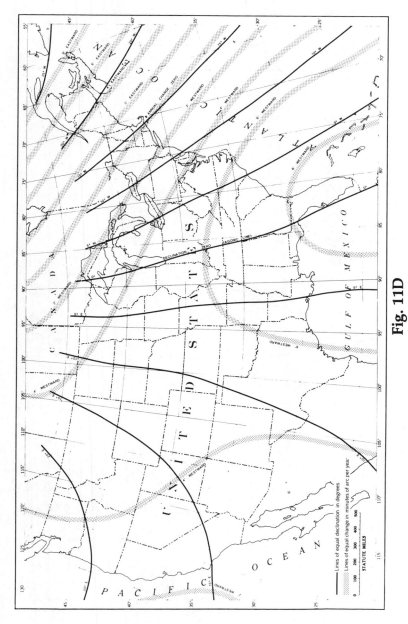

Fig. 11D

Magnetic declination in the United States for 1975.

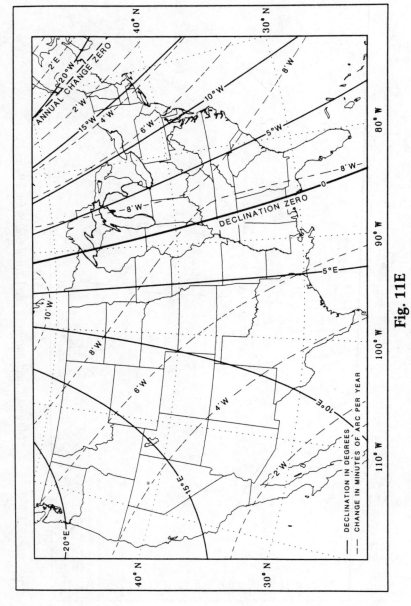

Fig. 11E

Magnetic declination in the United States for 1985.

Table 1

Degrees of Azimuth Cross Comparison Chart

0—0	60—240	
0—180	65—245	125—305
5—185	70—250	130—310
10—190	75—255	135—315
15—195	80—260	140—320
20—200	85—265	145—325
25—205	90—270	150—330
30—210	95—275	155—335
35—215	100—280	160—340
40—220	105—285	165—345
45—225	110—290	170—350
50—230	115—295	175—355
55—235	120—300	180—360

This table can be used as an aid when various azimuth degrees are given, e.g. 175 degrees of azimuth is the same as 355 degrees, but in the opposite direction. It has been mentioned that if a planet points in one direction, it also points to the opposite direction. Therefore, you can use this table for more exactitude.

Now comes the fun part. If your Local Space chart is on a transparency, then all you have to do is place it over the center of the floor plan and/or drawing of your home/office. You may want to get a transparency of the floor plan and put it over the Local Space chart. Another option is to draw in the planetary lines on the house map. To make sure you draw the correct angles you need a small plastic sextant which has the azimuth degrees (see Table 1).

You are now ready to "walk the chart." What I mean by this is to follow each planetary line from the center of your home and/or office and see what they intersect. These lines of force go in two directions. If a planetary line runs a few degrees south of west, then it also runs a few degrees north of east. If the line is due north, then it is also due south, etc. (see Table 1). At this point in my understanding of Local Space planetary lines, I'm assuming that both directions are equal in strength. It is entirely possible that the actual direction in which the planet lies has a stronger influence.

There are ten planetary lines plus the Nodes; some of these lines will be close together, others far apart (see Figures 9 and 10). Each planet reacts differently because of its own particular qualities. These

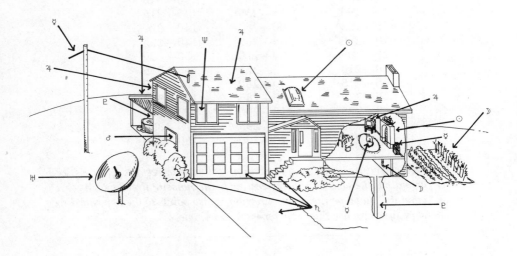

Fig. 12
*Planetary correspondences to fixtures and objects
within and outside of the home.*

qualities do not differ from the basic meanings familiar to most astrologers. The qualities of two or more planets will begin to blend at about five degrees of orb, using only the conjunction and opposition aspects. (These aspects cause a fusion of energies because the planets occupy the same or opposite direction, respectively, in space along the horizon, which is different from aspects that form planetary connections by angles, i.e., 60°, 90°, 120°, etc.). The closer they are to one another, the more blended their energies will become.

42

The objects and fixtures throughout your home or office also have a planetary signature. Each of them can be linked to a certain planet (see Figure 12 and Table 3). What we have then is planetary lines of force radiating outward, into and through objects and fixtures in the home. (To get a better idea of what others have experienced, turn to Table 2, page 45, for some of the survey results.)

Planetary energies have distinct traits, and are also linked to one of the four elements. This can cause either attraction or repulsion. When planetary lines hit certain objects that are antagonistic to them, we have a potential problem. Let's say the Pluto line intersects an object connected with the Moon; what effects should we expect? In this case effects have been shown to be inharmonious. The major reason for this is that a planetary line making contact with an object acts just like a conjunction. The conjunction is the most powerful of all aspects, and even though the Moon and Pluto are both Water planets, this is one example where the blend is mostly inharmonious. Look at Table 3 on page 46 and you will see which planets cause problems with different groupings of objects/fixtures.

Take your time in walking your chart, and when you are finished, go back to the center of the house where you started and think about what you have learned.

The Saturn line seems to cause most of the problems. It's best not to locate delicate objects in its path. Mars, Pluto and Neptune can also cause problems. The particular combinations in Table 3 represent only those that have been discovered. There are, in fact, many possible combinations, some difficult, some not.

Beneficial influences generally don't attract much attention because things remain somewhat normal. This is especially true when a planetary line runs through an object that it is naturally associated with, for example, Jupiter with valuables, Saturn with doors and stairs, etc. (see Table 4 and Figure 12).

Since we are talking about planetary actions and reactions we must not forget the aspects in the regular birth chart and how they are used with the Local Space chart (aspects in the Local Space chart are covered in Chapter 3). A basic truth in astrology, no matter what technique you are using, is that no extra input can override the birth chart assessments. If Saturn is well aspected, and/or the individual has made a concerted effort to work positively with Saturnian energy, then many of the adverse effects will not transpire.

Everyone is different, and some planets are more easily understood than others. Because of this you may be able to devise a healthy strategy in dealing with them. Other planets tend to be more imbalanced, and are therefore challenging and often destructive. If you already practice astrology, you know that it takes a certain amount of honesty and objectivity to admit that certain planets are more difficult than others. If you are not familiar enough with your birth chart, consult a professional astrologer. If you're unsure of how to find one, a metaphysical bookstore can put you in contact with a local organization or with qualified professionals. (Llewellyn Publications also offers astrological services—write for their free catalog.)

Table 4 is a list of the planetary lines in and around your home, and what you might expect from them. Each planetary line points to a particular area. The planetary influences are most helpful when they intersect the objects and fixtures that they are harmoniously associated with, as listed in Table 3.

Dividing your living area into astrological houses can also be used to better understand your living situations; however, they comprise a larger area and therefore are not as definitive as the planetary lines. These houses can be used with greater reliability if they lack planets. This is more common nearer the equator, where only the First, Seventh, Twelfth and Sixth Houses contain planets in Local Space horizon charts.

One other important factor about the planetary lines in the home relates to their altitude. You will recall that planets on the horizon have an altitude above or below that horizon. When the altitude is above or below 60 degrees it may point to an influence above or below ground. Planets below the horizon may point to events in the basement or under the house. Those above 60 degrees of altitude relate to occurrences in the upper rooms, attic or on the roof.

When you encounter an inharmonious situation the simplest remedy is to move the object to a better location. But what if it is a permanent fixture which can't be moved without a hefty financial investment? In these cases we can use some of the time-tested methods suggested by Feng Shui. See "Important Pointers from Feng Shui" at the end of the previous chapter.

Table 2

Case Examples of Planetary Lines Throughout the Home

SATURN line through Moon objects: Poor gardens, has to work hard on plants, frozen pipes, bad water pressure, doesn't water plants enough, poor sewer line, small garden.

SATURN line through Sun objects: Damper on fireplace broken, skylight leaks, hard to keep wood stove warm, cramped children's room.

MARS line through Mercury objects: Phone replaced a number of times, verbal fights, many old books, radio needs to be fixed, negligence about books, irritated by the radio, radio cracked, radio tuner out.

PLUTO line through Venus obejcts: Beat-up furniture, beautiful objects damaged, child abuse in guest room, very promiscuous person in the guest room.

SATURN and NEPTUNE lines through Mars objects: Old tools, car battery problems, rusty tools, vents closed off, not enough tools.

SATURN line through Jupiter objects: Uneven patio cement, doesn't use porch, rarely uses T.V., bad picture tube, large tree pushing against porch and cracking it, porch cracked, very selective in watching T.V.; with Neptune line included, either watches T.V. for a very short or very long time.

SATURN line through Saturn objects: Of no consequence.

PLUTO line through Uranus objects: Bad wiring has led to blown circuits, fuses blow out fairly often, poor T.V. reception.

SATURN line through Neptune objects: Broken windows; with Uranus line, too tense to meditate, and also distractions and uncomfortable in meditation. Bad reactions from drugs, medicine went bad (no data for MARS line).

MOON line through Pluto objects: Had to replace bathroom floor, bad water faucet, had to rebuild bathroom which was complicated and took a long time, clogged drains, hides things under water bed, a wall had to be removed because builders got garbage into drain, roof over bathroom leaks.

Injuries and Accidents: Mars and Uranus conjunct on west direction, broken ankle. On Uranus line, cut toe. On Mars and Saturn lines, cut left knee, broken nose. On Mars and Uranus lines, fire in attic.

45

Table 3

Planetary Intersections with Objects and Fixtures in and around the Home

♄* MOON objects: A. Main on and off water control. B. Majority of potted plants. C. Garden plot. D. Washer. E. Swimming pool. F. Allergic substances. G. Small boats.

♄ SUN objects: A. Skylight. B. Child's room. C. Wood stove, fireplace. D. Warmest part of the house.

♂ MERCURY objects: A. Telephone(s). B. Books. C. Radio. D. Dogs, cats and other small animals.

♇ or ♀ VENUS objects: A. Things of beauty. B. Most used furniture (not including bed). C. Guest room. D. Musical instruments. E. Wood pile. F. Women's clothes. G. Middle levels.

♄—♆ MARS objects: A. Furnace. B. Car. C. Tools. D. Machines. E. Driest part of house. F. Firearms.

♄ JUPITER objects: A. Valuables. B. Porch, patio, balcony. C. T.V. D. Master bedroom. E. Men's clothes. F. Upper levels, e.g. attic.

n/a SATURN objects: A. Little-used or unused areas. B. All stairs, beams and doors. C. Large wood or concrete structures including large trees. D. Lower levels, e.g. basement. E. Coldest part of house.

♇ or ♀
♂—♄ URANUS objects: A. Fuse box. B. Antiques. C. Electronic/electrical equipment, e.g. computer, ham radio, etc. E. Wind damage. F. Ventilation.

♂—♄ NEPTUNE objects: A. Drugs and/or poisonous substances. B. Major windows. C. Where you reflect or meditate. D. Horses, cows, and other large animals. E. Water damage. F. Bacterial and infectious substances. G. Large boats.

☽—♀ PLUTO objects: A. Main sewer outlet. B. Main bathroom. C. Hidden things. D. Septic tank. E. Hot tub. F. Garbage cans. G. Bedroom.

♅ TRANSPLUTO objects: A. Kitchen. B. Food storage. C. Dining room.

symbols in this column indicate adverse influence

Table 4

Planetary Lines in the Home

SUN: This corridor adds a sense of importance to things, so they are noticed. Objects are personalized and this is a personal spot. Round objects and those that are gold or orange are enhanced.

MOON: A positive place for living things, plants, animals, etc. May cause fluctuations and sensitivity. It is a natural and passive spot which helps anything with irregular curves or waves, as well as concave objects. Opal, silvery and pale blue colors are best.

MERCURY: This area has the ability to reveal meanings. It speaks to people—signs are read, phones get answered, letters get sent. A work area and message spot. Thin, clear objects do best along this line.

VENUS: On this line the beauty and desirability of items are brought out. This area also increases togetherness; it's a congenial spot. Things that are softly curved and colored or tinted with pastels of sky blue, green and yellow are best. Copper and brass objects do well.

MARS: Energizes and increases all activities. This can be a traffic corridor. It's an assertive spot. Anything that protrudes or has sharp angles (made of iron) does well. Red, carmine are good colors.

JUPITER: This area adds a protective influence. It promotes enjoyment, and things appear luxurious. For most people and most activities it is the best spot. Large, full objects and those colored purple, violet and deep blue do best.

SATURN: A stabilizing and supporting place, it may age things and definitely slows down activities. Often it is the empty spot. Things made of wood, compressed forms, black and darker colors do best.

URANUS: Objects are perceived as being more unique and antique. This is not a stable area, but certainly adds excitement. Odd-shaped things that are multi-colored are advantageous. The different spot.

NEPTUNE: Mystifies, obscures, may give false appearances. The mysterious spot. Gray, lavendar, and sea green colors are good.

PLUTO: Tests and hides things. Objects seem newer and renewed. This is the recharging spot. Scarlet, luminous pigments do well here.

TRANSPLUTO: Makes things more practical, valuable, edible and sensual. The earthy spot. Cloth and fabrics are accented.

Planetary Lines in the Community

The planetary lines that radiate out in all directions in your home keep right on going outside the house in their respective directions. You have a center in your home, and in turn your home acts as a center for the whole community.

Obtain a large and detailed city or county map and pinpoint where you live. Then place the center of the Local Space chart transparency over that point on the map. You can also draw in the planetary lines on the map using a sextant. Once this is done, it won't take long to discover why certain areas evoke certain emotions and trigger different experiences (see Figures 13A and 13B).

The list in Table 5 (below) can help you locate important areas throughout your community.

Table 5

1. Direction of work is _____.
2. The most frequent direction other than work is _____.
3. Direction of education and/or learning is _____.
4. Library _____.
5. Exercise _____.
6. Supermarket _____.
7. Restaurants _____.
8. Relaxation, meditation _____.
9. Family members _____.
10. Bank _____.
11. Lover _____.
12. Gas station _____.
13. Injuries _____.

The line that you travel most frequently is important because you are continuously under its influence. If this line happens to be that of a planet that is strong for you, then you will benefit, because its energies will be drawn into your life. If a musician practices at a place where his or her Venus line runs, s/he will tend to be more productive. However, if a construction foreman has his Venus line running through the job site, he may find that his workers tend to procrastinate, which causes delays. It all depends on the nature of the activity and how the attributes of the planetary lines work for or against you.

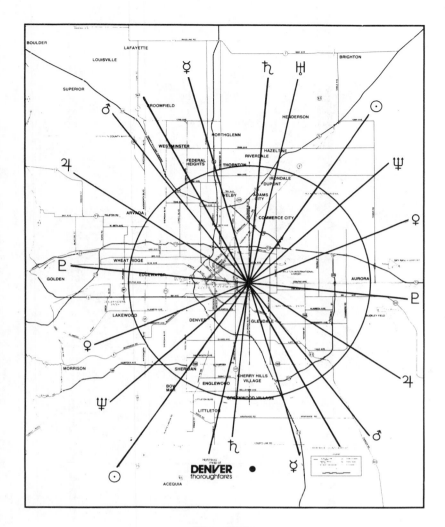

Fig. 13A

Planetary lines radiate throughout a metropolitan area.

The line that you travel on most often is not necessarily the most powerful influence. If any planet is within three degrees of the cardinal directions or five degrees above or below the horizon (altitude), it will be strongly felt. When either is less than two degrees, they can become a dominant influence (more on this later).

A woman I know must travel on her Neptune line 90% of the time. She lives in the southwestern part of town and her Local Space

49

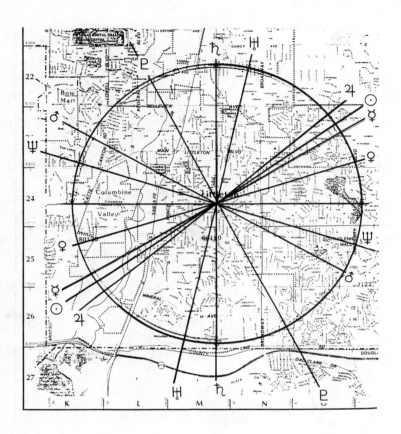

Fig. 13B
Planetary lines on a city map.

Neptune is northeast. If she wants to get anywhere in town she must travel northeast. This same person also has Jupiter within a degree of due west (Local Space Seventh House), so even though she gets disoriented and confused from the Neptune line, it never causes any serious problems because of her dominant Jupiter. A civil engineer working on a high-rise had his Mars/Saturn line pointing toward his quarrelsome boss. When he changed departments, the same boss was on his Jupiter line and the situation calmed down considerably.

The line that runs from your home to where you work often describes the type of work you do, or it may reflect your attitude about your work. It is an important line not only because it has to do with how you support yourself, but also because you travel on it frequently. If there is no line within a mile of the work location, it could mean that you have more freedom. It may also indicate that your job has no great meaning in your life at this time.

The other lines and locations are important depending upon various life situations. The line closest to the bank has an added importance when you apply for a loan; the library when you are doing research; the lover when you seek companionship, etc.

Reminder: Be sure and look in *both* directions, using Table 1. Follow closely the lines on the chart, comparing them (in azimuth) to your city or county map. The relative strength or weakness of the planets in your birth and Local Space chart will strongly affect the planetary lines (see Figures 13A and B).

If you know that a planet causes problems for you when you travel on or near its line, does it make sense to travel in a zig-zag pattern to your destination to avoid adverse affects? The answer may be yes, because traveling different routes to a certain place can lessen the influence of a planetary line. However this solution is only a temporary one, because you are still going from point A to point B, and point B will always be in the same direction from A, unless you move. So you can lessen the effects, but not altogether stop them, as long as the direction remains the same. The other option besides moving is to no longer go to place B, which could be easy unless it happens to be where you work. Remember planetary directions stay the same no matter where you are in your home or community. If Mars is due east and Jupiter is due north, then *every time* you travel in an easterly direction, you are on your Mars line, just as you are on your Jupiter line when you travel in a northerly direction.

It has been my experience that if you change your residence within your community, your whole orientation can change along with it. If, for example, you were living on the west side of town and you moved to the south side, your Local Space chart would stay the same. However, you would be traveling on different lines. Your starting point would now be in the southern area. Going to various places would require traveling predominantly north. In the beginning you would probably frequent many of the same places that you did while living at the previous location, but after a while there would be a

Table 6

Planetary Lines in the Community

SUN: Along this line you are apt to be self-contained, positive and consistent. A great sense of self-identity can develop. You are certainly more in touch with your inner power, so you can lead and/or express your individual creativity easily. It is not wrong to feel proud and important along this line, since you do in fact have a slight edge over others because of your increased willfulness.

Driving Tips: Very few auto problems encountered. Don't hog the left passing lane. If travel is to the east or south, situations are improved; to the west or north, influences are mildly weakened.

MOON: This particular pathway usually makes one aware of internal and external rhythms. Memories rapidly pass through your mind and you may be able to grasp subtle messages displayed in nature. It is common to be passive, moody, receptive. Experiences seem to evoke marked emotional responses.

Driving Tips: Chance of running out of gas. Fuel pump problems and flat tires are possible. Difficulties may arise from not driving defensively, or driving over-defensively. Movement to the north or west is best; the south or east is not as good.

MERCURY: Following this route will definitely enhance mental and communicative potential. It may be advantageous to car pool, for the added purpose of having someone to talk to. Keep a note pad handy to write down ideas at the red lights. You may prefer listening to talk radio and/or book cassettes.

Driving Tips: Use the turn signals and be aware of forks in the road. South and east are the best directions; north and west are somewhat weaker.

VENUS: On this path you become more attuned to that which brings pleasure. Art, music and all things of beauty seem to stand out. Since your need to socialize is accented, doing things with others can be rewarding. It is generally a peaceful and often relaxing line, however problems can arise when you allow indulgence and procrastination to take hold.

Driving Tips: Generally only minor problems, but avoid sightseeing when you are at the wheel. East and south directions are favorable; north and west are only slightly different.

MARS: Along this line you feel assertive; at times even combative. Direct involvement is stressed. If you need to get some place in a hurry, you can do it on this line, but you may be taking a chance. Remember, your car can be a weapon.

Driving Tips: Traffic tickets and accidents may be common, and car problems seem to be prevalent here. Buckle up! South is best; north the worst, and east and west variable.

JUPITER: This is most certainly a route in which you get a lot out of life. Activities are enjoyable because you feel relaxed and safe. Under these conditions it is very conducive to expand your horizons. This can be done in a variety of ways, and two of the most enjoyable are through recreational and educational activities.

Driving Tips: Since you rarely feel tense on this line driving is usually uneventful, although breaking technicalities of the law is a possibility. All directions have about the same influence.

SATURN: Quite naturally it will take you longer to get where you are going on this route. Situations demand that you think and act pragmatically. There is a tendency to think about matters in a serious vein, often causing worry and frustration.

Driving Tips: Physical as well as psychological obstacles are in your way. Be prepared for delays and detours. Car problems may be numerous. Watch out for detours on the road. The south can help matters; the other directions may have little effect one way or the other.

URANUS: Events occur suddenly around you and to you along this path. The element of the unexpected is ever present, sometimes adding excitement, and at other times causing irritation and upset. On the other hand you could get some of your best original ideas on this route.

Driving Tips: This is an out-of-the-ordinary sector. Accidents are likely. All electrical areas of the car are apt to cause problems. Often it's the battery, spark plugs, or ignition. Any little odd driving habits may be magnified. Be alert when it is windy. South and east are best. North and west may be more problematic.

NEPTUNE: On this line your imagination and fantasy life are activated, which can lead to inspiring small journeys and also to some confusing jaunts. Although you can get away from it all on this line, unclear appearances and false expectations are still present. Intake of drugs or alcohol can be deadly.

Driving Tips: Make sure you get understandable directions to new locations. When possible avoid driving in the rain or snow. To be on the safe side, keep things off the seats and lock your car, because thievery may be likely in this area. The radiator, fuel pump, and condensation on the points could be some of the more common car problems. For most people the northerly directions will be the most difficult. Influences of the other directions vary greatly from one individual to the next.

PLUTO: On this line you tend to waver a great deal. You feel that you are an integral part of the masses, or on other occasions you can feel distinctly removed from everyone. Although you discover things about yourself here that you never knew, it is still a somewhat compulsive and demanding pathway. For some people there is a certain amount of mystery and intrigue along this direction.

Driving Tips: This is certainly the place where a heavy foot and rude habits need to be controlled. Mechanical problems, when they do happen, can be major. Driving at night may prove hazardous. Directions have a wide variance from person to person.

TRANSPLUTO: This route predisposes you to think about your everyday concerns. Practical and financial matters take precedence. You may often frequent fast-food drive-ins.

Driving Tips: Overly conservative driving habits can cause problems on this route. You may have a fine car, but questions of comfort often arise. It seems that north is the best direction, with east being the least favorable.

Nodes: The nodes simply allow you to make contacts, form alliances with others. They are strongly influenced by close planetary aspects to them.

---

change. Let's say Neptune and Saturn were in an easterly direction at the old address, which meant that you had to travel on those lines most of the time. Traveling on Saturn and Neptune lines is not a pleasant experience for most (but not all) people. In the same Local Space chart, Jupiter and Venus are in the northerly direction. Since the home is now in the southern part of town, you would probably travel more extensively on the Jupiter and Venus lines, i.e. from south to north. The Jupiter and Venus lines would then become more influential. The Saturn/Neptune influence would change to a Jupiter/Venus one because of your new location. In most cases this would indicate an improvement in employment, income and social conditions. Even if you went to the same bank, restaurants, and friends' homes, your attitude would be different, because you would be traveling on new planetary lines.

There are three other ways in which the planets on the horizon have an influence.

Solstice and Equinox Azimuth Degrees

When the astronomy of ancient civilizations is examined, it is seen that there are four recurring observations used by nearly every culture that watched the sky. The astronomer/astrologer priests kept a record of these important dates—the spring and fall equinoxes and the summer and winter solstices. It didn't seem to matter how complex or simple their astro-mathematical model was, because these dates always played a very significant role in the culturally based cosmology.

In the Tropical/Seasonal Zodiac it is known that each of these points coincides with 0 degrees of the cardinal signs (Aries, Cancer, Libra, Capricorn). The seasons on Earth are measured by these four important points. Because of the 23.5° tilt of Earth's axis, and the orbit of the Earth around the Sun, the Sun's position with respect to the equator (declination) has four critical points throughout the year. At the times of the spring and fall equinoxes (Aries and Libra), the Sun is at the equator. Its declination is moving northward at the spring equinox and southward at the fall equinox. The Sun's position at the equator makes the distance from the poles about equal, hence the word equinox.

The Sun's equivalent position at these times coincides with azimuth observations, which are almost the same for all latitudes north and south. The Sun will rise very near due east on the mornings of the spring and fall equinoxes. The relative uniformity of these events indicates that the cardinal directions of east and west are crucial in astrological and geomantic practices.

The renewed heat of the Sun at the spring equinox indicates a time of new beginnings, a time when each person begins to reach out and communicate. New cleaning, planting and construction were the most common outlets for this Arian fire-of-action. This fire is fed by the Air element, which was also strong at this time. Air and the direction east and the Local Space Seventh House dominate in the springtime. Partnerships are renewed and new bonds are forged through sharing.

When the Sun enters Libra at the fall equinox, the harvest is well underway; not only a harvest in the fields but also a harvest of human ideas. Nature is about to rest and there is a turning inward. Each individual must face the transformation of autumn alone. The emotional Water element and the Local Space First House are activated at this time. (The difference in east and west is explained in Chapter 3.)

Solstice means "to stand still," and that is exactly what the Sun appears to do at the solstices. Because the Sun's declination is either to the extreme north or extreme south at these times, we do not have an equivalent situation. Each latitude north and south will be different (see Table 7).

In order to determine the azimuth of the Sun at these times it is necessary to calculate the chart for the exact sunrise closest to 00 degrees of Capricorn or Cancer, i.e. the winter and summer solstices, respectively.

If you observe the summer solstice sunrise at latitude 25 N 00 and someone else is observing it at 45 N 00 there would be a difference of about 8.5 degrees of azimuth. These particular degrees of azimuth at the solstice have a powerful influence on other planets that are within three degrees of conjunction or opposition (see Table 7).

The Sun's stationary position was a sacred time for the ancients, a time filled with power and mystery. The two solstices work differently, since they occur at different times of the year (they are, of course, reversed in the Southern Hemisphere).

The summer solstice and the beginning of the sign Cancer are looked upon as a time of growth and abundance. The fields are filled with growing crops and game is plentiful. This abundance is also signified by the fullness of emotional expression, warm feelings and direct actions. This time corresponds to the long days of the solar fire, and the direction south. This direction is the Local Space Tenth House, the house of one's profession and position. It is a time to fulfill one's destiny. Planets within three degrees of the summer solstice azimuth will be more productive in terms of allowing things to move toward their fullest potential. These planets will also act as guardians of inner visions. They will play some part in your quest for self-realization. The emotions evoked can either help or hinder affairs suggested by this solstice point.

The winter solstice is a time of sacrifice and austerity. In this quiet and calm time of less sunlight, you can organize your thoughts, and find answers. There is more darkness than light (in the Northern Hemisphere) for only three days out of the year, and those days are December 22nd, 23rd and 24th. On the 25th, light conquers darkness and the Sun (Son of) God is reborn. At this time, a silent birth also takes place, and a new year begins. This is also the Local Space Fourth House. You stay in your home so that you can better realize your internal world. The earthy stability of Capricorn can overcome the mysterious and oppressive forces of the north. Planets located within three degrees of the winter solstice azimuth point will tend to be foundation builders, bringing powerful learning experiences of maturity and stability. Correct timing is both a friend and foe at this solstice.

The following table will help you find the solstice degrees in your Local Space chart. Use the latitude of your present location or any other latitude you wish to check; use south latitude for the Southern Hemisphere. The fall and spring equinox points are very close to due east/west, so a table for them is unnecessary.

Table 7

Summer Solstice:

    25 N 00 — Azimuth is approximately 64/244.
    30 N 00 — Azimuth is approximately 61/241.
    35 N 00 — Azimuth is approximately 62/242.
    40 N 00 — Azimuth is approximately 59/239.
    45 N 00 — Azimuth is approximately 57/237.

Winter Solstice:

    25 N 00 — Azimuth is approximately 116/295.
    30 N 00 — Azimuth is approximately 117/297.
    35 N 00 — Azimuth is approximately 118/298.
    40 N 00 — Azimuth is approximately 121/301.
    45 N 00 — Azimuth is approximately 123/303.

Due north is 0 degrees azimuth.

Magnetic Declination

It has been shown that the cardinal directions of east and west are given added importance because of the Sun's position (sunrise) at the spring and fall equinoxes, and an even greater importance at the solstices.

What about the north-south axis? What contributes to its energy and importance? One answer is found by studying the influence of the magnetic pole, which is a deviation from true north.[1] This deviation is called magnetic declination and it almost always differs from true north/south. In the United States, it ranges from 23 degrees east of north to 23 degrees west of north.[2] (See Figures 11A-E.)

The north-south magnetic pull is one way in which the Ch'i flow can be detected. Feng Shui geomancy has four major rings or plates that concern themselves with Ch'i.* The Earth ring which has the correct cardinal directions is used to determine the general direction or path of the Ch'i. The two Heaven Rings measure the worth of the Ch'i, how vital/rich or torpid/poor it may be. The Man Ring shows how the flow affects man during a twelve-fold cycle: from conception to burial.

---

*—In the traditional Feng Shui geomantic circle there is a minimum 16 rings, but it can have as many as 38 rings. Each ring has its specific purpose just like the cross-cultural information contained in the Local Space geomantic circle.

The Heaven Rings are measured in accordance with magnetic declination. Therefore any planet within three degrees of the magnetic north-south line will take on a greater significance, because it will pick up the magnetic charge.

Look at your Local Space chart and see if any of the planets are in the Third, Fourth, Ninth or Tenth Houses (which could put them near the degree of magnetic north of your locality), using a 3-degree orb. The basic nature of the planet will describe the grade or worth of the Ch'i flowing into your life. If this planet has been helpful in the past, then so will the Ch'i. If it is a planet that tends to cause problems, then the worth of the Ch'i is diminished. So you can have good or bad Jupiter Ch'i, good or bad Saturn, Pluto or Venus Ch'i, etc.

Altitude of the Local Space Horizon Planets

Another important position in the Local Space chart is the planet that is closest to the horizon. Secondary is the planet with the highest altitude or elevation. Although all the planets are measured in azimuth on the plane of the horizon, each one is at a different altitude in the sky. (Remember the cardinal directions are on the assumed flat plane of the horizon around you, and altitude is measured above and below this flat plane.) Directly above is the zenith, directly below is the nadir; the altitude is 0 to 90 degrees above or below the horizon and a + (plus) or - (minus) is used to indicate it.

The planet that is the lowest or closest to the horizon is thought to be most significant. Any planet + or - 7 degrees can have a very strong effect on that locality. Often (but not always) the very same planet(s) will conjunct the Vertex/west or Anti-Vertex/east. In equatorial regions all planets are close to the horizon, so the effects are insignificant. However, when you shift the planets to the Campanus/Prime Vertical system they no longer remain bunched, but are dispersed along the Great Circle which connects the zenith and nadir directly above and below. (See Chapter 3 for more details on how to use the prime vertical in equatorial regions, i.e. between 30 degrees north and south latitude.)

Planets with an altitude above or below sixty degrees are also important, but they seem to be a distant second in importance to those close to the horizon. (There is a similar correspondence in natal astrology, where a planet close to the Tenth and Fourth House cusps is considered descriptive of your inner nature and objectives. However, natal Tenth and Fourth Houses are *not* the same as the zenith and nadir. The zenith is directly above and the nadir is directly below, whereas the Tenth and Fourth cusps are due south and due north, respectively.)

In any locality the extreme altitudes of a planet, i.e. 60 degrees above or below, is significant. A planet above the horizon (+) helps describe your goals and outward activities. The planet that is the lowest (-) will be descriptive of your inner or unconscious process and development.

Whatever its altitude, a planet will tend to be located toward one of the cardinal directions. For example, if a planet has a low altitude and is generally in an easterly direction, then the descriptions in Chapters 3 and 4 can be used. If a planet happens to be in between two cardinal directions, e.g. southwest, then there will be a blend of the influences of both south and west. Referring to Tables 10, 12 and 13 will prove helpful.

In summary the most important positions in the Local Space chart for any locality are:

1. The influence of planets closest to any of the four cardinal directions is felt at 5 degrees of orb, but it is generally not a major influence until it is less than 2 degrees of orb. Include conjunctions to the standard Ascendant/Descendant. (This is covered in Chapters 3 and 4.)

2. The influence of planets with the lowest altitude (closest to the horizon) begins at 7 degrees and becomes increasingly stronger as the orb decreases.

3. Planets in close conjunction or opposition in the Local Space chart, under 3 degrees of orb, especially those that closely aspect the Local Space positions at the birthplace.

4. The planetary line you travel on most frequently in your community. Usually less than 1 mile orb or two degrees of orb.

5. Other close aspects (less than 2 degrees in the Local Space chart).

6. Planets near the solstice (3 degrees orb).

7. Planets near magnetic north or south (3 degrees orb).

8. The planets that have the extreme altitudes, e.g. 60 degrees above or below the horizon. The planet that is highest followed by the

planet that is the lowest will have a mild influence. Experiment with Figures 10 and 13, and Table 8.

9. Don't forget to compare your planetary positions with the geodetic Ascendant and Midheaven (this is explained in Chapter 7).

10. Please see pp. 154-155 for another summary of locality guidelines.

Notes

1. Newitt, Larry, "The Magnetic Pole on the Move Again." *The Denver Post*, Denver, CO, December, 1984.
2. "Values of Magnetic Declination," prepared by the National Geophysical Data Center, Boulder, CO, December 12, 1982.

CHAPTER 3

RELOCATION AND
LONG DISTANCE TRAVEL

When people travel across the planet or settle down in a new locality, they immediately begin to take notice of different physical and psychological changes. For some individuals, definite unconscious and spiritual changes occur as well.

When people talk about a new environment, they tend to explain the new events in terms of their own emotional responses. The major reasons for relocation, such as marriage, divorce, college and military service, are often de-emphasized because relocated individuals are busy dealing with the emotional impact of the new environment. Descriptions of the new location in general terms are common. Statements like "It feels good to me," "The place has good vibes," "I like the climate" or "The people seem friendly" are often used. These general, non-descriptive statements are attempts to explain all the new stimuli.

This is not to say that these are incorrect expressions. But we tend to rely too often on our first impressions and gut reactions without really knowing for certain how the new place will affect the totality of who we are. Sometimes these first reactions are correct, but there comes a point when initial expectations must give way to a more complete understanding of the situation.

It is true that no matter how far you travel from the birthplace you still carry an original imprint of that location (with the aspects between planets remaining the same). The important point is that you can modify your birth chart to some extent by changing where you live! Therefore the actual planetary influences at work, when properly understood, can give you a unique opportunity to develop plans and maximize your potential more directly, often in a short period of time.

When you change where you live, the physical surroundings will change. More importantly, however, your subjective interpretations also change. You begin to perceive the new place in accordance with the new planetary emphasis for that location. The longer you stay in a particular location, the more dominant this planetary influence will become.

If you never move from your birth location, it is necessary to make the best of the situation through a greater understanding of the Local Space planetary lines. In many Third World countries and countries where relocation is restricted, people don't have the advantage of changing the angles of the chart.

In the final analysis, any location is what you make of it. By overcoming difficult problems and drawing out the potential around you, it is possible to maximize your growth and happiness. We all know of some people who are miserable despite their beautiful and prosperous surroundings, while other individuals can be productive and happy in some of the most depressing and chaotic locations.

Each individual's Local Space lines start at the center of the home, then pass through the home and radiate out into the community. They don't stop there, but keep right on going across the surface of the Earth. (On a physical level they start in the human body at the tip of the sternum. More on this in Chapter 5.)

Because these lines are traveling on the round surface of the Earth, they form a curving wave motion. A planetary line when projected due west will begin to bend southward until it has covered about six thousand miles. Then it will begin to swing northward again. The planetary lines only *appear* to travel in straight lines in your home or community. In fact, they are slowly curving northward or southward. This bending effect becomes noticeable after about 50 miles. Because of this phenomenon, plotting with a graphic display program was developed (see Figures 14A, B and C). At the end of this book, there are instructions on how to use these programs as well as information

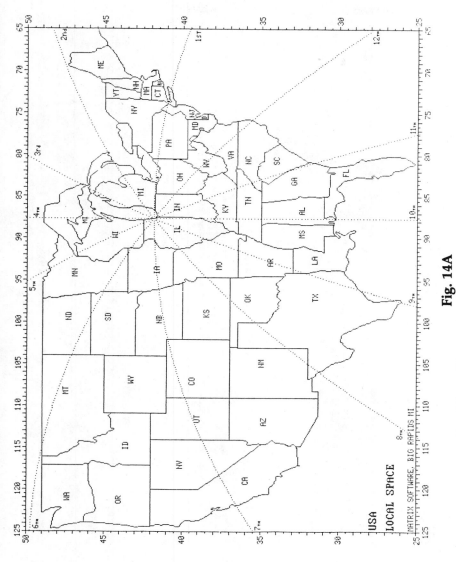

Fig. 14A

Local Space Houses are plotted from a central location.

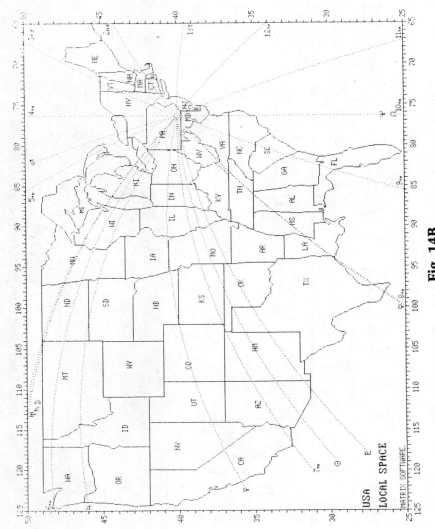

Fig. 14B

*Planetary lines and Local Space houses radiate outward
from any given location.*

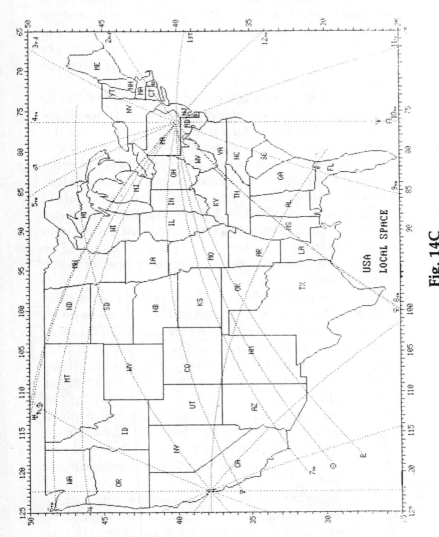

Fig. 14C

Planetary lines intersect when projected from two locations.

on where to order a copy of your Local Space chart and/or graphic map, including the Astro*Carto*Graphy® map.

In my initial survey of friends and clients, one of the questions I asked was about important relocations in their lives. In almost 100% of the cases, the movement from one location to another followed the direction of a certain planetary line(s), i.e., the direction of travel and certain planetary line(s) matched. Keep in mind that the planetary line goes in two directions—the azimuth of where it originates and towards the opposite azimuth or direction.

It was discovered that the line(s) traveled on seemed to describe an *overriding need* present at the time of travel and/or relocation. If, for example, your major reason for moving is to attend college, then it is likely that the best line for you to travel would be that of Mercury or Jupiter. This is true unless you are actually attending college in order to find a mate or play football—then romantic Venus and active Mars, respectively, would be more descriptive. What if your life is one in which your energies have been scattered due to excesses and overindulgence? Your need would then be to gain greater control over your life, and to become more responsible and organized. Traveling on your Saturn line to a new and temporary or long-term location would be a possible way to achieve this.

If you can isolate your true life needs before relocating, then by comparing them with the appropriate planetary lines, it may be possible to know in advance in what direction you are going! On the other hand, if you are already in a new location, the knowledge of what planetary line you traveled on can prove very helpful in clarifying what situations caused the move, along with added objectivity in assessing present goals.

Keep in mind that when you travel on a planetary line, it means that city A is connected to city B by this line. No matter how you get from city A to city B you are still in effect traveling on that particular line, because the cities are both connected by this direction in azimuth (see Figures 14A, B and C).

What if you feel that your needs are expansion, growth, success, etc., and you wish to travel on your Jupiter line, but don't know where? If your present location is Boston and the Jupiter line is on the east/west axis, then you would know that you must travel east or west. Suppose you decided to travel west. Looking at the Local Space graphic display, you observe this line going through Indianapolis, St. Louis, Santa Fe and on to Los Angeles. How would you know your destination? The standard method would be to check a series of relocation charts for various points west. (Although the standard relocational methods are valid, the number of choices can confuse matters.) Thanks to the Astro*Carto*Graphy® and Local Space maps you will be able to see what aspects there are to your angles, i.e. the I.C., M.C., rise/set, Ascendant/Descendant, or Vertex. Neither method is 100% accurate, due to birth time errors. When *both* are used together you can improve your chances of pinpointing a beneficial geographical location. (For more details on these and other methods, see Chapter 6.)

The descriptions in Table 8 can be helpful in clarifying needs and to show what you can expect generally when traveling to relocate or on vacation on various planetary lines. (Traveling on these lines in the home and community was covered in Chapter 2.) Keep in mind that the prominent planets in the Local Space chart for a particular locality, i.e. planets conjuncting the Imum Coeli, Medium Coeli, Vertex, Ascendent, etc., basically determine the influences for any location.

Choose the planetary line that is closest to your destination. If it is more than 200 miles (and/or more than 8 degrees of azimuth) from this selected location, it should not be used.

Table 8

Travel and Relocation on Planetary Lines

MOON: Moving along this line will certainly involve your basic emotional drives in a variety of ways. Home, land, parental and domestic security needs generally seem to be pronounced. The Moon very often takes on the qualities of the sign and aspects it has in the birth chart. Close aspects from planets in the Local Space chart are very important. Therefore with the Moon you will most likely feel a mixed influence. Awareness of your intuitive feelings and receiving guidance from the natural environment can occur on this line. Past emotional conditioning is the key to understanding how this line will manifest. Your general need is to feel more emotionally secure so you can grow on different levels.

SUN: This line has to do with your basic selfhood and sense of individualism. A contained, positive and consistent way of life can be realized by relocating on this line. The Sun line seems to add importance to any other line it is connected with, personalizing the other planet. Individualism is the key to understanding this line. Your need is to get in touch with your essential self-identity; then you'll be able to know what is important and what isn't.

MERCURY: Mercury is similar to the Moon, taking on the qualities of the sign it is in and its close aspects in the birth and Local Space charts. The major difference is that the other planets take on a mental quality rather than an emotional coloring, which happens with the Moon. The Mercury line always involves the intellect in some way; it also can pertain to professional skills. Educational and business travel may be other reasons for following this pathway. Learning is the key to understanding this line. Thinking, learning and teaching needs are developed through the sharing of ideas; thus, on this line you find deeper meaning in life, which can lead to self-knowledge.

VENUS: Naturally with the planet Venus, affairs of the heart will somehow be involved. You may want to move to improve your social situation, to search for a lasting partnership, to bring more beauty into your life or to express a talent. Keeping your desires in balance is the key to understanding this line. The need may be to reduce stressful conditions so that you can realize inner harmony.

MARS: Assertiveness, boldness and courage are needed to move forward and begin some purposeful activity. In some cases impulsiveness and acting prematurely can place you in dangerous situations. An energetic push is the key to understanding this line. Only through definite action are you able to attain your goals.

JUPITER: Following the direction of this line in most cases improves your situation regardless of what your need and/or problem may be. Movement along this line usually means that health, wealth and social improvement is in the offing. Expansion, not excessiveness, is the key to this line. The need is to step into the arena of success so that a lasting happiness will take place.

SATURN: When more self-control, organization and responsibility are needed in your life, Saturn will point the way. Relocating along this line means that you may experience some hardship or delay. At the same time, sober and realistic experiences will bring solid development and maturity. Concentration is the key to understanding this line. You need to make a serious commitment to self-development.

URANUS: Suddenly breaking away to start a new adventure is common with this line. Certain rigid and restricting circumstances periodically need to be altered, and if you are traveling along your Uranus line, something will always get changed. While change can certainly be unsettling, at the same time you may look forward to greater independence. Freedom is the key to understanding this line. Your need is to start something new, so that you may perceive the world in a new way.

NEPTUNE: You need to be reminded that there is more to life than what meets the eye. Why else would you search out the mystical and mysterious unless somehow, in some strange way, you could be made aware of different realities? Even though this line can be confusing and deceptive at first, it often allows for an inner awakening to take place. Refinement is the key to understanding this line. Your need is to attune to your inner life where true inspiration and unselfishness dwell.

PLUTO: Power, force and pressure. . . too much of it or too little in your present situation can cause you to follow your Pluto line to a new location. Definite objectives drive you forward. Depth perception is the key to understanding this line. Escaping from pressure and/or being pushed to the limit can cause transformation.

TRANSPLUTO: This planetary line indicates that there are very set and determined behaviors and motivations. This is a down-to-earth movement and one where emotional and/or financial factors play an important role. Steadfast persistence is the key to understanding this line. Your need is for pragmatic stabilization.

THE NODES: This line indicates that there is some connection, or association between locations. The connection can be a telephone "WATS" line, a branch office, a relative or even the direction your dream (astral) body can travel at night. The Node, even more than the Moon and Mercury, takes on the qualities of any planet that is close to it in the Local Space and birth charts.

When two planets are within 5 degrees of one another, i.e., in conjunction or opposition, the *overriding need* will be a blend of both planets. Certain qualities of each planet will remain, but new meanings will also develop. The following descriptions should prove helpful. This table can also be used for travel in the community, and for other close aspects between planets. (This table borrows heavily from R. Ebertin's *Combination of Stellar Influences*).

Table 9

Two-Planet Combinations

Sun/Moon: Very personal and important undertakings.
Sun/Mercury: Personal thinking; involved, creative ideas.
Sun/Venus: Personal and physical love/attractions.
Sun/Mars: Personal effort and leadership.
Sun/Jupiter: Personal creative advancement and success.
Sun/Saturn: Personal hindrance and/or concentration.
Sun/Uranus: Personal progressive reforms and/or rebellion.
Sun/Neptune: Personal deceptions, also imagination/mysticism.
Sun/Pluto: Personal objectives, force, egotism.
Sun/Nodes: Important male or authority contacts.

Moon/Mercury: Thoughts with feeling, emotional thinking.
Moon/Venus: Affection, tenderness, joy.
Moon/Mars: Frank, forceful, emotional actions and beginnings.
Moon/Jupiter: Happiness and generosity.
Moon/Saturn: Duty, loneliness and control of the emotions.
Moon/Uranus: Exciting and unusual emotions.
Moon/Neptune: Introspective, subtle tendencies. Gullible.
Moon/Pluto: Deep feeling and emotional extremes.
Moon/Nodes: Important spiritual (female) contacts.

Mercury/Venus: Balanced, funny, harmonious thinking.
Mercury/Mars: Very active (rash) thinking.
Mercury/Jupiter: Positive ideas and learning.
Mercury/Saturn: Problem solving, serious thinking.
Mercury/Uranus: Nervous, quick (technical?) thinking.
Mercury/Neptune: Intuitive and/or unclear thinking.
Mercury/Pluto: Mental challenges, overbearing thinking.
Mercury/Nodes: Mental and/or younger contacts.

Venus/Mars: Creativity, passion.
Venus/Jupiter: Sociable, enjoyable, wealthy qualities, overindulgence.
Venus/Saturn: Reserved, setting limits, dutiful.
Venus/Uranus: Social upsets, sudden attractions and desires.
Venus/Neptune: Romance, dreams and illusions.
Venus/Pluto: Strong sexual and artistic expressions.
Venus/Nodes: Pleasant, comfortable contacts.

Mars/Jupiter: Ambitious, enterprising, courageous, impulsive.
Mars/Saturn: Determination to overcome obstacles, anger.
Mars/Uranus: Stressful, hurried efforts.
Mars/Neptune: Inspired actions, exploitation, irritability.
Mars/Pluto: Confidence, force and compulsion.
Mars/Nodes: Energetic or physical contacts.

Jupiter/Saturn Economic considerations, slow/stable progress.
Jupiter/Uranus: Optimism, fortunate ideas.
Jupiter/Neptune: Speculation, imagination, idealism.
Jupiter/Pluto: Organization, leadership.
Jupiter/Nodes: Successful efforts.

Saturn/Uranus: Separation, tensions, toughness.
Saturn/Neptune: Sacrifices, limitations, discipline.
Saturn/Pluto: Challenging work and research, cruelty.
Saturn/Nodes: Depressive contacts, separation from others.

Uranus/Neptune: Unusual inclinations, very different ideas.
Uranus/Pluto: Transformation and a totally new start.
Uranus/Nodes: Sudden contacts, a new network of friends.

Neptune/Pluto: The unknown, presentiments.
Neptune/Nodes: Strange contacts.

Pluto/Nodes: Fateful and powerful contacts.

There is no fast and simple way of understanding all the possible combinations of planetary lines. The best advice is to use the basic attributes of the planets outlined in Table 8, regardless of the number of planets that are bunched together. Then use Table 9 to further understand the planetary combinations.

Planets on the Local Space Angles

The Local Space chart for your present locality or any locality you may visit (or speculate about visiting) is liable to have one or more planets close to the major directions (i.e., north/Imum Coeli, south/Medium Coeli, west/Vertex or east/Anti-Vertex), either in azimuth or altitude or both. Any planet within three degrees of a cardinal direction will have the predominating influence in that particular locality.

Two of these cardinal directions are the equivalent of the standard birth/natal angles. In the Northern Hemisphere, due south is the same as the Medium Coeli/Tenth House cusp, and due north is the same as the Imum Coeli/Fourth House cusp. The Ascendant is in an easterly direction but not usually due east, as is the Anti-Vertex. Likewise, the Descendant is usually in a westerly direction, but rarely due west as is the Vertex.

Even though it is rare that the Ascendant and Anti-Vertex are in the same place, a planet can set off both. Any planetary body when conjunct or opposite the Ascendant also triggers and/or includes the Vertex. Likewise, when the Vertex or Anti-Vertex is aspected (conjunction and opposition only), it may trigger and/or include the Ascendant/Descendant. The horizon and ecliptic are intimately related to each other, so they always work inclusively rather than exclusively (see Chapter 6).

When the Ascendant/Descendant is receiving the aspect, the effects are likely to be more subjective and psychological; dealing with your *attitude,* outlook and personality inclinations. When the Vertex/Anti-Vertex is aspected, the influence may be more objective and *event*-oriented. The Vertex is a highly localized point; in a sense it is right in front of you, ripe and ready to manifest. (For a more concise geomantic/symbolic meaning, see Chapter 5.) Both angles *must* be used to get a complete picture. Therefore the Astro*Carto*Graphy® method of Jim Lewis and the Local Space methods work together (see Chapters 4 and 6).

When you are looking at your Local Space chart, the houses appear in reverse order from the standard horoscope (refer to Figure 2). The four sectors or houses that are most important in the Local Space chart are the Fourth/north, First/west, Tenth/south and Seventh/east. The planets occupying different houses will have various meanings similar to the standard interpretations of planets in Houses—similar because at this point there just isn't enough information on how the planets in Local Space Houses may differ from the standard. See the end of this chapter and Table 11.

The accepted practice of "the closer the orb, the stronger the influence" applies. If you have Jupiter 1 degree from the north and Saturn 4 degrees from the east, then Jupiter would be the predominating influence. This is not to say that you would not feel the influence of Saturn, but that it would not be as significant as that of Jupiter.

The closer your present location is to the equator, the more the planets will tend to cluster either east or west. Two and even three and four planets can be very close together, producing some complex effects. Therefore it is suggested that the Prime Vertical/Campanis chart should be used for equatorial latitudes. Aspects and interpretations are the same, but keep in mind that you are dealing with a circle that goes east to west, above and below you, connecting the zenith and nadir. The Fourth/zenith, First/west, Tenth/nadir and Seventh/east are the positions of the angles.

The following descriptions are to be used for planets conjunct the Ascendant or Anti-Vertex, Descendant or Vertex, Imum Coeli/north or zenith and Medium Coeli/south or nadir. Specific descriptions relating to planets on the Local Space geomantic compass are in Chapter 4, and Figures 8 and 9. I strongly suggest the reader use *both* when reading about a particular planetary line. See Figure 15 and Tables 12 and 13.

Table 10

Interpretations of Planets on the Angles

SUN ♂ Ascendant/Anti-Vertex

Because the Sun rises in the east, you realize that there is a special strength in this location. You can easily take on an attitude of confidence and determination. Your will is strong and therefore you are able to deal authoritatively with life's problems. Your health can improve and this vitality effects your way of meeting life. Some vanity and arrogance may creep in, but you are able to deal with it in a positive way. If there's a battle to be fought, you have a good chance of winning.

SUN ♂ Medium Coeli/Tenth House

This placement suggests that your leadership and influence can crown you "king of the mountain." You will find it easy to achieve your ambitions. Certain over-estimation of self can occur, but your creativity and will can certainly make things happen in this locality.

SUN ♂ Descendant/Vertex

The ability to share your sense of individuality with others can cause positive social interaction. A very candid type of cooperation can develop. The strength of stable relationships will go a long way in overcoming all types of people problems.

SUN ♂ Imum Coeli/Fourth House

Here the healing light of the Sun enters your home and can make your personal life glow. Self-contained enthusiasm can guide you toward an objective understanding of your basic needs. Family life becomes playful and a creative source of joy.

MOON ♂ Ascendant/Anti-Vertex

In this area your natural instincts take over, allowing you to encounter life in a sensitive and receptive manner. On the surface your moods and psychic perceptions change quickly. This may seem inconsistent, but in fact it is this changeable quality that helps you to remain flexible. When you feel confronted by conflicting forces, you will be able to use your sensitivity to adapt to or avoid situations *before* they happen. Adopt a "wait and see" attitude.

MOON ♂ Medium Coeli/Tenth House

Here spiritual ties and deep aspirations guide you toward your goals. A dedication to public life can develop, yet outer achievements are seen as symbols of internal growth. Your reputation and career can easily fluctuate, indicating that you should look within as a way of dealing with external uncertainties. Empathy and supportiveness are constant themes.

MOON ♂ Descendant/Vertex

Strong emotion and sympathy through involvement with others is common in this locality. Yet being pulled into others' lives can cause problems. They may seek you out for protection and emotional support, yet in time, you may find that you are the one who needs protection from them. In spite of all this, you feel drawn toward others; thus relationships become an abundance of giving and receiving.

MOON ♂ Imum Coeli/Fourth House

Home and family life are paramount in this place, and your roots tend to run deep. You may find yourself becoming very protective, maternal, even clannish. You may find it easy to hide in your own private little shell because your home is a source of such rich feeling and productive activity. If you get too wrapped up in domestic matters, however, it may lead to child-like indulgences, worry and insecurity. Responsiveness to natural forces can lead you to an understanding of personal life cycles.

MERCURY ♂ Ascendant/Anti-Vertex

Life may become a maze of "data in, data out." Knowledge is catalogued and pieces of the puzzle are found. Internal reasoning may improve your learning ability. Sometimes you find yourself tangled up in restless and worrisome dilemmas. This locality offers you the resources to learn and express your professional skills.

MERCURY ♂ Medium Coeli/Tenth House

Here is where your particular brand of knowledge goes to work for you. Communication of your skills and an understanding of your mental framework entitles you to a new type of professionalism. What you write and say may cause others to think along different lines. All kinds of knowledge flow toward you, so you can't help being more versatile. The only problem encountered here seems to be acquiring a "head trip" (being overly intellectual), which could make you unresponsive to the emotional and subtle feeling parts of your life.

MERCURY ♂ Descendant/Vertex

A lively exchange of ideas occurs in this spot. Verbal contacts, agreements and negotiations seem to be an ongoing affair. Learning reaches its peak in this place, because your understanding of what others can offer is so clearly defined. You are in a learning situation no matter what the general circumstances dictate. Generous amounts of talking and communicating are accepted as part of the spirit of inquiry. In some cases you may be surrounded by young and/or intellectual people.

MERCURY ♂ Imum Coeli/Fourth House

In this locality a dialogue opens up between the past and the present, the inner self and the intellect. You question your natural surroundings and in turn nature instructs you. Ideas become highly personal, causing your immediate family to serve as your direct source of information. Indecisiveness can plague you because you see things from a rather introverted viewpoint.

VENUS ♂ Ascendant/Anti-Vertex

This is a place where you find the surroundings and/or the people beautiful. This locale has a relaxed and calming effect, so naturally you are more affectionate and cooperative. Your personal charm is strong, and consequently this attracts others who enjoy being around you. Some people can become "pleasure-bent" in this area because attractions abound. Keeping a balanced and harmonious outlook seems to be the proper thing to do, and by so doing you may avoid many hardships.

VENUS ♂ Medium Coeli/Tenth House

This is a place where the expression of real talent can find a profitable outlet. One reason for this is that you enjoy what you are doing. Your social network is filled with interesting people and places. You can be known for your style and grace. A fair share of popularity and wealth can come your way and along with it a certain frivolousness, which may result in too much high living. Following the dictates of your inner heart will avert major difficulties.

VENUS ♂ Descendant/Vertex

The need for a mate and/or partner is very pronounced in this locale. If you are not married but want to be (or even if you don't want to be), this is the place to live. The spirit of compromise and cooperation is such that any previous differences with partners will decrease. There seems to be a constant interaction between you and others. You expect more from all types of partnerships, so it is necessary for you to give more and put more into them.

VENUS ♂ Imum Coeli/Fourth House

In this place the family intermingles with attractive, talented and congenial people, so advantageous meetings take place fairly often. It suggests a down-to-earth lifestyle, where you enjoy the simple things of life. Affections are openly displayed, because you feel that friends and family are a priceless commodity. Depending on your basic make-up, both relaxation and practicality can flourish.

MARS ♂ Ascendant/Anti-Vertex

There is nothing indirect about your actions in this place. People may think that you are overly bold and this may be true, but you do get things done. Your physical strength and stamina are very pronounced; you have a self-reliant and assertive attitude. Therefore, this is where you meet life head-on. Your actions may get out of control to the point of causing destruction of the very things which you have fought for. Even though this place is filled with adventure, the stress and strain built around a need to fight and compete may at some point force you to leave.

MARS ♂ Medium Coeli/Tenth House

The extra effort you expend here can keep you advancing toward your goals. You may be known for your energy, enthusiasm and confidence. Although fighting for a position is easy here, you also have to learn when to be patient and wait for your efforts to pay off. People can only be pushed to their particular limits and not beyond. Knowing these limits in others as well as in yourself can prevent defiance and aggravation.

MARS ♂ Descendant/Vertex

This is a combative place with a fair share of potentially dangerous situations. (It's what you would expect to find in a chart of someone in a war zone). It can certainly bring out the worst in people you have to deal with everyday. You need to develop forthright and bold tactics when dealing with others. This seems to work because this is what they understand. . . force. After a certain period of time your argumentative confrontations with others will begin to toughen you, unless you take care, and you could become overly coarse. Then you find it necessary to relocate.

MARS ♂ Imum Coeli/Fourth House

In this locale you tend to be actively involved with family matters and domestic concerns can become a source of anger and frustration. This may manifest in family feuds or accidents in the home. The trick is to find an outlet to direct your aggressive energy. Practical and physical projects can serve as healthy outlets. You may feel a strong drive to protect and improve your personal life, but hasty actions can prevent any lasting good from developing. There may be cases where Mars will work for and not against you, but in most cases this line does not allow for a happy family life.

JUPITER ♂ Ascendant/Anti-Vertex

This location promotes the very best of what you have to offer in life, and the returns are abundant. Your capabilities are enhanced because of a healthy optimism and an attitude of expansiveness. If you can truly radiate wealth and success, then wealth and success *must* flow into your life. This is where it becomes possible to realize this. Personal growth through a broader understanding of the universe makes life under this influence truly satisfying, humorous and enlightening.

JUPITER ♂ Medium Coeli/Tenth House

Generally speaking this place offers the best of the best. You find objective goals will manifest easily. Recognition breeds achievement; conversely achievements add to your recognition. With this process going on, your income and community standing can continually reach new heights.

JUPITER ♂ Descendant/Vertex

Here you feel that you are in the right place at the right time; call it luck, fate, or good karma—what really matters is that this location stimulates success. Since everyone is dependent on everyone else, here is where that right person can walk right into your life offering needed advice, and/or money.

Good business partnerships and happy marriages can unfold. It is not so much how this happens as the fact that it does, and your life is greatly improved.

JUPITER ♂ *Imum Coeli/Fourth House*

This is a wonderful place to raise a family, build a home, explore nature and honestly live the good life. When there is peace in the home and life's basic needs are met, internal growth naturally takes place. Mother nature is kind to you here, and if you pay attention, you may become aware of many sources of hidden wealth.

SATURN ♂ *Ascendant/Anti-Vertex*

You have the potential to learn a great deal in this area; in some ways it may be seen as attending the school of hard knocks. We all learn to adjust to difficult circumstances, yet this location demands a lot, and may cause you to be more personally responsible and committed. You may perceive this Saturn influence as the opposite of a sociable, warm and friendly place, but it is where you realistically have to deal with the practical side of life. It can function as ground on which you pay your dues and then move on to put what you have learned into action. Avoid blocking your own efforts, because time is on your side in the long run. The only way to deal with what *seems* to be delay and denial is to fulfill your obligations through patience and perseverance.

SATURN ♂ *Medium Coeli/Tenth House*

This is where you feel the full weight of authority bearing down on you. It may be represented by the responsibilities of your own position or suppression from higher-ups. Your ability to endure functions well here, and you certainly can put in long hours. These factors will definitely solidify a maturation process. The drawback is that you have to act within narrow bounds of conventionality. Although you may attract some notoriety, fame or position, you still have to deal within a confining structure.

SATURN ♂ *Descendant/Vertex*

There is real irony in this area. You have to depend on others, but when you do, they seem to limit you in some way. Dependable partnerships can develop, yet most dealings with others have to be handled with the utmost diplomacy to avoid repercussions. Dealing with dull, thick-headed people can get old very quickly. If you give in to your inhibitions, it may aggravate the situation. There has to be a certain amount of acceptance on your part, when control is not in your hands. You learn humility and simplicity as a strategy for cautious involvement.

SATURN ♂ *Imum Coeli/Fourth House*

This can be an incredibly stable, yet lonely place. Harshness seems to infringe upon your home life, feeding a variety of fears. Fear is a tremendous motivator, but it isn't something that you want to deal with continually. A dutiful adherence to family matters can cause a certain degree of enslavement toward those that you love. Living in an environment filled with limitations may foster a bad attitude—a state of mind which can easily submit to pessimism and emotional melancholy. You will find that hard work and methodical planning can be a passport out of this place, or a way to endure.

The Transaturnian Influence

The transaturnian planets have a special complexity all their own. For most people they work almost entirely on an unconscious level. Because of this fact there are powerful consequences for us all, unless we somehow grasp that Uranus, Neptune and Pluto are really attempting to awaken our inner potentials. When we try and repress, divert or otherwise remain ignorant of their intentions, they seem to be the enemy, when in fact they are only different types of teachers. Life can never be normal under their influence, for normality means stagnation and non-growth. These planets, more than any of the others, reveal the degree of spiritual growth that you have attained. They are truly mirrors of your self-conscious awareness.

The Influence of Uranus

Under the Uranus influence, people with pronounced technical abilities, independent people and those who travel frequently don't seem to experience as many problems. If you are really a free thinker and progressive in any number of ways, then Uranus has less to disrupt and change. Society seems to be becoming more Uranian all the time and this process accelerates many of the upsetting and erratic qualities of Uranus, while at the same time causing you to perceive life in new ways.

Uranus in many respects is a mental planet, i.e. it deals with thoughts and ideas. Mental discipline therefore is vital in channeling the new and unexpected thoughts and ideas. All freedom exists within limitations!

URANUS ☌ Ascendant/Anti-Vertex

This locality may bring out a wild and rebellious part of your personality. You can feel very restless because you are stimulated in a variety of ways. Your personal magnetism is accented here and original ideas are quite common. Your individual freedom becomes a big issue, so it may be necessary to adopt some unconventional tactics to preserve it. There is nothing boring about this place, however too much excitement can periodically scatter your energy, leading to unstable and undependable behavior.

URANUS ♂ *Medium Coeli/Tenth House*

Instability can be experienced here due to the fact that your goals may change so rapidly. If you run your own business or function in a position with a considerable amount of autonomy, the inventive and entreprenurial side will have its needed outlet. The problem with most jobs is that they do not allow you to express individualism in a resourceful way. Many people become rebellious and indifferent in this area because of the frustrating situations they encounter with various structured livelihoods. At some point you need to make the right chances by yourself, and for yourself. Your wealth of creative ideas needs to be channeled and this could be the place to do it, even though the prospect of going it alone and the thought of financial independence is unnerving and unsettling.

URANUS ♂ *Descendant/Vertex*

This locality offers you an assortment of novel and unpredictable encounters with people. From the altruistic to the perverse, the associations you form are anything but conventional or common. People pop in and out of your life, causing surprising insights, as well as sudden tensions. You may try to be uncommitted to others, yet at the same time you seek the excitement they bring into your life.

URANUS ♂ *Imum Coeli/Fourth House*

This location can give you the opportunity to approach family matters in a progressive way. Peculiar and strange reactions may crop up from time to time, making you somewhat on edge about your home and family. Using new avenues of approach to deal with the humdrum routine of family life is a possibility. You may experience a strange aloofness which causes tension. Odd situations never seem to totally calm down and this irregularity around your home tends to promote discontent. Highly technical, unmarried or travel-oriented people may find this place less disturbing.

The Influence of Neptune

How realistic is your belief system? How clearly have you identified bad habits? How well do you understand your dream symbolism? These are three of the most important questions concerning Neptune. Over-impressionability and enticing desires can run rampant, promising satisfaction but not always delivering. Not only does your imagination work overtime, but your susceptibility to so many influences creates the feeling of a need to escape. Some forms of escapism can lead to addiction or unhealthy behavior. You may be treating internal problems with external answers. Only by directly confronting your complexes on the level where they exist (the unconscious) will you be able to sort out your internal puzzle. Through the process of meditation and exploratory therapy, you may be able to unravel the mystery of your personal symbolism.

However, if unrealistic expectations, misguided beliefs and temporal intoxicants sway you, self-deception will have the upper hand. Therefore, at some point you have to take the sword of discrimination and cut through your illusions, stop the dream machine and reject falsehood. Long-term meditators, and people involved with the arts or any other creative expression, will have less of a problem with Neptune. In the final analysis, self-discipline and/or dynamic creativity can keep Neptune in balance.

NEPTUNE ☌ Ascendant/Anti-Vertex

Susceptibility to a variety of influences can be confusing. Your imagination works overtime in a place like this, projecting outward subconscious ideas about what reality should be like. Unless you have a well-developed inner awareness, you can expect to be surrounded by deceptive circumstances. Appreciation of abstract concepts and dynamic creativity help keep Neptune in healthy perspective. You may be attracted to metaphysical teachings, but there is no guarantee that they will be authentic. If you can work through the indulgent and unrealistic side of Neptune, you have a greater chance of establishing an intuitive and mystical approach to life.

NEPTUNE ☌ Medium Coeli/Tenth House

This is definitely a difficult place to sort out dreams from reality. It is more likely that your dreams will be your only reality. There are usually disappointing episodes concerning your career. Often it is a case of not seeing eye to eye with the company and/or with cultural values. On the other hand, once your belief system is ignited, devotion to goals (be they true or false) will lead you onward. Different crusades, inspired ideals, and strange career motivations continually interweave here.

NEPTUNE ☌ Descendant/Vertex

Things are not on the up and up with partnerships, and for good reason: you simply do not see others as they are; possibly because you as well as they keep projecting expectations and assumptions that are in all likelihood false. This produces a lack of trust, and disillusionment. You must be very prudent in business and personal relationships, because an overdependence on others, or conversely letting them depend on you, may only make things more false and confusing. In some cases this area allows you to feel the problems and suffering of others, and compassionate actions can result from this sensitivity.

NEPTUNE ☌ Imum Coeli/Fourth House

There can be something physically and/or psychically toxic about this place. The problem is that the danger is not usually detected early on. These problems can subtly undermine your sense of security. Delving into your past and the mysteries of nature can be one of your best therapies in this place. Uncontrolled sensitivities and helpless, hopeless attitudes will only feed a general depressiveness. Leading an ethical and contemplative lifestyle can be very helpful and healing.

The Influence of Pluto

Pluto is the prime mover of the unconscious, and nothing passes its way without somehow being redefined, recycled and renewed. It also is the key generational planet, and one of its major functions is to connect the personal unconscious to the collective unconscious.

One of the significant issues with Pluto is the proper use of power. The abuse of its power can unleash a destructive torrent, laying to waste the very things that it has built. If you have enough internal integrity, then you will somehow start again, but with a transformed outlook. It's advisable to use Pluto's power to help others; not only will this increase its depth, but it will allow the transforming process to proceed at a comfortable pace.

Expect to be pushed beyond your self-imposed limits to a place where being and doing are the same. Pluto demands a great deal, but at the same time much can be discovered. The common problem with Pluto is that it is difficult to be moderate; your reactions are too black-and-white, and often extreme.

PLUTO ♂ Ascendant/Anti-Vertex
Personal power is developed in this place. You can feel very alive and invigorated here. You are certainly more tactful and able to use the force of persuasion. You can completely withdraw from involvement with the same intensity that you jump into experiences. Your emotions are pulled to extremes and this can lead to problems if you don't discover how to defuse them. This place compels you to redefine and re-evaluate your life.

PLUTO ♂ Medium Coeli/Tenth House
This is unquestionably a place where you can attain recognition and demonstrate power over others. The corrupting aspects of power can be very much alive in activating the obsessive and fanatical parts of your personality. Pay special attention to the type of strategies and maneuvers that you employ; there is a strong likelihood that something will get out of hand. Allow your goals to take on contrasting demands; in this way you will directly benefit from the transforming energies at work.

PLUTO ♂ Descendant/Vertex
Partnerships and people in general can drive you to either excellence or destruction. This is the place where a petty tyrant can play upon your weaknesses until you master them. If you resort to continual hostility against others, you'll only wind up depleting your energies and punishing yourself needlessly. Of course, partnerships are intense, complex and often demanding. Teamwork is needed, so that instead of battling with others you could be urging each other toward excellence.

PLUTO ☌ Imum Coeli/Fourth House

Active intervention by outside forces into your personal life can be demoralizing, yet this is a typical happening in this area. The influence here is too unconsciously provoking for most, producing compulsive behavior which continually interferes with the promotion of a normal family life. Fight-or-flight reactions continually surface over a variety of domestic issues. For most people the constant struggle in clearing out discordant forces eventually compels them to leave.

What about Transpluto?

Transpluto can be described in a number of ways. The way that I have found to be most descriptive is to view it as a Taurus planet, or Venus in Taurus. In this way, many of the key words associated with Taurus can be used in describing the influence of Transpluto. It can also be described as an earthy-Pluto-type planet, which has led researchers like Hawkins to say that Transpluto has to do with the visible powers (not the invisible like Pluto) that enable you to do what you normally couldn't.[1] You can expect Transpluto to cause some breakthroughs, yet because of its earthy nature, don't assume it will happen overnight. Whether it is with your outlook, job, partnerships or in the home, Transpluto can provide the ability to endure and enjoy life, while at the same time making you somewhat more stubborn and obstinate.

Houses in the Local Space Chart

In the Local Space chart the controversy of House systems is avoided because the horizon is always measured equally. The 360 degrees of azimuth on the horizon around you can be used all throughout the middle and upper latitudes. It is most effective at the polar regions and least effective at the equator.

The 360-degree constant allows for each sector or House to be exactly 30 degrees in length. Take a look at Figure 2 (page 4) and it will be apparent that the Local Space houses are in reverse of the standard horoscope. The Seventh House is to your left (west), and the First to your right (east); also, the Third and Fourth Houses are at the top (north) and the Ninth and Tenth are at the bottom, which is south. On all maps and compasses, this common figure is displayed:

N

W+E

S

The Local Space Houses have no rotation; they remain fixed in their directions. However, the transiting planet positions do change continuously throughout the day, placing them in any one of the 12 Houses, 16 directions, and in different degrees of azimuth. Remember that they are also at different degrees of altitude (0 to 90) above and below the horizon.

Traveling within the community or for longer distances does not always mean that a planetary line will be followed. Sometimes you may travel into a sphere of life's activity, i.e. into one of the Local Space sectors (Houses). Keeping within the standard meaning of the Houses, let's say you wanted to meet other people while traveling to the west-southwest, the Local Space Seventh House (see Table 11). Moving in a northwesterly direction would put you in the Local Space Fifth House, a place where you could meet a lover or take your current lover to the movies. What if you just wanted to be by yourself? You could travel into your Local Space Eighth or Twelfth Houses. As long as you are not within 7 degrees of a planet, the Local Space Houses will generally describe the activities. When you get closer to a planet, its particular energy will override the general meaning of the House.

Besides the personal uses of the Local Space Houses, there are some apparent historical implications. The westward movement of civilization along with the destructive concept of "manifest destiny" seems to fit in with Sixth and Seventh House matters. The Seventh House is "others" and it can be viewed as the greener grass on the other side of the hill. The migration of people westward caused wars, intermarriage between various groups, new legal problems, temporary alliances, etc. These all fit very clearly with the standard meanings of the Seventh House: open enemies, marriage, litigations, partnerships. The westward movement also caused the spread of diseases, the interbreeding and domestication of many animals, the development of new skills to meet the challenge of the frontier, the necessity for large armies, etc. These happenings correspond to the Sixth House: health matters, small animals, job skills, hard work, military service.

The great civilizations of the past and present predominantly conquered to the south; this is the Tenth House, where power, leadership, authority, position, fame are manifested. Isn't this what war and conquest is all about? The Ninth House is also to the south; after the conquest, the new rulers introduce their philosophy, which caused the educational system and laws of the land to change. Throughout history the northernmost culture and/or the one with a higher elevation has conquered and easily maintained the land and peoples to their south.

The previous examples dealt with past historical migrations of many people; however the personal applications are many. You can travel into friendships by going southwest, or into money through the northeast. So Houses definitely work in Local Space astrology, but in a more general sense than planetary lines.

Table 11

The Twelve Local Space Houses, with special emphasis on Home & Travel

First House: Outlook, outer personality, early environment, general constitution, physical appearance, love affairs on long trips (as Fifth from Ninth), children's long trips (as Ninth from Fifth), friends' short trips, grandparents.

Second House: Finances, holdings and possessions, memory, value system, home of friends and friends of the family (as Fourth from Eleventh), short trips of hidden enemies (as Third from Twelfth), long trips connected to health or job skills (as Ninth from Sixth).

Third House: Short trips (1-2 hours), everyday thinking, communications, primary education, neighbors; homes, non-relatives that live in your home, friends of children (as Eleventh from Fifth), long trips of spouse (as Ninth from Seventh).

Fourth House: Least dominant parent, family affairs, property, meditative and sexual experiences on long trips (as Eighth from Ninth), cars.

Fifth House: Love affairs, children, sports, gambling, entertainments, creativity, short trips of brothers and sisters (as Third from Third), long trips of grandchildren (as Ninth from Ninth).

Sixth House: Health awareness, employees, work skills, armed forces, long trips of most dominant parent and for business (as Ninth from Tenth), small animals.

Seventh House: Marriage, partnerships, the public, open enemies, short trips of children (as Third from Fifth), long trips of friends (as Ninth from Eleventh).

Eighth House: Meditation, sexual energy, secrets, sleep, death, money of others, short trips connected with health (as Third from Sixth), job skills, long trips of hidden enemies (as Ninth from Twelfth), major problems on long trips (as Twelfth from Ninth).

Ninth House: Long trips (2 hours by air), higher education, legalities, higher mind, foreign lands, grandchildren, short trips of spouse (as Third from Seventh).

Tenth House: Profession, standing, goals, gains, most dominant parent, authorities, long trips for money (as Ninth from Second).

Eleventh House: Friends, group awareness, hopes and wishes, stepchildren, long trips of brothers and sisters (as Ninth from Third).

Twelfth House: Troubles, seclusion, crimes, large animals, short trips of most dominant parent (as Third from Tenth).

Notes

1. Hawkins, John, *Transpluto or Should We Call Him Bacchus?* Dallas: Hawkins Enterprising Publications, 1976.

CHAPTER 4

THE GEOMANTIC CIRCLE

W hen you study Figure 15 on pages 92-93, notice that ring number 2 shows each of the four elements relating to a specific direction. Ether, the fifth element, is located above at the zenith, while the individual occupies the bottom pole of the center line, the nadir. Everyone has the four elements within them, biochemically and psychologically. Understanding how these elements help and hinder your progress is one of the most important keys in the proper use of the "geomantic circle."

The first step in using the geomantic circle is to ascertain which of the four elements has been the strongest or most helpful in your life. Typically, one element will stand out. Its qualities come naturally to you, thus the statement "He's in his element." Another element will be the weakest, with the other two elements falling somewhere in between. There are a few cases where two elements are strong and two are weak; less frequently all four are about equal. (A balance is an indication of a highly developed person.) The average person will have a 1, 2, 3, 4 ranking—a rating of elements from strongest to weakest.

I caution the reader not to attempt to rank the elements by simply looking only at the birth chart. The chart constitutes a complex maze of relationships, especially as regards the elements. Each sign is assigned an element, and each planet has an elemental assignment, with the Houses and aspects also having their correspondences. A seasoned and intuitive astrologer may be able to determine the ranking of the

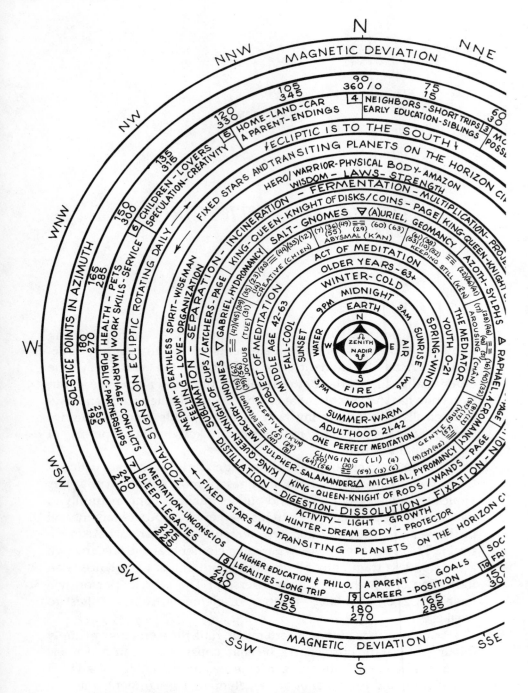

Fig. 15—*The Geomantic (Local Space) Circle*

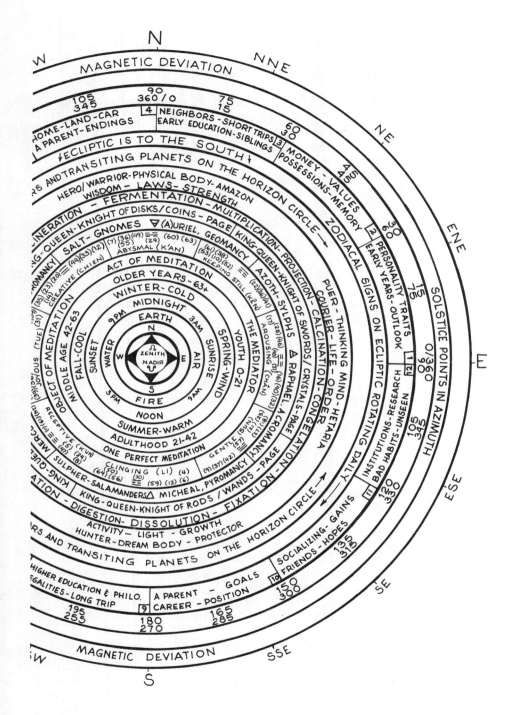

93

The Rings of the Local Space Geomantic Compass

○ *ONE.* The zenith is directly above you and the nadir is directly below you. The ancients used the Dragon's Head/North Node for the zenith and the Dragon's Tail/South Node for the nadir. There are 90 degrees of altitude between the horizon and the zenith and another 90 degrees below the horizon to the nadir. Planets with a low altitude (+ or -10 degrees) have a dominant influence in that particular locality.

Note: In rings one to seven, *only* north and south are reversed for the Southern Hemisphere.

○ *TWO.* The four cardinal directions used on the compass. These are loosely connected with the signs of the zodiac: Aries/east, Libra/west, Capricorn/south and Cancer/north. It is important to remember that the signs are not stationary, but appear to rotate daily as the Earth turns.

○ *THREE.* The four major elements that are agreed upon or strongly implied by almost every system studied. Additional information is contained in Table 13, which is taken from the Chinese Feng Shui system.

○ *FOUR.* The apparent universal system of time correspondences.

○ *FIVE.* The seasons and weather that seem to be consistent.

○ *SIX.* The stages of life were mostly taken from the Feng Shui system, but they are implied by others. The Hindus would use childhood, student, householder and renunciate.

○ *SEVEN.* The basic Kriya Yoga meditation formula. To explain it, the meditator is represented by the east, where the Sun rises. The process leads to the west, where the Sun sets: the Not-Self. The energy and wisdom of the north is tapped and the perfect meditation merges with the personal divinity, which is God and/or realizing one's true Self: south. In actual practice the meditator would face east.

○ *EIGHT.* The later heaven arrangement of the I Ching is used. The eight houses of trigrams are placed in the proper directions. For the first time, we have a designation for directions other than the major four, i.e. northeast, southwest, etc. Contained within these eight major trigram houses are the corresponding 64 hexagrams in the entire I Ching. In the Southern Hemisphere it may be necessary to reverse all positions, since the trigrams are derived from the Chinese view of seasonal change (i.e. in the Northern Hemisphere).

○ *NINE.* In this ring the symbols for the four elements occupy the center. These symbols are taken from Western astrology, magic and alchemy. (In the Chinese system, Earth is in the center, wood is in the east, Fire/south, metal/west and Water/north). In the Western system the fifth element, ether, is in the center. In the yoga system of psychic centers, or chakras, the first center along the spine is Earth, the coccygeal area. The next center up is Water, and it is the sacral. The third center is Fire and it is the lumbar. The next center is Air, at the dorsal vertebrae. This puts the element ether at the fifth center in the cervical area. The two head centers, medulla and cortex/mid-brain, is the zenith point. The nadir represents dormant centers below the coccygeal, i.e. the tail. Also contained in this ring is the Archangel place in Western magic and folklore. (In Levi's Hebrew system and in the Gnostic there are some different placements and names). The names for the lower order of angels or elementals are given. These forces are the builders and maintainers in the biosphere of Earth—the hidden intelligence behind the nature. They have been represented as elves, fairies, pixies, leprechauns, ewoks and protective spirits in Western folklore. The four basic substances of alchemy are included along with the four divinatory systems (north and south reversed in the Southern Hemisphere).

○ *TEN.* The royal names for the four suits of court cards in the Tarot. The Knight cards typify the four directions with the particular suits (elements) being a general indicator for the directions. There are an additional 10 cards for each direction, making a total of 56 cards in the minor arcana (4x14=56). The minor arcana cards are used similarly to the astrological houses and aspects in astrological interpretation. The 22 cards of the major arcana (56+22=78 total) correspond to the signs and planets. The signs and planets are always moving and this is the reason they are not assigned a specific direction. (Reverse north and south if south of equator.)

○ *ELEVEN.* The alchemical stages or process as it relates to the cycles in nature, directions, etc.

○ *TWELVE.* In this ring the various geomantic correspondences are linked with a variety of indicators from various sources. The central position takes into consideration the four functions or four states of man's awareness: the physical body/awake state, thinking mind/awake and asleep, the dream body in deep sleep and the essence or spirit in a self-realized state. The key words to either side of the center are the male and female archetypes taken from the depth psychology system of Wolff. For a more complete description of these archetypes, see the explanations in Table 13. Directly below the central words are the four basic key words used in Western magic systems and strongly implied by other sources. The other key words on either side are taken from Amerindian and Mesoamerican sources like H. Storm and Don Juan. In Table 13, more information is given (reverse north and south in the Southern Hemisphere).

○ *THIRTEEN.* This ring is for the positions of the planets, fixed stars or whatever else you may be looking at in the Local Space circle. Ring sixteen gives you the azimuth degrees; fixed positions as well as transiting positions can be observed and compared for any locality. Rings thirteen and sixteen can be used together or thirteen can be used for the transiting positions and sixteen for the birth positions.

o *FOURTEEN.* This ring is a reminder that even though we are concentrating on the horizon circle around us, the ecliptic, the path of the Sun and the signs of the zodiac are always to our south in the Northern Hemisphere.

o *FIFTEEN.* These are the abbreviated versions of the standard astrological houses. It may seem odd to see the Fourth House at the top of the chart, but remember that the Fourth House cusp is pointing to the north in the Northern Hemisphere. If you face east with your Local Space chart in hand and parallel (flat) with the horizon, then the First House is the first 30 degrees of azimuth on the horizon moving north. 22.2 degrees of azimuth north of east is east-northeast and it is in the first Local Space House. Northeast along the horizon is in the center of the Local Space Second House, and so on around the chart (see Figure 15).

If your locality is below 30 degrees north latitude (or above 30 degrees south latitude in the Southern Hemisphere), then face north and hold your Local Space chart up, vertical to the horizon. Look to the east along the first 30 degrees above the horizon (toward the zenith); over your head is the First Campanus House on the Prime Vertical.* More on this in Chapter 5.

o *SIXTEEN.* The 360 degrees of azimuth are listed twice in this ring, because some astrologers prefer to start counting in the east. But it is standard for the compass to start at the north. This ring is used to take note of where the exact positions of the planets are in azimuth. (Refer to your Local Space map/chart).

o *SEVENTEEN.* This ring is used to indicate if any planets are near the azimuth degree solstice points. These points will only be in the east and west portions of the circle (see Table 7).

o *EIGHTEEN.* In the north and south portions of the circle, the points of magnetic declination are listed (see Figure 8).

o *NINETEEN.* The final ring includes the 16 major and minor directions on the standard compass.

See notes at the end of this chapter for source material.

---

*The Houses are the twelve-fold division of the Earth's surface, and in the standard astrological chart (ecliptic system), the zodiacal signs are placed or laid over the Houses. The proportional distribution of signs placed over the Houses depends on the distance from the equator. The greater the distance, the greater disproportionate alignment there is between the signs and Houses. At the equator, the signs and Houses are close to equal, because the ecliptic and equatorial planes are closer together. As one travels above 40 degrees north or below 40 degrees south latitude, an entire sign can be contained within the boundaries of a House and near the polar regions. Two whole signs or more within one House is possible, while in the opposite area of the chart a single sign is stretched over three or more House cusps).

elements, but it does not come easily for most. An Earth planet can be in a Fire sign within a Water House, in Air aspect to a Fire planet which is in an Air sign in an Earth House!

Thankfully, there is a faster and easier way to discover your strong and weak elements, a method which makes it much easier to avoid error. Think of your childhood and the relationship you had with the four elements. I have found that the weakest element has a way of revealing itself in a number of common childhood experiences. The strongest elements usually do not produce any alarming, fearful or irritating experiences. Sometimes, however, the energy of the element is so powerful that as a child your initial reaction may be fearful. This may be a way in which additional time is obtained to adjust to the force level.

When you look back at your early years, some of your childhood learning and play experiences seem to be spontaneously understood, while others evoke caution and fear, and create a challenge. Most children in the process of growing up participate in a large variety of activities. These activities depend a great deal on the family structure and also upon your culture and geographic location. What has to be determined is not so much your actions but your unique *re*actions: the levels of your ease/enjoyment, or of frustration/pain.

Almost all children like to play with sand and water, but it would be wrong to say that they are strong in Earth and Water, because we don't know the amount of time they spend with these activities, nor do we know the level of enjoyment they attain. Childhood memories are usually quite vivid, and you may be surprised at how easy it is to relive certain emotional responses. Only *you* know what you liked and disliked. It won't take long to sort things out, and once you have done this you will be able to make better use of the "geomantic circle."

If Earth is a strong element for you, then playing extensively with dirt and things of the Earth may have occupied much of your play time. These activities may have included: planting a garden, building things with wood, collecting rocks, learning how to cook, saving money in your piggy bank. In their earlier years some (not all) Earth children have the tendency to eat the crust from their noses and to briefly contemplate their solid waste. I realize this is crude, but Earth *is* crude. If Earth is not strong within you, you may have had an aversion to or avoided the above activities. If you didn't like to get dirty and/or muddy, Earth is not your strong element.

Air children enjoy writing notes to one another, learning how to use the telephone, climbing high in trees to feel the wind, flying kites, and making paper and plastic airplanes. They also like books at an early age. If there are rocks or old food under an Earth child's bed, you're likely to find pens, pencils and plenty of paper under the Air child's bed. Many Air children talk themselves to sleep. In fact, mothers and fathers agree that they talk much more than is necessary. If Air is not strong for you, you may not feel that these activities were all that important, or you could have been annoyed with them. When the wind blows and howls, how do you react?

Fire children unfortunately like to play with matches and generally enjoy watching fire. They love the heat of the Sun, and often take on leadership roles among their playmates. They are inclined to "play doctor," as sexual themes are stimulating to them. Whenever there is friction, emotional or physical, they are drawn to it. When you were burned for the first time, how traumatic was it? All children have a fascination with fire, but only a Fire child will get in there and actually play with it!

Water children love to swim, and many learn how at an early age. Caring for pet fish, fishing, sailing and generally anything that involves the Water element attracts them. Water children are noted for their intense emotional responses—crying, laughing or just carrying a mood for an extended period. If being in or under water bothered you, then Water may not be strong in your chart. How much fear was produced when you went in over your head for the first time?

Now that you have some important clues about your childhood encounters with the elements, let's look at the ranking of elements in the present and how they have affected your adult life. All you need do is return to some basic astrological knowledge.

As an Earth-type person, you tend to be involved with life on a practical level. All of us need to be practical about some matters, but Earth people are generally more comfortable and successful with money matters and material concerns. Earthy people can be boring and thick-headed, and may often carry a self-created burden with which they continually hassle. You are rarely the life of the party, but could be the one paying for it.

As an Air-type person, you certainly stress communication in some form or fashion. You usually know how to get a point across through speaking and/or writing. You can be somewhat "bubble-headed," i.e. more head and less heart.

Fire signs are fire starters. You instigate, lead or cause some sort of friction or action, and have the energy to *do*, but carrying objectives to a successful completion is not one of your strengths. You usually are a starter, and not a finisher.

As a Water person, you love moods, emotions and feelings, which you often use in conveying your intent. In fact, you may have a hard time containing your emotions. You also enjoy escapism, because then you can just "feel." You often indulge in an active dream life, and accept intuitive powers more readily than other people.

An important point to remember is that you are always drawn toward or into your weakest element. Circumstances in life that afford you the opportunity of learning about a weak element will prove valuable, as will involvement with people, places and skills that are characteristic of that particular element. This is one of the best ways in which you can begin to deal with your weaker elements.

Time after time I've observed that in personal relationships, she needs him because he's down-to-earth (strong Earth) and stable, or he needs her because Fire energy makes him feel more alive. I've seen Air people search out Water people because they desperately need to understand their emotions.

This concept of balancing the four elements also holds true for relocating. If the cold planets (Saturn, Uranus and sometimes Pluto) are dominant in your chart, you will have a tendency to move to a warmer climate. If the hot planets (Sun, Mars, Jupiter and sometimes Pluto) have the upper hand, then you can tolerate cold weather, and may even enjoy it. In one sense, tropical beaches are for cold-planet people, and snow skiing is for hot-planet people.

The possible combinations of elements are numerous, but one important point remains clear. As long as you have a very weak element, it will control you more than you can control it. Once you grasp its message and incorporate it into your whole personality, you will be able to use it to your advantage.

In reviewing what has been said, ask yourself: "Do I seem to always be in need of money, stability and practical know-how?" That is weak Earth. "Do I have problems in talking or writing about what I feel or think?" Then you could be weak in Air qualities. "Does the energy and drive to start new things seem to be lacking?" If so, Fire may be your weak element. "Am I in the habit of repressing my emotions, and does someone expressing their emotions puzzle me? or do I see them as out of control?" This may indicate that you are weak in the Water element.

The whole process of finding out which elements are strongest and weakest can reveal which directions will help or hinder your life. If Fire happens to be your strong element, then you probably already know that your energies are higher at noontime, and that you may be more productive in the summer months. Things in the southern part of your home or office will tend to have more power (see Figure 15 and Table 13).

A strong direction is valid everywhere and anywhere you go. It can protect you from the adversity which results from having certain antagonistic planets in that direction. (Planets in different directions are covered in Chapter 5.) The planets in your Local Space chart will change as you change localities, but your good direction will always be helpful. Unfortunately, the difficult directions will continue to challenge you.

Practical Use of the Geomantic Local Space Circle

If you already have your Local Space chart, then you will be able to line it up with the cardinal directions in the geomantic circle. You'll be able to draw some interesting comparisons. This chapter offers a start in the use of the cardinal directions, but it also offers a solid method of getting people to explore and experiment on their own.

In order to get the most use out of the "Local Space Geomantic Magical Circle," it is imperative that you think differently about your relationship with nature. Some people who spend a great deal of time outdoors, like surveyors, nature guides, rangers, hunters, etc. often develop (consciously or unconsciously) a special relationship with the forces of nature and with certain directions, if they are so inclined. In agriculturally based societies, natural forces and horizontal directions are part of the prevailing folk wisdom.

The majority of people who are modern urban dwellers are up against a difficult problem. Urban people are removed from most animal life, isolated from the forces of nature, and are generally insensitive to the night sky. The natural learning process and communion with nature takes place too infrequently to really be of any lasting help. The situation is not hopeless; it can be worked on and changed.

In addition to what you have read, keep in mind that certain elements are antagonistic or complementary to each other. If you look at the geomantic circle (Figure 15), you'll see that there are Earth, Fire, Air and Water planets. Basic astrology teaches us that Earth and Water get along, and that Fire and Air are compatible elements as well. It is also known that Earth puts out Fire and also clashes with Air, while Water turns Fire to steam. Therefore in a general sense the north and west directions work together. Isn't it true that almost all of the valuable moisture moves out of the north and comes across from the west (a wet and cool direction)? South and east work in unison, too: the heat flows from the south and the temperature rises when the Sun comes up in the east (which is dry and warm).

Because of the planet-element-direction connection, the Water and Earth planets—Saturn, Transpluto, Neptune, Pluto and the Moon—will be more constructive when thay are in the northerly and westerly parts of the Local Space chart. Likewise the Fire and Air planets—Mars, Jupiter, Venus, Mercury, Uranus and the Sun—will function better when contained within the southern and eastern parts of the chart.

Prior knowledge of astrology and occult principles will be extremely helpful in working with this system. Yet geomancy is just like any other system—the more you reflect upon its meaning and put it into practice, the greater the benefits.

Each ring represents a different system of knowledge; some are quite simple, but not unimportant. Take for example the four directions, elements or seasons. They are just brief statements, yet when compared with other systems, many insights into their significance are possible in Local Space astrology. If you are more comfortable with the Western magical path than with the alchemical, Tarot references may prove valuable. If you use the I Ching, it too is represented. Amerindian and depth psychology are also included. By the way, for Table 13 the (non-graphic) rings 15 to 23 are explained in more detail in the accompanying table.

The various meanings of the planets on the four directions relate specifically to the geomantic circle (compass). In Chapter 3, the planets on the four angles were described in a more traditional sense. In my opinion, you should consult both to get a complete viewpoint (Tables 10 and 12). The focus in this chapter is on the physical and symbolic meaning of the four directions. The mystical flavor is added without excluding the practical indications.

The real beauty of the geomantic circle (a static and universal form of the Local Space chart) is that it allows for a direct interplay of the intuitive and rational worlds as well as providing access to many areas of knowledge not readily available in standard charts. The cross-cultural and multi-level approach brings forth an unlimited number of possible interpretations, each pertaining to a variety of life experiences (see Figure 15 and Table 13).

When explaining the horizon compass directions (especially the Vertex/west and Anti-Vertex/east), one is inclined to encounter actual events. The Horizon System places you on the Earth's surface, thus grounding all activities. The events of everyday reality can no longer just be passively observed, which is often the case with the Ascendant/Descendant axis. A greater frequency of direct involvement and interactiveness can be expected. Events in the form of confrontations, challenging involvements, and learning experiences are highly probable.

To position yourself properly (generally above 30° north latitude or below 30° south latitude), simply hold the geomantic circle and/or your Local Space chart flat and parallel to the ground (as on a table). It is now on the same plane as the horizon around you. Use a landmark that you know to be correct—a map aligned to any angle of the circle, and/or a chart with a direction, i.e. N, S, E or W.

Using east as an example, first align yourself in that direction. Then check and see where your Local Space planets are (in azimuth) on the geomantic circle, remembering that it represents the horizon surrounding you. The houses on the chart divide the horizon circle into twelve equal parts. The First House is to the east, the Seventh is west, Fourth north, and Tenth to the south (in the Northern Hemisphere).

Below 30° north or above 30° south in the equatorial latitudes, a different positioning is necessary. The Prime Vertical circle is used because of the bunching effect on the horizon in the equatorial latitudes. Face due north or south and hold the circle and/or chart upright, i.e. vertical to the horizon. Now the Local Space Houses will be on the Prime Vertical circle from east to west, above and below you. Instead of the Houses being in a circle around you, they are now directly above and below you in a circle. The Local Space First House is just above east, the Second House is above it, and the cusp of the Third and Fourth Houses are directly overhead at the zenith. The Ninth and Tenth Houses will be directly below you (at the nadir), with the Sixth and Seventh to the west. Take note of any planets that are very low or very high in amplitude, i.e. near the zenith or horizon. They will have the strongest influence for a locality.

Planetary Positions on the Local Space Geomantic Compass

Life energy (Ch'i or Prana) is always changing around us due to the fact that the transiting planets are continuously moving while the Earth rotates. In order to truly understand if the electromagnetic forces that flow through nature are good or ill, you need to be thoroughly acquainted with the principles of Feng Shui and the Local Space geomantic circle, and have a working knowledge of astrology. There are many other specialties that are important, but you don't have to be a specialist to begin. (Even with some simple facts in a Boy Scout manual or from dowsing, you could discern many hidden facts from the natural surroundings. Of course, a special sensitivity to nature is always extremely helpful.)

Please keep in mind that your dominant planetary positions for any locality will influence your interpretations. To illustrate: suppose you had Jupiter in the north and also in this direction lay an undisclosed toxic waste dump. Jupiter, being what it is, would somehow protect you from this adverse influence. You may not be in the direction of the prevailing wind, or you may get bottled water before anyone else, etc. On the other hand, Neptune in the same direction would be very harmful because of its connection with toxic substances. Seeing the world through Jupiter or Neptune eyes can be quite different.

What if you had a waterfall ¼-mile to the west of you, and Saturn was in the west? You would not be able to receive the healing benefits due to certain limiting circumstances caused by Saturn. Whatever the quality of the natural or man-made surroundings, their effect ultimately depends on the positions of your planets in that particular locality.

All the planetary positions listed in Table 12 are for planets within 3 degrees of any cardinal direction. The altitude becomes increasingly important below 30° north latitude or above 30° south latitude, due to the east/west bunching effect described in earlier chapters.

These descriptions can also be used for any planet which is less than 7 degrees above or below the horizon, and generally positioned in the vicinity of any cardinal direction. Say that Jupiter is at an altitude of 2+ degrees; this would make it quite important. Jupiter with its low altitude could be in any one of the four major, or twelve minor directions. If Jupiter happens to be closer to the east than to any other direction, you can look to the indications below pertaining to "Jupiter in the East."

What if a planet is not near a major direction but lies northwest or southeast, etc.? Then you have to rely on the aspects, Houses, solstice points and magnetic declination to properly understand how the planet would function. However, don't limit yourself to just these indicators, because there are many other possible correlations possible . . . the seasons, meditation stages, I Ching, Tarot and the elements, to name just a few (see Figure 15 and Table 13).

The question may arise: Just how realistic are the "Keynote Event" statements in the following descriptions? They are intended to give a symbolic approximation of a major event or series of events. The probability of events occurring in the exact way described is remote, however the symbolism remains as correct as possible. In fact, these statements are open to numerous meanings.

In your home, the persons or events can literally come into your life. These events can take place on your property or in your home and often they will correspond to, and happen, in a certain direction. In the community, it can be the direction you are taking when certain encounters happen, or the direction out of which someone contacts you. "Out of the west" could be someone from Japan or just a neighbor from down the street; it all depends on the planets involved and on their aspects.

The poetic content in the "Nature Signs" was simply the most comfortable form of expression for the author. The wording, seemingly abstract, may not become clear until such a time when an experience (or memory of an experience) jells, matches up, or is otherwise found to be similar or significant. It is likely that these statements will make the most sense to people who are experienced in observing nature, including human nature.

Consult Figure 15 and Table 13; also check with the descriptions in Chapter 3. Please reverse north and south for the Southern Hemisphere.

Table 12

The Planetary Positions

SUN in the East

Here is where your self-identity is fed by the wind of the east. Air always feeds a flame, and quite naturally your spiritual and physical vitality is vibrant because of it. Your *will* to communicate in new ways seeks a creative expression. Each word has a power all its own, and this knowledge can clear your mind as well as inflate your ego. There is a definite focus on individual development pertaining to leadership. This locality demands identification of your personal power and creativity. You may have to deal with a certain degree of narcissism, and arrogance within yourself and/or in others.

Nature Signs: Read the shadows on the hills. Partake of the orange heat, cerebral petals unfolding, the dance of photons and infra-reds—telling personal stories.

Keynote Event: On a warm and windy spring morning, an honorable and attractive young man comes out of the East with an important message.

SUN in the South

The spotlight of outer importance and the inner light of self shine brightly. It is here where external prominence and internal realization support each other. Attainment of goals and creative growth abound. Authoritativeness is a big issue. Corporate egos and conceit could pose some problems. Don't let the gravity of who you are, or what others represent, deflect your clarity.

Nature Signs: The white flames of sunlight brighten a landscape that is reclaiming moisture, dispersing shadows. Reflecting heat mirages stimulate the imagination, time for the cool-within—the siesta, the silence, the spinal nectar.

Keynote Event: On a sunny summer afternoon a man comes from the South to help with a new plan of action.

SUN in the West

The depth of experience in others reflects back to you, causing an evaluation of needs. You are confronted with egotism, blind ambition and selfishness from the people around you. Overcoming the strong influence of others will bring forth fresh approaches and friendships.

A connectedness with others will then allow a light to shine in dark places. . . making the unconscious conscious, the unknown known and the unseen seen.

Nature Signs: Long shadows, rain leaving, life force calming, the pink twilight slips into blue, into stars, a fire is built near the medicine wheel.

Keynote Event: On a cool autumn evening a mature man from the West silently reveals hidden facts about others.

SUN in the North

Your home life can become a creative activity, a statement of your character. Make no mistake about it, what you will for yourself strongly affects the family around you. The strength of your self-identity demands that you give the best of what you have. Parents, children and even friends rely on you to set standards and maintain the household honor. You can easily be a big fish in a small pond, but sometimes the pond may grow and the fish has to do the same.

Nature Signs: Pale light, star bright, the battle of fire and ice, other Suns twinkle in the darkness. Hear the cosmic reverberations, the Aurora Borealis— a movement in stillness.

Keynote Event: On a cold night in the winter, an older practical man is observed to the North, where he has taught.

MOON in the East

Objective understanding of your strong emotional life and your mood changes is necessary so that you won't be overly defensive. Certain impressions of the man-made and natural forces in your surroundings can cause a variety of emotional responses. Fear and uncertainty may crop up, yet it is also likely that your presentiments will fortify your decision-making abilities.

Nature Signs: Breezes on water, dew in the air, it's morning in the valley; man and beast erupt with excitement.

Keynote Event: On a moist morning a young woman delivers her message from the East.

MOON in the South

Involvement with the moods of the masses is somehow emphasized. Circumstances dictate that you learn how to flow with and adapt to different attitudes, goals and lifestyles. Adaptation is not surrender; protect yourself, then navigate beyond the emotional storms.

Realize that the outer life will always change, but inner life stays the same.

Nature Signs: The fullness bursts forth, multiplying, spinning threads of moonlight, weaving new baskets of creation.

Keynote Event: An inspired woman and a small child from the South advance in a search for meaning.

MOON in the West

People you come in contact with seem to leave an emotional imprint upon you. Quite often their emotional condition is discordant, leaving you in a somewhat defensive posture. Playing defense without following another is exactly the challenge that is presented, i.e. in the sea of emotions it is necessary to keep your head above water. Allowing others to cling or meddle in your life, or doing the same yourself, can create dependencies which never really help relationships.

Nature Signs: Water, whirling, churning, turning, splashing ions, onward, downward, inward, a carrier of feeling.

Keynote Event: On a rainy day a mature woman from the West mirrors the unconscious, triggering introspection and inspiration.

MOON in the North

Strong bonds with family and home can override your own personal dictates. (By family, I mean parents, close relatives, brothers and sisters, wife and children.) This is not an advantageous position to be in, especially when your personal decisions are always filtered through what the family would think. There certainly are times when decisions as well as sacrifices are a necessity and an important ingredient of family life, however, learning to draw the line somewhere is also important. I suppose it's the difference of working with the family or being worked over by them.

Nature Signs: Ice crystals hang, and the cool rain enters the Earth, moist semi-dormant places.

Keynote Event: On a cold night an older woman from the North spins the wife's (wise) tales that nature has taught her.

MERCURY in the East

Discovering the powers of thought and development of skills is a major issue in this place. Circumstances continually prompt you to say what you feel and speak your mind. Flexible thinking helps open up a world of ideas to be thoroughly explored.

Nature Signs: Buzz words, key words fall into place, a word is a symbol and a thing. Objects and thoughts intermesh in a wind of re-definition. Small creatures, each in its own way, display their routine and a message is delivered.

Keynote Event: A young and fluent person from the East speaks his piece; it's news you can use.

MERCURY in the South

Those around you (professionally) can't disregard what you say; your words seem to stick in their minds. Therefore the choice of words, how you say them, and when you say them, is an important concern. Problems could develop if you become a little too intellectually cute and clever for your own good.

Nature Signs: The endless activity of movement in this eco-system. Each stage within a cycle tells its own story.

Keynote Event: A younger person out of the South speaks in ways that offer fulfillment and direction.

MERCURY in the West

A smorgasbord of facts, thoughts and ideas are entering your awareness. Your mind will become more discriminating and thought-provoking. You'll find that you need to know the difference between talking at people and talking to them. You may discover that pondering upon something long enough helps it to become reality. Therefore you need to search out the most advantageous ways of only giving the proper ideas energy. At times, what you say and write can get you in and out of conflicts.

Nature Signs: Interludes between work and play, stillness and movement, dark and light, a time of deeper thought.

Keynote Event: A younger person from the West whispers (as if in a dream) ideas most difficult to express, saying things that aren't usually said.

MERCURY in the North

Small worries can add up to mental distress. Establishing a system whereby you put your daily affairs in order can be the difference between peace of mind or mental frustration. Learning to be more objective is helpful, because quite often highly personal ideas harbor narrow perspectives. Periodically, petty distractions can interfere with your concentration level.

Nature Signs: In its own time the Earth teaches each person in a direct way knowledge of the soil, the value of minerals, defining the specific functions of living things, classifications and orderings.

Keynote Event: A younger person from the North displays the virtues of patience and studiousness.

VENUS in the East

The expression of talents, sociability, and congeniality is focused on in this place. The question then arises: are you ready to express talent, to be congenial and sociable? There is no guarantee that the beauty of Venus will find an outlet; it is possible that indulgence and a "party time" mentality could lead to a sort of empty social life. In order to maintain a balance you need to relax, but not collapse; to give, but not completely give in. A lot depends on the quality of your desires. The philosophers have said: *we bring the beauty to the sunrise.*

Nature Signs: The contours, curves and pleasant rounded shapes revealed on the canvas of life. The silent language of color seeks to merge with its complements.

Keynote Event: An attractive and talented young man from the East longs for companionship, as words do for a melody.

VENUS in the South

Popularity sometimes means that those around you may be attracted to the quantity of your success rather than the quality of who you are. The glamour that comes with greater popularity should be secondary to the inner joy that comes from increased acceptance. Don't let career satisfactions lead to laxity or sidetrack your giftedness. Balanced cooperation and sharing moments of happiness with others can become quite common, yet it is possible that a narcissistic aloofness could develop.

Nature Signs: The light of one to another, the passionate embraces of plants to the Earth. The symmetry and fragrances of the landscape explaining things to the heart.

Keynote Event: A spirited young man from the South desires love and attention.

VENUS in the West

The strong desire for the right relationships and business partnerships becomes paramount. Wishing to please or be pleased and generally bending over backwards can be overdone. Developing positive bonds with people is a two-way street of sharing, yet seeing others for what they really are is not the easiest thing to do in this location. Many enticements pass your way, and they must be balanced with the right amount of trust and realism so you can avoid letting opportunities slip away.

Nature Signs: Everything blends near water, even the particles of earth roll under its surface. The perfected crest of the wave, its mist, is reversed before the pulse on the shoreline.

Keynote Event: A young woman from the West shows the deep ties she has with others.

VENUS in the North

The strong emotions that you can feel for your immediate family are a definite source of strength. Complications develop when this relative harmony becomes a dependency. That which is comfortable is not always the best path to follow. You can get stuck in your little niche. Naive and superficial tendencies can definitely tarnish an otherwise loving home life.

Nature Signs: The laws of the land; the chemistry of the soil. The quiet eco-cycle, digesting and fermenting.

Keynote Event: A young maiden from the North displays her wares, and cooks up a bounty of needed nourishment.

MARS in the East

The energy and drive in this place is more than enough to get things done. You can feel sure about your abilities and want to improve upon them. You may display impulsive and headstrong qualities, making you more aggressive then need be, and this may be harmful to your accomplishment. It is almost too easy to become self-centered and competitive, walking around with a chip on your shoulder. Healthy outlets for mental and physical aggression will not only keep you from overheating but will also improve your attitude. Feeling that something has to be fought for is quite common under this influence, however you will need to put some energy into dealing with your own shortcomings.

Nature Signs: The internal heat, the friction of doing, muscles and machines performing the rolling, crushing, and turning momentum that shapes and harnesses natural forces.

Keynote Event: A vigorous and bold man from the East starts activities through confrontation, stamina and struggle.

MARS in the South

An untiring effort toward goals is promised. Getting things done in a brisk and intense manner becomes the norm. You may have to undergo life in the fast lane, along with some problems with authority figures. The issue of someone stealing your thunder can easily crop up. Exercising tolerance and knowing when to act is something that must be observed. Apply yourself to the tasks at hand and keep a safe distance from all the big egos with, often, weak personalities.

Nature Signs: Rising temperature, thermo waves dance in the field of vision. A burning dryness is present.

Keynote Event: A strong and capable man from the South takes charge and exercises authority.

MARS in the West

To put it quite simply, people you come in contact with in this locality can be argumentative, obnoxious, even violent. Under certain circumstances you could find very honest and straightforward comrades, but it's the exception rather than the rule. This is a war zone of sorts and you need to toughen up in order to survive.

Nature Signs: The clashing drums of thunder as the extremes of high and low pressures meet, the furious storm pounds onward. The ongoing combustion of fossil fuels altering the atmosphere.

Keynote Event: A reckless and potent man from the West evokes intense emotions and stirs up trouble.

MARS in the North

The natural forces around you are a source of energy holding potential destructive powers. Sometimes it is necessary to buckle down, mobilize and struggle to keep what you have, or to get what you need. There is a struggle to protect and provide those tangible and intangible necessities of life. Family activities can be emotionally explosive and there may be a lot of in-fighting.

Nature Signs: The dominating providence of natural forces encounters and overwhelms weaker defenses. The mark of man across the land.

Keynote Event: An imposing and knowledgeable man from the North subjugates resources, demands structure, and imposes rules.

JUPITER in the East

There's no doubt that this place is filled with great and good things; the only question is whether you will be able to avail yourself of the abundance offered. It's probably easy to get spoiled here, taking too much for granted. Extravagance is a waste of money, often translating into a loss of time and energy as well. People may trust in you more here, and without knowing it you could take unfair advantage of them. Certainly you can take chances here, but it is unwise to press your luck too far.

Nature Signs: Fair and dry, high, thin clouds disperse in the morning.

Keynote Event: A teacher/benefactor from the East brings clarification and understanding.

JUPITER in the South

Goals can be achieved, lucrative and important positions are attainable. In situations that promise so much, it is vitally important that you attempt to give back to life, as a means of sharing your good fortune, also as a safeguard against corrupting influences. Be on guard for conceit and dogma; they can definitely cause a lack of respect, and lead to certain miscalculations.

Nature Signs: A beautiful day brings the idea of success and faith in the natural order of things, as well as the vision of what can be done.

Keynote Event: A teacher/benefactor from the South explains great ideas and ideals; expansive progress ensues.

JUPITER in the West

Tolerance is an amazing tool in dealing with others; it can help them relax, while motivating them to do their best. Mutual acceptance is alive in this area and can be turned into profit and satisfaction. You will undoubtedly meet your fair share of big mouths, snobs and fat cats along with generous and kind people who will see fit to help you. Pompous fools still abound, so learning how to choose properly is directly related to how fortunate you can become.

Nature Signs: The clear burning trail of sunset; the promise of a fulfilling tomorrow.

Keynote Event: A teacher/benefactor from the West heals conflicts, and unites factions.

JUPITER in the North

A relative prosperity predominates in this setting. A rewarding family life based on understanding and dignity is indicated. There is, of course, a tendency to sit back and assume things will take care of themselves; this can be folly because those "sins of omission" can come back on you. The honest, healthy lifestyle this area can promote is a tremendous boon to whatever you wish to accomplish.

Nature Signs: The harshness of nature is held back and diverted, thus fragile ecosystems can create new life.

Keynote Event: A teacher/benefactor from the North brings the wealth and influence of the land.

SATURN in the East

In this place more than any other, you can get a realistic sense of what you need to work on. This work will ultimately make you a better person, but at times you'll probably feel that experiences in general are much too hard and heavy. Many of your fears and undeveloped qualities seem to be played upon until you apply proper concentration. Self-effort, discipline and organization continually come into focus as a path that must be followed. There is, of course, the potential problem that you will become too rigid in your outlook. In the process of learning about limitations, you may underestimate yourself.

Nature Signs: Hot and cold weather and wind on rocks turns them into sand; pressure on sand turns it back into rock—the ancient cycles of time. The notch in the rock marks a calendar of light.

Keynote Event: A mature person from the East patiently helps to turn the abstract into reality.

SATURN in the South

The laws of the everyday world are made strikingly clear. Orthodox and straight-laced conventionality are all around you. Work can be hard and thankless, and the pay below average. In some cases the job is dependable, yet very boring. Important situations depend on you. Duty and obligations are pressed upon you, and in time your experience and forebearance tends to bring even greater responsibilities. Undoubtedly, a place where you can attain solid maturity, holding on to what you have learned for a lifetime.

Nature Signs: Baking flat rocks, heated quarries, petrified pictures, static and sublime.

Keynote Event: A mature older person from the South adheres to the structure that allows perseverance to flourish.

SATURN in the West

Exercising caution and reserve in your encounters with others becomes a necessity. By observing the actions of those around you, learn what *not* to do. When you deal with others, there always seems to be something lacking. Although some stable and simple relationships can transpire, most are weighted down with emotional and/or financial deficiencies. Disappointments and the narrow-mindedness of others may cause you to withdraw; sometimes this can mean a sparse social life.

Nature Signs: Cool shadows of rock, sacred formations damp and low lying, somber solitude.

Keynote Event: A mature person from the West solidifies relationships and dissolves attachments.

SATURN in the North

Dealing with limitations and making a little go a long way is customary. There always seems to be some ordeal or impending difficulty which complicates an already toilsome existence. You are called upon to provide structure and security for others. An inability in making ends meet can put you between a rock and a hard place. Any progress is gradual, and slowly it is possible to overcome some of the (self-imposed?) boundaries. One way to do this is almost too obvious: relocate!

Nature Signs: Mountain chains, hilly borderlands defining regions. Monoliths indicating the ancient pathways, the network of the past.

Keynote Event: A mature person from the North controls, restrains and consolidates resources.

URANUS in the East

Ready or not, your personality will awaken to new and original ideas. There is quite a bit of restless energy that accompanies this combination and no guarantee that you'll be able to channel all of it into practical use. Do you want to be a reformer or a troublemaker? Do you easily scatter your mental energies? Even though you have all kinds of exciting ideas, will others still see you as digressing all over the place? Many of the things you do and say seem to be progressive, yet if you'll stop long enough to be objective, you may find that in many cases you've only learned to be different, simply deviating from one thing to the next. Is the freedom of unrestricted expression worth the price?

Life will never be complacent here, remaining turbulent in an attempt to find a fulfilling outlet for your erratic and anxious energy.

Nature Signs: Sudden winds rush across the upper atmosphere, the shifting jet stream alters its route.

Keynote Event: Without notice a stimulus from the East interrupts and alters your stream of consciousness.

URANUS in the South

Your independence is on the line and the big issue is: How can you make the best use of your talent? In your sphere of activities there could be people with empty or unworkable idealism, while others may have developed into magnificent leaders of lost causes. You have it in your power to be the catalyst for change and you must rely on your own ingenuity to pull it off. Gathering your forces will not be simple. Uncertainties seem to hang around, yet you have the willful attachment to bring about unique innovations.

Nature Signs: Flashes of electromagnetic force spin across the subtropics, pumping and channeling ions.

Keynote Events: Suddenly out of the South comes exciting and extraordinary aspirations and directions.

URANUS in the West

Dealings with people can be quite hectic and disruptive while paradoxically awakening fresh and innovative vistas. Although it's hard to categorize people in this locale, you could find yourself not being able to live with them without certain associations. Partnerships may lack a mutual give-and-take that is vital for a continuing healthy endurance. Conflicts arise because demands are made without the commitment to carry them through. The abrupt and alarming behavior of others can, at times, cause some sort of estrangement.

Nature Signs: The purging storms, thunder crashing and lightning recharging the atmosphere.

Keynote Event: Unexpectedly a person from the West with a contrary but inventive personality brings forth ingenious and extraordinary ideas.

URANUS in the North

Here your personal life is anything but typical. Unusual conditions come into play requiring you to alter standard behavior and traditional beliefs. Another way to look at this place is where the needs of family (or personal lifestyle) come up against your impersonal, selfish attitudes. Those in your immediate circle (including yourself) can be caught in a kind of future shock situation. The onrush of new ideas and technology may cause a variety of uncertainties and insecurities. These rapid changes impose irregularities on your domestic life, possibly causing you to question the foundations of what you stand for.

Nature Signs: Arching mesas as natural fortresses. Faults and fissures marking the Earth's mantle, the flexible and rigid crust of electromagnetic crystal.

Keynote Event: A stern and revolutionary influence from the North divides and conquers.

NEPTUNE in the East

Abstract, mystical, and deceptive influences pervade this place. Sensitivities which you may have been unaware of are now felt, seemingly for the first time. Your psyche is often flooded with many impressions which are not easy to sort out or understand without some confusion developing. Your personal charm is pronounced here, but so are feelings of inferiority and possibly a poor self-image. You need to use your perceptions to protect yourself from all the unseen, yet real delusions that are present. Your dream life should be more active and in time you may develop into a medium and/or mirror for others.

Nature Signs: The early breeze across the water, humid vapor softening and moisturizing.

Keynote Events: Subtle and complex feelings from the East inspire a receptive spirit.

NEPTUNE in the South

The ethics of the workplace and the soundness of your goals are tested. Humanitarian justice is a big issue not easily resolved; in other words it is important for you to feel right about your livelihood. All kinds of intrigue and scandal are possible if you allow yourself to commit to false ideologies. You may feel close to what you consider spiritual, yet without proper guidance these feelings can give way to escapism and fanciful longings.

Nature Signs: Insect larva on the lake, plankton on the ocean, surfaces that reflect and feed the chemistry of life.

Keynote Event: Devotional impressions from the South help develop compassion and an inner knowing.

NEPTUNE in the West

There's a whole assortment of ambiguous and mysterious circumstances awaiting you here. In this locality it may be quite easy to feel that you are surrounded by a host of devils and angels. People have a strong effect on you and they can be a source of spiritual uplifting as well as great disappointment.

Relationships may have a strong undermining influence; the habits of others and various skeletons in the closet interfere with your ability to trust others. It pays to be very discriminating, because quite often you'll find that people aren't what they appear to be.

Nature Signs: Great waves and currents steering and driving the oceanic planetary pulse.

Keynote Event: An undefinable force from the West reveals in a dream the meaning of certain symbols of reality.

NEPTUNE in the North

This is a somewhat reclusive place with an atmosphere of psychic escapades. Chronic family problems can surface, leading to depressing situations. A life of quiet desperations is promised unless some other positive factors counteract it. You can find yourself pondering the past while being receptive to the healing and hidden powers of nature. There seems to be much more suffering involved in your everyday living, and your problems seem to require more energy to resolve. The need to get away and a general sense of escapism is ever present.

Nature Signs: The weight of the polar ice, the cycles of freeze and thaw, snow slides rumbling downward. A dense fog hides the material world but condenses on the spiritual.

Keynote Event: Out of the North a transcendental mystery becomes a reality; imaginative designs are made concrete.

PLUTO in the East

Under this influence the best and worst qualities of your personality are expressed. You live life to its fullest, reacting intensely to many issues. It is quite easy to overshoot objectives and suffer the consequences, burning out and bouncing back again. The testing of your limits in different areas will occur, making it possible to really learn about your own resources, and seeing if you have the "right stuff." There is definitely a need to continually enforce your position because of a sense that you are always fighting someone or something. The common tendency is to be more compulsive, pushy and nervy, thus evoking the anger and resentment of others. Your outlook will tend to be too black and white—cut and dried. Finding ways to relax and cool down is not only healthy, but mentally uplifting.

Nature Signs: Pelting rains, steaming mornings, water rising to its limits.

Keynote Event: A force out of the East deciphers cryptic messages from the unconscious.

PLUTO in the South

In this locality the transforming and corrupting influences of power await you. It is common to be involved with some type of hierarchy that rewards and punishes with impromptu swiftness. You may encounter an assortment of despots and petty tyrants, as well as highly specialized and dedicated people. Under this influence you may live in a world of your own creation or manuever in the corporate world. You somehow have to control your desire nature in order to get to (what you consider) the top.

Nature Signs: Steaming vapors, a dripping humidity breeding life and consuming life.

Keynote Event: A dynamic onrush of power from the North transforms and consumes, altering destinies.

PLUTO in the West

Psychological preparation, like speaking softly and carrying a big stick, is very appropriate in this place. Anything from mass hysteria to total isolation is possible. Periodically you will find it difficult to separate yourself from the inclinations and destinies of large groups. You can play the game of one-upsmanship, feeling many types of undercurrents which are both manipulative and divisive. Others may literally try to reverse your life for better or worse.

Nature Signs: Great volumes of water: the tidal wave, hurricanes. Vast aquifers and tidal basins, pools of storage and life.

Keynote Event: In a deep silence a force from the West reaches inward, drawing out feeling and renewal.

PLUTO in the North

That which is vital and full of personal meaning is eventually uncovered in this locality, but not without hardship. Often you'll feel deep unconscious stirrings. You may have to become accustomed to living with an ample amount of pressure. You may feel threatened here and this could explain why you react defensively in personal matters. Strong reactions and outbursts revealing your innermost feelings can occur.

Nature Signs: Bubbling outpouring of mineral hot springs, cleansing and purifying. Crystal ice structures mirrored in still waters; a frozen, timeless world.

Keynote Event: The forces of providence from the North controlling, dominating, transforming the form and structure.

Table 13

II. Cross-Cultural, Multi-Level Geomantic (Local Space) Circle

	North	South	East	West
1	North	South	East	West
2	Midnight	Noon	Sunrise	Sunset
3	Winter	Summer	Spring	Autumn
4	The Laws	Light	Life	Love
5	Techniques The Act of Meditation	Self-realized One Perfect Meditation	The Self The Meditator	The Not-Self Object of Meditation
6	Earth Ch'i paths of Air & Water	Fire Electromagnetic/Lightning	Air Wood/Vegetation	Water Metal Conductors
7	Cold and humid	Warm and dry	Wind	Wet and cool
8	Older years, 63+	Adult, 21-42	Youth, 0-21	Middle age, 43-63
9	Winter/Solstice	Summer/Solstice	Spring/Equinox	Autumn/Equinox
10	Saturn, Transpluto	Sun, Mars, Jupiter	Mercury, Venus, Uranus	Moon, Neptune, Pluto
11	Frontal shield Disks/Coins	Power objects Rods, Wands	Magic weapons Swords, Crystals	Spirit catchers Cups
12	Auriel, Pandochus	Michael, Thoth	Raphael, Horus	Gabriel, Elurus
13	Gnomes, Body, Salt Geomancy	Salamanders, Soul/Memory, Sulphur, Pyromancy	Sylphs, Spirit, Azoth Aeromancy	Undines, Mind, Mercury Hydromancy
14	4th-3rd Houses Home and land Basic thinking A parent, car	10th-9th Houses Higher mind Education Profession; a parent	12th-1st Houses Personality Outlook Early years; habits, limits	6th-7th Houses Public Partnerships Marriage; work methods

#				
15	Patience/purity Renewal needed	Love/friendship is needed	Energetic/earth work is needed	Teaching/leading Evaluation needs Introspection
16	Powers and Wisdom	Innocence, Trust, Growth	Sees far and wide Reflects laws	Changing
17	Bad influence, barren, the dead, mystery	Good influence, growth, fertile	Good influence, new birth, abundance	Indifferent, decline
18	Wife	Travel	Life	Children
19	Business gains	Fame	Good family	Children's fame
20	Strength Resourceful, blunt, direct, tenacious woman.	Growth Nurturing, loud and shy, warm woman.	Order Optimistic, light-hearted, smooth, persistent woman.	Feeling Introspective, remorseful, sly, cunning, fierce, loony woman.
21	Knowledgeable Scholarly, noble, calm, dependable man.	Active Highly volatile man.	Courier An assistant; a silent, somber man.	Organizer Mysterious, unknowable and secretive man.
22	Amazon Practical, supportive, strong, capable, efficient.	Mother Protective, caring, nurturing. Compassionate, forgiving.	Hetaira Gifted mind, cultured, artful, loving, promiscuous.	Medium Prophetess, seeress, visionary. Intuitive, inspiratrice, creative.
23	Hero/Warrior Businessman, influential, soldier, statesman. Courage, drive.	Father/Hunter Supportive, sheltering, family values. Protecting, reassuring.	Puer/Intellect Youthful, airy, flighty, Flexible, changing mind, spirited.	Wise Man Insight, vision, creativity. A magician.

The Cross-Cultural, Multi-Level Geomantic Circle

The correspondences and correlations that could be added to this table are quite numerous. Therefore in constructing this geomantic circle, I had to be selective and include the most important cross-cultural data without excluding any vital points. The information in the basic system offers an excellent place to expand from, if the interested reader feels the need to add information. In some cases I've added, taken away or substituted one or two words. This was done for the purposes of clarification, and because of space constraints.

All the systems used in the construction of the circle were in agreement with one another, with only minor discrepancies. This is really remarkable, since in most cases the data used is from sources which are far removed from each other geographically and culturally.

There are a number of items that I was unable to add either because they did not fit into the directional format, or because it was found that they were culturally derived and therefore not universal in nature. Two examples of these cultural items were colors and animals which almost always differed from place to place.

Explanation of Geomantic Source Material

o *ONE.* The standard cardinal directions used on the compass.

o *TWO.* Apparent universal system for the Northern Hemisphere.[1] In the Southern Hemisphere noon would be midnight; also, in the Toltec system noon and midnight are reversed.

o *THREE.* Reversed in the Southern Hemisphere, i.e., summer is winter and spring is fall. This is another universal designation, but the source for this was the European magical tradition from Gray's book.[2]

o *FOUR.* A standard Western magical system taken from Gray.[3]

o *FIVE.* Basic Kriya yoga meditation formula.

o *SIX.* The four major elements are those agreed upon or strongly implied by almost every system. The additional information is from the Chinese Feng Shui system.[4]

o *SEVEN.* Weather Ch'i taken from the Feng Shui system.[5]

o *EIGHT.* Another taken from Feng Shui, but implied by others.[6]

o *NINE.* The seasonal/cardinal signs, for the Northern Hemisphere only, i.e., the winter solstice/Capricorn, spring equinox/Aires, summer solstice/Cancer and fall equinox/Libra.

○ *TEN.* In reviewing all the sources for the geomantic circle nowhere were all the planetary relationships mentioned for the ten known and two unknown (i.e., not observed) planets. After much deliberation, I have assigned the planets to where they seem to fit best. The planets follow the weather and element patterns; they do not necessarily follow their respective signs. Even though the planets have not been assigned places, keep in mind that in *actual* practice they are the variables and can be found anywhere around the Local Space circle.

In the Feng Shui system, the planets are given directions but seem out of place when they are compared to the other directional correspondences. Only when we take the Feng Shui placements as an equivalent of the Western Exaltation and Fall does it begin to make sense. Mercury in the north would mean that you have to teach and talk about the mysteries of the north. Mars in the south means that you have to take action for trust to develop, and for growth to occur. Venus in the west suggests that calm and balance are needed to deal with the emotions involved with subtle and abstract realities. Jupiter in the east could indicate that travel and expansion are necessary for intellectual and artistic development.

In the Feng Shui system, Saturn occupies the fifth direction, the center indicating a central structural permanence and stability of the physical brain/body and ego.[7]

○ *ELEVEN.* These are combined categories from Gray's magic ritual methods,[8] and Don Juan's Toltec System.[9]

○ *TWELVE.* The standard placements for the Archangels in Western magic and folklore.[10] Both Egyptian and Christian are given. Levi's Hebrew and Gnostic Archangels are different in a few cases.[11]

○ *THIRTEEN.* These listings come from Levi; they have an ancient Egyptian and Greek origin.[12]

○ *FOURTEEN.* Abbreviated versions of the standard houses that occupy the four directions in the Northern Hemisphere.

○ *FIFTEEN.* This listing comes from Sun Bear's Native American "Earth Astrology." I have taken the liberty of adding the word "needed," since the implication is evident when these listings are compared with the others.[13]

○ *SIXTEEN.* This group is from H. Storm's "Seven Arrows" system.[14] The correct name for this system is the Medicine Wheel, a common tool of self-discovery and divination among Amerindians.[15]

○ *SEVENTEEN.* This is the overly simplified version of Aztec astrological assignments as interpreted by Tunnicliffe.[16]

○ *EIGHTEEN.* This is the ancient eight-house Octopus System used by the Greeks and brought to light by C. Fagan. It is speculation on my part that this system had a use in the area of Local Space. However, the orientation toward direction is indicated, and therefore I felt that it had to be included.[17] In addition, this slot contains the Feng Shui eight-house system.[18]

○ *NINETEEN.* These are the I Ching correspondences taken from the Feng Shui system.[19] The entire set of trigrams are included in Figure 15.

○ *TWENTY.* These are the four corners of winds that females are drawn toward. Given by Don Juan in the "Rule of the Eagle."[20]

○ *TWENTY-ONE.* These are the male counterparts to the female directions. Although the males are not assigned a specific direction in the Toltec System,[21] they all fell into one of the directions quite comfortably. This is primarily due to their distinct characteristics.

○ *TWENTY-TWO.* These are the four types of women according to the Western depth psychological system of Wolff.[22] They can be viewed as the anima, the inner female half of the male unconscious or psyche. In both the male and female, the words in the beginning describe the general characteristics along with what is called the "bright face." The concluding words describe the "dark face" qualities.

○ *TWENTY-THREE.* These are Whitman's four male types and also the inner male half of woman, called the animus.[23]

Notes

References used for Figure 15:

Chu, W.K. and Sherrill, W.A., *The Astrology of I-Ching.* York Beach, Maine: Samuel Weiser, Inc., 1976.

Gray, Edin, *The Tarot Revealed.* New York: Bell Publishing Co., 1969.

Hall, Manly P., *The Secret Teaching of All Ages.* Los Angeles: Philosophical Research Society, 1977 (Reprinted from the 1929 edition, Crocker Co., San Francisco, CA).

Wilhelm, Richard, *The I Ching or Book of Changes.* Princeton, NJ: Princeton University Press, Bollingen Series XIX, 1967.

1. Gray, William, *Magical Ritual Methods.* Cheltenham, Engalnd: Helos Books, 1969, p. 59.
2. Gray, p. 59.
3. Gray, p. 59.
4. Skinner, Stephen, *The Living Earth Manual of Feng-Shui.* Boston: Routledge & Kegan Paul, 1982, p. 58.
5. Skinner, p. 58.
6. Skinner, p. 58.
7. Skinner, p. 58.
8. Gray, p. 59.
9. Castaneda, Carlos, *The Eagle's Gift.* New York: Simon and Schuster, 1981, p. 120-127.
10. Gray, p. 59.
11. Levi, Eliphas, *Transcendental Magic.* New York: Samuel Weiser, 1972, p. 61.
12. Levi, p. 228-236.
13. Bear, Sun, *The Medicine Wheel.* Englewood Cliffs, NJ: Prentice-Hall, Inc., 1980, p. 127-149.
14. Storm, Hyemeyhosts, *Seven Arrows.* New York: Harper & Row, 1972, p. 6.
15. Storm, p. 6.
16. Tunnicliffe, K.C., *Aztec Astrology.* Essex, England: L.N. Fowler & Co., 1979, p. 85.
17. Fagan, Cyril, *Astrological Origins.* St. Paul, MN: Llewellyn Publications, 1971, p. 163.
18. Rossbach, Sarah, *Feng Shui.* New York: E.P. Dutton Inc., 1983, p. 109.
19. Skinner, pp. 58 and 62.

20. Castaneda, p. 175.
21. Castaneda, p. 176.
22. Wolff, Toni, *Structural Forms of the Feminine Psyche.* Bern, Switzerland: Herausgeber G.H. Graber, 1956.
23. Whitmont, Edmund, *The Symbolic Quest.* New York: G.P. Putnam's 7 Sons, 1977.

CHAPTER 5

THE LOCAL SPACE CHART
AND PHYSICAL HEALTH

*T*he Local Space chart can provide a map to unravel the mystery of how any locality affects your physical, emotional and mental functions. Geomancy and mysticism alike have taught that man is a part of nature, and *not* apart from nature. This fact is one of the principles that we are constantly being reminded of in locality astrology.

When dealing with your physical body it is important to keep in mind that you are composed of the same substances that you find in your back yard. Your body is, in fact, a system of tubes and biochemical interactions, and in many respects you are an organic computer, capable of responding to the most subtle of stimuli. Your mind even registers an average brain wave pattern of 13 to 15 cycles per second, which happens to be the same frequency as that of the ionosphere.

Although medical science has increased the life expectancy 25 years in the last 50 years, and cured many age-old diseases, there are many physical problems that can't be changed at present. This being the case, you have the viable option of getting the right amount of physical exercise and eating fresh and wholesome foods, along with an awareness of the effects of your immediate environment. In attempting to really live a more healthy lifestyle, it becomes necessary for you to make changes, and in doing so you come up against old mental habits, as well as ingrained behaviors and emotional patterns.

Astrology says that these unhealthy habits can be traced to certain aspects in the birth chart; furthermore, we know that the birth chart is constructed according to the exact locality (latitude and longitude) of birth. Sociology tells us that most people are products of their environments. If you change this environment, can you change the product as well, and improve its health and productivity? locality astrology responds with a resounding "yes."

Using the Local Space map for any locality provides you with the necessary insights on how the planets will affect your health, thinking and inner life. Examine Table 14, which gives basic correspondences of planet, sign and sector to a general body area.

The Local Space Houses correspond to the signs and planets, e.g., Mars/Aries/First House, etc. It has been my experience that the twelve divisions of the horizon—the Local Space Houses—have a mild or weak effect on physical health. Close planetary aspects have the most influence.

Generally speaking, the two planets which promote physical health are Jupiter and the Sun. When they are close to the angles, or low in altitude, that locality will tend to upgrade health. Any soft aspects with the Sun or Jupiter in the Local Space chart can also prove helpful, but often to a lesser extent. Mars and Pluto can be quite helpful with body vitality; however, they need soft aspects to them, and it helps if they are constructive in the birth chart.

Mercury and Venus by themselves may not be strong enough to consistently affect health, however in most situations they can be counted on as a positive influence. Saturn and Neptune usually cause problems of one sort or another.

What I'm proposing is a theoretical outline of how stellar and planetary energies relate to the human psychophysiology, and how the vital force (Ch'i or Prana) in the universe functions on the Earth and in man.

Whether you stay in or near your birth locality, or relocate to other places, or are in the process of travel, the physical and non-physical parts of yourself are always oriented toward the four great circles. These circles, the equator, ecliptic, horizon and Prime Vertical, are measuring systems whereby man can locate the positions of the planets and stars. Each system was developed under a different cultural emphasis and during a different time in history. The Chinese and Egyptians developed and favored the equatorial system, perhaps as early as 2000 B.C. The Greeks developed the ecliptic system around 600 B.C. The Arabian and Mesoamerican cultures developed and worked with the horizon and Prime Vertical between 700 A.D. and 1300 A.D. The cultural and metaphysical orientation of each circle is

Table 14

Anatomical & Physiological Correspondences with Planets & Signs

SUN/LEO: Heart, spine in general, overall constitution, circulation, right eye, left brain, frontal cortex center.

MOON/CANCER: Pscyhosomatic reactions, skin, fat/water content, allergies, stomach, blood, sleep patterns, left eye, right brain, medullary center.

MERCURY/GEMINI: Arms, lungs, parasympathetic nervous system, upper throat, normal thinking, cervical center (right side).

MERCURY/VIRGO: Hands, upper intestine, sympathetic nervous system, upper throat, concrete thinking, cervical center (left side).

VENUS/LIBRA: Ovaries (right), kidneys (right), small of back, buttocks, bronchial tubes, dorsal center (right side).

TRANSPLUTO/TAURUS: Ovaries (left), kidneys (left), thyroid gland, throat, neck, salivation, sweat glands, dorsal center (left side).

MARS/ARIES: The head in general, muscular system, body temperature, overt sexuality, white blood cells, adrenals, lumbar center (right side).

PLUTO/SCORPIO: Covert sexuality, reproductive organs, rectum, colon, fight or flight reactions, swellings, lumbar center (left side).

JUPITER/SAGITTARIUS: Hip bones, liver, thighs, recuperative abilities, fat cells, sacral center (right side).

NEPTUNE/PISCES: Feet, pineal gland, lowered resistance, dreaming function, sacral center (left side).

URANUS/AQUARIUS: Ankles, pituitary gland, aura, spinal nerves, coccygeal center (right side).

SATURN/CAPRICORN: Bones, knees, teeth, general skeletal structure, inner ear, coccygeal center (left side).

NODES: Polarity functions of the astral/dream body.

undeniable. The very fact that each system causes one to view the sky in a different way relates directly to one's own psychophysical health.

It is a precept of Western metaphysics and of East Indian and Chinese medicine that human beings unconsciously function on four different levels. Each one of these levels in turn corresponds to a state of consciousness. The first level is the physical, and it relates to the waking state of consciousness. For most people, this state applies only to the five senses. The second level is the astral body, which relates to the dreaming state of consciousness. The third is the higher mental body, which relates to the deep-sleep state. The fourth and final level is the deathless/spirit or higher-self, relating to the cosmic consciousness state.

According to yogic theory and practice the four states of consciousness function within and through a series of chakras, or wheels. These chakras, or psychic centers (as they are called in the West), are a complex system of interrelationships on various levels of consciousness. Each of the non-physical centers is located along the spine and is connected to a physical nerve plexus. The vital life force for any individual flows from the higher levels of consciousness into the spinal centers, where it becomes a kriya/kundalini current—the active vital force in the human body, measured as nerve impulses.

Although the physiological and psychic functions of each center are known, the exact locations, size, and degree of potential balance in each center will vary depending on the birth chart, which in turn is modified by location.

In the following Table 15 the standard twelve-House system (with six centers) is listed. There are five dual and two single centers. The single centers are the Sun/Leo/male at the cortex between the eyebrows and the Moon/Cancer/female center at the medulla in the back of the head. The remaining five centers are dual, with the Water and Earth signs on the left/female side of the spine, and the Fire and Air signs on the right/male side.

The way the four circles work relating to the states of consciousness depends on the position and location of the physical body, and on the amount of self-conscious awareness that you as an individual have attained.

Table 15

Spinal Section	Located at	Plexus	Planets	Sign/House
Coccygeal	Base of spine	Sacral	Saturn	Capricorn/10th
			Uranus	Aquarius/11th
Sacral	Genital level	Prostatic	Neptune	Pisces/12th
			Jupiter	Sagittarius/9th
Lumbar	Navel level	Tepigastic	Pluto	Scorpio/8th
			Mars	Aries/1st
Dorsal	Heart level	Cardiac	Transpluto	Taurus/2nd
			Venus	Libra/7th
Cervical	Throat level	Pharyngeal	Mercury	Virgo/6th
			Asteroids?	Gemini/3rd
Medullary	Eyebrow level	Cavernous	Moon	Cancer/4th
			Sun	Leo/5th

The sixteen system is looked upon as a semi-dormant system predating the above in the evolution of consciousness. Here there are nine centers—seven dual and two singular. The singles are the Nodes, with the north Node at the top of the head and the south Node at the (now non-existant) tail: the dragon's head and tail! The Moon was a dual center in the head. The Sun (dual) was at the sternum between the Mars and Venus centers.

The equator is really only a geographical measurement of the Earth; therefore it represents the connectedness of spirit with the physical body in any position or orientation.

Table 16

Correspondences of Three Systems

Ecliptic

Observed Tract: 180 degrees, tilted; the tilt-a-whirl.
Type System: Solar, i.e. the Sun's path, relating to the celestial.
State of Consciousness: Awake, everyday awareness, five senses.
Psychic Centers: 12 system, 6 centers; five dual and two single.
Directions: North/south (zodiac belt), faces opposite ecliptic.
Body Positions: Vertical; sitting or standing.
Rotations: Both clockwise and counterclockwise.

Horizon

Observed Tract: 360 degrees around; the merry-go-round.
Type System: Lunar; relating to terrestrial happenings.
State of Consciousness: Sleep state, dreams, desires.
Psychic Centers: 16 system, 9 centers; seven dual, two single.
Direction: East/west, sunrise/sunset, east preferred.
Body Position: Horizontal, lying down.
Rotation: Only clockwise.

Prime Vertical

Observed Tract: 180 degrees, directly overhead; a Ferris wheel.
Type System: Planetary and stellar influences.
State of Consciousness: Deep, dreamless sleep.
Psychic Centers: Upper four.
Direction: Above the head, zenith; below the feet, nadir.
Body Position: Vertical in meditation but horizontal in sleep.
Rotation: Only clockwise.

The *observed tract* is the orientation as viewed by the observer; the *type system* the main astrological concentration; the *state of consciousness* the corresponding states induced; the *psychic centers* the etheric and physical ganglia activated; the *direction* the advantageous (natural) body position; the *body position* the description of this position; the *rotation* the observed planetary and stellar movement.

From Table 16 it can be seen that when the physical body is parallel, i.e. horizontal to the Earth's surface, sleep is induced. On the other hand, keeping the body vertical to the surface promotes deeper and more aware states. Thus good posture is not only physically advantageous, but it also allows the spinal current to lift properly through the centers. Therefore all meditation positions are vertical to the surface. If they are horizontal, then dreams and astral projections can take place; they may not be as productive as meditation, but on the other hand, they are necessary for rest.

From Table 14 on page 129 you can ascertain what part of your body will be sensitized by a significant planet. In Table 15 on page 131 you can see how a prominent planet will affect your psychic system. In Table 16 on page 131 you can find out how the planets in the three systems operate in a variety of ways.

Different views of the cosmos have been created because the great circles are, in the final analysis, a blend of cultural and religious beliefs along with personal preferences. In regards to health the ancients have said: What a man thinks, so he is. Mind rules body and form follows function.

The following are planetary pairs used primarily for conjunctions and oppositions—the two planetary aspects which affect health more adversely than any others. With squares, the orb must be two degrees or less. This is *not* a diagnosis.

1. *Saturn/Neptune*—Inert and inactive physiology, slow recuperation, persistent blockages, lingering problems, hampered progress, adverse reaction from most drugs.

2. *Mars/Neptune*—Very susceptible to infectious diseases, strong adverse reaction to drugs, build-up of toxins, mucus, or pus.

3. *Mars/Saturn*—Destroyed vitality, breakdown of organs, incisions into the body, muscle and joint problems.

4. *Neptune/Ascendant (Anti-Vertex)*—Psychosomatic problems, illusions of the senses, infections, oddities.

5. *Saturn/Ascendant (Anti-Vertex)*—Defective organs and/or glands, hereditary problems, depressed functions.

When three or more of these planets and/or points appear together in the same sector/house, then the probability of health problems increases. Other planets involving hard angles to those same planets in the natal or Local Space charts will compound the situation.

CHAPTER 6

RELOCATION TECHNIQUES

*T*he most commonly used system is the Ecliptic, the particular plane of reference of which is the Sun's path across the Earth's surface—which is another way of saying the Earth's orbit around the Sun. The measurements along the ecliptic are in zodiacal longitude from 0 to 360 degrees in an easterly to westerly direction; see Figures 16 (page 136) and 17 (page 138).

Declination is the term used for a planet's position north or south of the equator, measured from the ecliptic. Declination is measured from 0 to 90 degrees both north and south. In relationship to the seasons on Earth in the Northern Hemisphere, the Sun is 23 degrees 26 minutes declination south on December 20th, and 26 degrees declination north on June 20th. On the 20th of March and 20th of September, the Sun is at 00 degrees declination—at the equator.

The 360 degrees of the zodiac are derived from the fact that the ecliptic when viewed from the Earth passes through twelve groupings of stars called constellations. These groupings of stars have been subsequently divided into twelve equal parts called the signs of the zodiac. There are two major zodiacs, the Tropical/Seasonal and the Sidereal/Constellational.

The most common zodiac in use is the Tropical. It is based on the Earth's rotation and orbit, which determine the seasonal variations. When the Sun is at its furthest point in the Northern Hemisphere (see Figure 16, page 136), we experience the longest day of the year in the

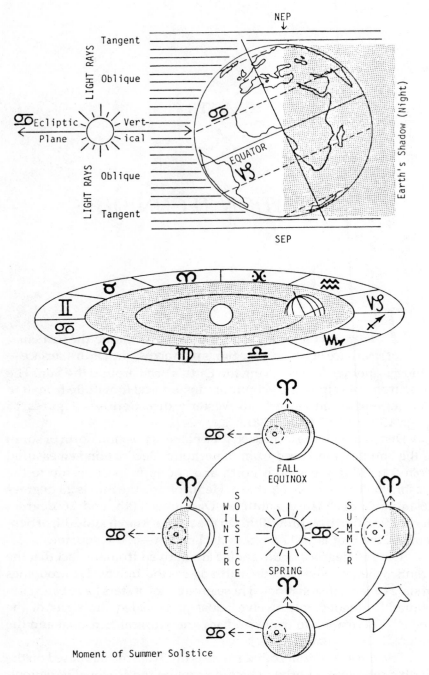

Fig. 16—The Ecliptic, the Signs and the Seasons

Northern Hemisphere: the Summer Solstice (which means "standing still"). The Summer Solstice is also the beginning of the zodiacal sign of Cancer. In the Southern Hemisphere, this is the shortest day of the year, and the beginning of winter. When the Sun moves southward and is at the Earth's equator, the Autumnal Equinox ("equal night") is reached. This is the beginning of the Tropical zodiacal sign of Libra. When the Sun is at its furthest point south, then we have the Winter Solstice, which is the shortest day of the year in the Northern Hemisphere, and the beginning of winter as well as of the zodiacal sign Capricorn. (In the Southern Hemisphere it is the longest day of the year, and the beginning of summer.) To complete the circle, the Sun's energies are once again back at the equator, moving north, at the time of the Vernal Equinox; this is the beginning of spring, as well as the beginning of the sign Aries.

If the Ecliptic System coordinates are the ones that are used for calculating a horoscope, then how do we arrive at the major angles in most House systems? Look now at Figure 17 on page 138. You can see that the M.C. (Medium Coeli: "middle of the sky"), or the Tenth House cusp, is the point on the ecliptic where the celestial meridian and the celestial equator intersect in the southern direction. The I.C. (Imum Coeli: "under sky"), which is directly opposite the M.C., is at the same intersection but in the northern direction. There are a number of ways in which to measure the Ascendant, but the most common is the easterly intersection of the ecliptic with the horizon. Therefore the Descendant is the same, only in a westerly direction.

The second major system is the Equatorial System. Its particular plane of reference is the Earth's equator. The measurement along this plane is in degrees of right ascension, from 0 to 360 degrees east to west. The other name for right ascension is geographical longitude, east or west (see Figures 18 and 19C). A generic term for a line stretching in a north/south direction is a "meridian." The meridian at Greenwich, England represents the beginning of the series of time zones around the Earth, and the point of 0 degrees of longitude.

Distance north and south of the equator is measured in latitude, which is the equivalent of declination. Latitude is expressed as 0 to 90 degrees in both directions, north or south, from the equator. When a planet is in right ascension in the Equatorial System, it is not necessarily in the same place in the Zodiacal/Ecliptic System. If you study Figures 17, 18 and 19A and C, you'll see that the ecliptic circle and the equatorial circle run perpendicular to one another, except when a

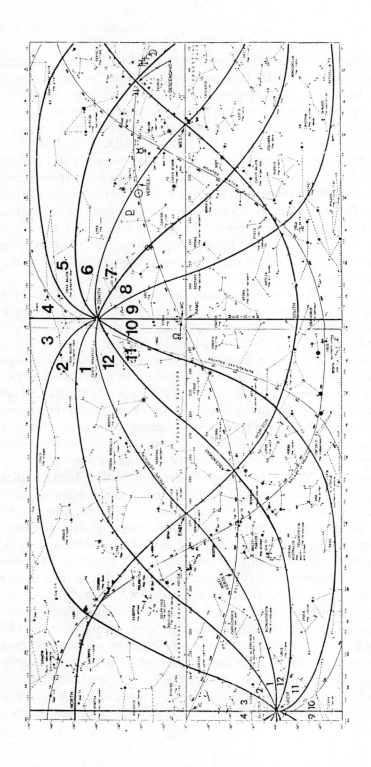

Fig. 17

The sky measured into twelve Local Space Houses and four systems.

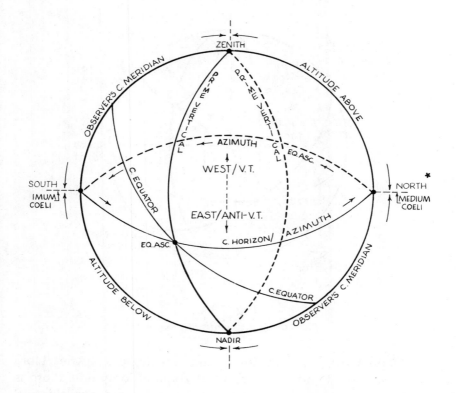

Fig. 18—*The Celestial Sphere**

*—*Medium Coeli and Imum Coeli are for the Southern Hemisphere;*
reverse for Northern Hemisphere.

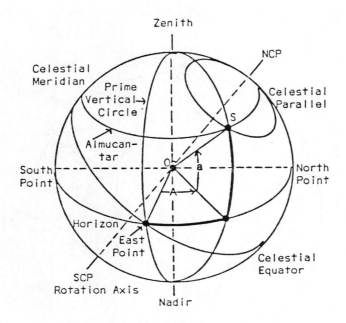

Fig. 19A

The Horizon Coordinate System

planet happens to be near the intersection at 0 degrees of Aries/Libra —which is both 0 and 180 degrees of zodiacal longitude. Pluto is usually the most out of line, due to its variable speeds in elliptical orbit.

Let's look at the Horizon System and see where it fits with the other two, and most importantly how it differs. The plane of reference in the Horizon System is the visible or sensible horizon. This means that if you were standing on the ideal surface of a flat plane, such as a desert floor, you could see an even horizon in all directions around you, assuming that there were no large mountains or hills in any direction. This horizon is in fact tangent to the surface. The complete circle around you is measured in azimuth, and it contains 360 degrees. The other measurement is called altitude and pertains to the elevation of a planet above and below the horizon, measured from 0 to 90 degrees. Regardless of the various altitudes of the planets, the important thing to grasp is that the planets are located within 360 degrees of *azimuth,* and therefore they fall in line with the cardinal directions of

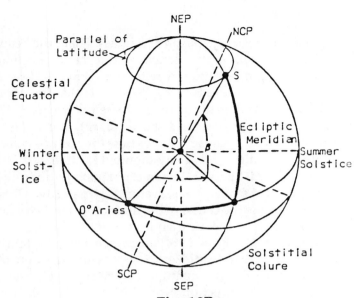

Fig. 19B

The Ecliptic Coordinate System

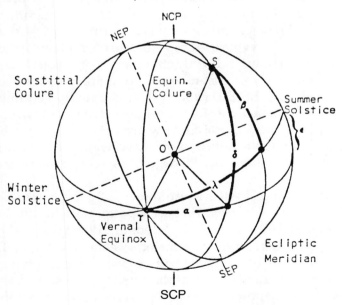

Fig. 19C

The Equatorial Coordinate System

north, south, east and west, just like on a compass. That's the beauty of this system: the movement of the planets in time, and the actual visible sky in any location, are united with the compass directions. Another unique feature of the Horizon System is that the zenith is always directly above your head and the nadir below your feet. This is an exact representation of time and space (place), and even more exact than the natal chart, because it shows how the cosmos is seen by an observer at any location and at any moment in time.

Therefore, the Local Space/Horizon is not just symbolically correct but actually correct from an observational perspective. To say it another way, *you* become the center of the horizon circle, because you are at all times the center of your own universe.

Looking at Figures 17, 18 and 19B, you can see that in the Horizon/ Azimuth System, due east (Anti-Vertex) is the intersection of the Prime Vertical and the celestial equator on the horizon. The Vertex in the west is in the opposite direction. Notice that the celestial meridian intersects the horizon at the north and south points.

There is one other coordinate system; although it is not usually considered one of the three major systems, it is a very important one. The plane of reference in this system is the Prime Vertical, the east/ west circle that is always 90 degrees vertical to the horizontal/horizon plane. This circle is always directly above and below your location; it makes a large circle from east to west and in doing so connects the zenith and nadir. The height factor is called amplitude. It is a measurement that shows a planet's position on either side, i.e. north or south of the plane of the Prime Vertical circle, which runs east to west directly overhead. Amplitude is measured from 0 to 90 degrees above and below the horizon, i.e., there are four 90-degree angles, two above and two below.

The Prime Vertical System is also known as the Campanus Houses, or mundoscope. It is very useful in Local Space work when the locality is below 30 north latitude (or above 30 south). When the locality gets closer to the equator, the three major systems converge. This is because the 23.5° tilt of the planet with respect to the ecliptic is not as obvious at the equator. You are at the center of the sphere and not toward either of the poles. Although the convergence is not exact, it does nullify some of the horizon's unique measurements. This is especially true of the Horizon System, in which the planets will bunch up in an east and west direction for a Local Space chart drawn near or at the equator. The Prime Vertical, however, remains intact at the equator, and the Local Space planetary positions can be shifted to this plane of reference (see Chapter 5).

Johndro gave some very descriptive terms for the above systems. He called the Horizon System the "merry-go-round," which gives a clear picture of what is represented: a circle on the horizon around us, with ourselves at the center. The "Ferris wheel" is the Prime Vertical placed 90 degrees to the "merry-go-round." We are still at the center, but the Ferris wheel is directly above and below us.

If the horizon and the Prime Vertical are the merry-go-round and Ferris wheel respectively, then the ecliptic has to be the "tilt-a-wheel." In the northern and southern latitudes, the plane of the ecliptic is tilted above and below the horizon. It appears untilted when we reach the equator, where horizon and ecliptic are very nearly the same.

Edward Johndro's Contributions

There's no more fitting introduction to relocation techniques than the work of L. Edward Johndro. His work in locality predates everyone except Sepharial. In 1929, Johndro introduced a whole group of theories which he had been using.[1]

It's very inspiring to know that back in the 1920's, locality astrology was already being practiced. When Johndro talked about various methods in locality astrology, he attempted to explain them by relating them to what were at that time the most advanced theories in physics and electromagnetism. Although he lacked the laboratory and extensive research to prove many of his theories, he nonetheless set forth some of astrology's most original and intriguing ideas.

One of his main points, the one he hammers home time and time again, concerns electromagnetism and the chart angles. He likened the Earth to a crystal*—as a charged body rotating in space. He pointed out that planet Earth's relationship with the cosmos is measured by astrological and astronomical great circles: the ecliptic, equator, horizon, Prime Vertical, and meridians.

He described the ecliptic, the Ascendant/Descendant axis, as basically "electromagnetic" in nature, and the right ascension M.C./I.C. as "electrodynamic." He further explained that when planets are aspecting the Ascendant/Descendant they manifest as psychological inducements, i.e. various attractions and repulsions. In Johndro's theory the Ascendant/Descendant reveals the "intensity of current"—the voltage in its static state.

---

*Similar to Buckminster Fuller's "spaceship Earth" concepts.

In reference to the M.C./I.C., Johndro makes a very important distinction. Planets in aspect to these angles are basically electrodynamic in nature; they "deliver the current," thus producing current events and/or the turn of events.

In making these distinctions, Johndro said that there are really two Ascendants: one electrical and one magnetic. Magnetic current is the standard Ascendant/Descendant, but the electric current is none other than the Anti-Vertex/Vertex employed in Local Space. Johndro maintained that anything connected with the ecliptic is usually an indicator of potential. However, anything relating to right ascension— M.C./I.C. or the equator—actually "causes" the events. Of course, when you're talking about the M.C./I.C., which is really south and north, you have to include east and west or the Anti-Vertex/Vertex of the Horizon System. This is one explanation as to why many astrologers have found the four directions/angles in the Local Space chart characteristic of direct events.

Johndro pointed out that the electromagnetic and electrodynamic currents and their flows are in constant interplay, producing many of the effects that astrology attempts to identify and place in time. In the matter of timing, Johndro recommended that an orb of 16' (minutes) be used, basing this on the fact that the Sun's light frequencies are 32' in width (the ecliptic is approximately 16' wide). He said that events usually occur at the beginning, the middle or the end of the orb, i.e. 0', 16', or 32'. He continued his analysis by saying that important factors are the type of event(s) and planet(s), the amount or degree of aspects involved, and what angle is highlighted at any given time. He called all the above "couplings," and likened these various systems and planets to the geometric and trigonometric problems of Einstein's "tangle of world lines" (see Figure 20).

Making the system more complete and at the same time more complex, Johndro also used secondary and solar arc directions, along with eclipses and planetary stations, to predict events.

Johndro's theories did not stop with planetary influences. In his second book, *The Stars,* he examined ways in which the fixed stars related to certain geographical areas. He didn't feel that the stars had specific qualities in and of themselves; instead he felt that they were points of radiant energy which were amplified by the planets aspecting them. He did point out that large magnitude stars were more important than the hundreds of visible stars and approximately 71,000 very dim stars. According to Johndro, the main function of the stars

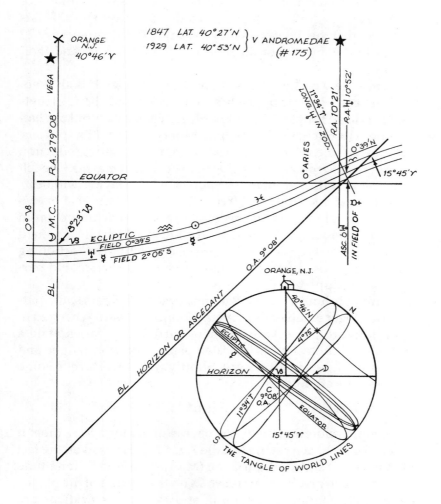

Fig. 20—*Johndro's R.A.-Ecliptic Star Location Lines*

was to amplify the good, bad or mixed influences of the planets in a given locality. He felt that in some cases, they could cause an influence to be felt for a longer duration than one would normally expect. This is due to the fact that the fixed stars move at a rate of 1 degree every 72 years. Later in this book we will return to the fixed stars and their various uses.

Johndro's view of the inner workings of astrology is both revolutionary and complex. He basically saw the Earth and all the planets as charged bodies. He described the Earth as a charged crystal oscillating at a certain frequency with the Sun, Moon and the other planets. Therefore, to him the solar system was in a constant state of induction with respect to electromagnetic fields of the charged masses.[2] He felt that each planet reflected many harmonics while staying within its own fundamental note/tone and frequency. He believed that events came forth from the various forms of electromagnetic induction in respect to the interactivity of planes and planets, which all happened at the speed of light. He also felt that because gravity was functioning within this set of coordinates, our rate of consciousness could perceive events as happening separately.

In honor of Johndro's achievements, every two years some outstanding astrologer receives the coveted Johndro Award (changed in 1986 to the Johndro-Jayne Award, in honor of the late Charles Jayne, a very versatile, technical and dedicated astrologer who taught and inspired many leaders in astrology). Shortly we shall return to some of Johndro's relocation ideas.

Relocation Charts and Astro*Carto*Graphy®

The simple relocation chart has been with us for a long time. It can be traced back to at least the Middle Ages, and is based on the fact that the Ascendant and Medium Coeli (M.C.) are found by longitude and latitude, which give an exact location on the surface of the planet. We know that geographic longitude and the time meridians are measured in right ascension. (The term "meridian" is used because this line always crosses the equator at right angles. The meridian/longitude is always vertical and 90 degrees to the horizontal equator.) Each time zone contains 15 degrees of longitude, with all time zones beginning at Greenwich, England. Each increment of 15 degrees is equal to 1 hour of sidereal time, so when you want to calculate a chart for a new location, you have to use the new longitude. Every degree of longitude east or west of your birth place will change the Medium

Coeli approximately one degree. In a manner of speaking, the birth chart will rotate when you move from any location—counterclockwise when the movement is to the west, and clockwise when the movement is to the east.

If you are interested in calculating a relocation chart yourself, you must first note the difference in longitude from the birth location to the new location. Longitude can be changed into minutes by multiplying 4x the number of degrees difference in longitude. This amount in minutes is then added or subtracted from the sidereal time at birth.

Example 1. If you were born at 90 degrees west longitude and you moved to 120 degrees west longitude:

$$120$$
$$-90$$
$$\overline{30}$$
   30   (difference in longitude)

   30x4 = 120' or 2 hours.

The 2 hours is then subtracted from the birth sidereal time, because the movement is westerly. If it were east of the birth place, you would add the 2-hour increment. The corresponding Ascendant is then found in a Table of Houses (for the new latitude). Remember that the right ascension or Medium Coeli (Tenth House) will be uniform, but the Ascendant will vary according to the latitude.

If you have a computer program, in most cases all you need to do is to enter the true time and date of birth, and then put in the new latitude and longitude; depending on the program, it may not be necessary to change the time zone.

Even though the longitude degrees of your birth Ascendant and Medium Coeli are *always* used no matter where you live, the fact remains that the chart does change or rotate when we move. The changing angles of the chart are, of course, the whole basis of what Locality Astrology is all about.

Lest we become too optimistic, keep in mind that the aspects between the planets do not change. How could they, since the aspects they form with one another are out in space, viewed from the Earth (viewed from the Sun they would be heliocentric aspects)? The natal/birth aspects remain fixed; this leaves us with the only choice: changing the angles, which includes the Anti-Vertex and Vertex. It is not possible to alter the time of birth after it has happened, but we can alter space by moving or traveling to another place.

A Mars conjunct Saturn in your chart may be in the Fifth House, affecting your children. If you didn't want it to affect your children, you could shift it to the Sixth or Fourth Houses. Moving west would put the conjunction in the Sixth House, because a westward movement backs the chart up. Moving to the east, it would be rotated to the Fourth House. You can't change the aspect of Mars conjunct Saturn; however after you are in the new location it will be out of the Fifth House, and your children may feel it less. Depending on which direction you moved (under 1,000 miles), Mars conjunct Saturn will either affect your health (Sixth House) or home life (Fourth House).

The option of relocating is taken for granted, yet it has only been in the last 75 years that a substantial number of people in the world had the economic and technological means whereby they could relocate or travel if they chose to do so. Today the economic and political realities in most countries still prevent the great majority of the world's population from relocating. Freedom of movement, like freedom of information, is most certainly a great blessing, offering a fantastic advantage.

Government statistics point out that on the average, each American over the last 40 years has moved at least four times from his/her birth place. Granted, some of these moves may have been only across the street, but as Local Space has shown, even a small move can make a *big* difference. In the future, Americans will tend to move less. The reasons are many, but the main factor involves the baby boom generation (90% have Pluto in Leo). They will be settling down because of ecological trends, with a standardization of services, and stronger feelings of regionalism. Also, travel may be temporarily restricted for economic or national security reasons. These trends should place a greater emphasis on the study of Local Space influence in the home and community. It should also encourage you to take a closer look at the influences you have to work with locally, whether in your birth place or in some other location.

Rotating the chart back and forth is in fact searching for the right channel of expression, the place where you feel tuned in and more alive. What if Neptune were on your Medium Coeli at birth? If you move east or west, every 50 miles would move Neptune approximately 1 degree farther away from your Midheaven. Let's say Saturn is in your First House, 10 degrees from the Ascendant; therefore if you moved too far east (clockwise rotation) and south, Saturn would come to the First House cusp. In effect you may get away from nebulous Neptune only to have solid Saturn clobber you. The problem with "dial-an-angle" logic is one that astrologers are continually confronted with by anxious clients. Questions like: "Where in the world is the all-round best place for me to be? What is the best South American city for my particular career?" These are not easy questions, but they are very important ones. In the past, the astrologer was faced with calculating many charts by hand to get the right answer to the above questions and others like them. It took time and energy and increased the fee, sometimes to a level that was more than clients were willing to spend. Fortunately, in 1977 Astro*Carto*Graphy® came to the rescue.

The Role of Astro*Carto*Graphy®

This method given form by Jim Lewis fulfilled the old adage that "a picture is worth a thousand words." The entire surface of the Earth can be viewed at once. The various straight and curved lines representing an individual's planets on the four angles can all be viewed on one printout.* The ten planets are shown in conjunction to the four angles, for a total of 40 different lines. This introduced thousands of people to the practical uses of locality astrology. It has also given professional astrologers a reliable and accurate tool to pinpoint the correct locations.

The Astro*Carto*Graphy® maps are calculated from right ascension *only*, i.e. the north/south meridians' intersections with the equator. These are called the mundane positions or "in mundo" (see Figure 21, pages 150-151). They work out fine for all of the planets in conjunction with the Medium Coeli or Imum Coeli. However, when it comes to planets conjunct the standard (ecliptic) Ascendant/Descendant, there is a difference not shown on astrocartographic figures. Pluto, Venus and the Moon show the greatest differences. These three bodies achieve higher latitudes than the others: the Moon reaches 5.5 degrees, Venus 8.5 and Pluto 18 degrees of latitude. (This is the measurement of how far planets are from, or off of, the ecliptic. Mars sometimes reaches 7 degrees and Mercury 5, but the frequency of these measurements is much less.) These extreme latitudes produce a 1 to 6 degree *difference* between the standard ascending position (ecliptic) and the equatorial ascendant, which is really the Ascendant at 0 latitude, always 90 degrees from the Medium Coeli.

---

*Similar figures plus Local Space maps can be generated on a home computer using Matrix Software's M-95 Astro-Maps program.

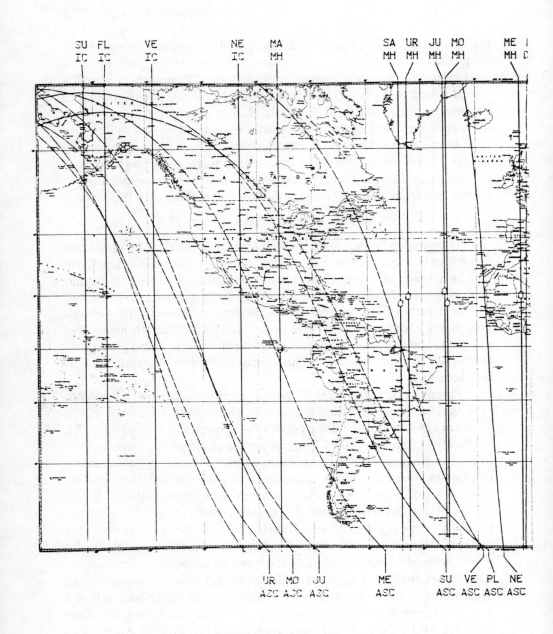

Fig. 21—*Astro*Carto*Graphy*®

MA   SU PL   VE   NE   MA   SA UR JU MO SA
DSC   MH MH   MH   MH   IC   IC IC IC IC ASC

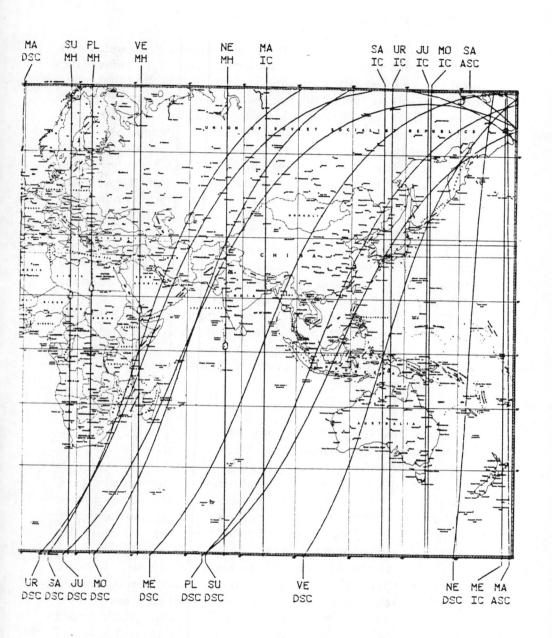

UR SA JU MO   ME   PL SU   VE   NE ME MA
DSC DSC DSC DSC DSC DSC DSC   DSC   DSC IC ASC

151

This can put the Moon off by about a degree, or 50 miles, and Venus by about 3 degrees, or 150 miles maximum. Pluto is *always* off, and it can be by as much as 6 degrees, which is around 300 miles difference—much beyond the suggested orb of influence (50 mi.=1 degree).* This means that there are *always* two Pluto lines/measurements and in some cases two lines for the other planets as well.

The lines you see on the Astro*Carto*Graphy® map are calculated from right ascension; they are the exact rise and set positions. The lines that are *not* on the map are the standard Ascendant/Descendant positions. You would get these if you did a (non-graphic) relocation chart. (Some services allow you to pick one or the other.) See Figure 22.

The standard Ascendant/Descendant lines are usually somewhere west of the right ascension lines on the map. Exactly how they differ, or which one works better, is a matter of opinion. Mundane astrologers will tell you that the rise/set positions work best. If we accept the Johndro theories, then the (ecliptic) Ascendant/Descendant position will show inducements while the (right ascension) equator rise/set will produce events. Personally, I would rather get Pluto inducements than Pluto events, or Jupiter events rather than Jupiter inducements.

Astro-Mapping

Astro*Carto*Graphy® maps show all ten bodies used in astrology in conjunction with rising, setting, Medium Coeli and Imum Coeli, representing the most significant places on Earth for the individual. It is common knowledge that the conjunction is a powerful aspect, because it unites, fuses and blends the energies of the planets and/or angles involved. Of course, other aspects can be formed to the angles; even though they will never be as potent as the conjunction, the fact is they exist for almost every location.

When an area seems blank on the map, it really isn't; there are *always* other aspects. Most will not amount to much. However, when they are a degree or less in orb and two or more of them are present, they definitely will be noticed. This is especially true if the soft or hard types predominate; i.e., two squares with no trines or sextiles, or two trines and one sextile with no squares, etc. (see Figure 22, page 153). (If the Local Space map is done for the same location we would,

---

*This orb of fifty miles east and west of a planetary line is really about 100 miles in *each* direction due to the common 1 to 2 degrees difference between the two systems.

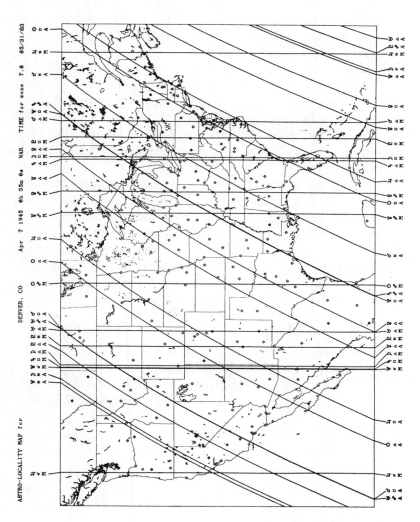

Fig. 22—Astro Locality Map with Aspects
by Astro Computing Services

no doubt, find a number of additional important positions.)

Keep in mind that the 40 planetary lines on the Earth's surface will remain fixed. However, you do not have to remain fixed in one place. Being in a new location for the first time may be a new experience, but the line has always been there. You can't move a planet from a location, but you always have the option of moving away from any planetary influence/location.

In looking over your map you may find that some potentially wonderful places run through the middle of the Atlantic or Pacific oceans; such is the nature of your chart. Of course, if you sailed near these lines you could have a great time. There are also potentially favorable lines in countries that are either too far away or offer a hostile political climate. It's equally true that places you hear about as being exotic and/or filled with opportunity are not going to be good for you if there is a difficult line close by. It takes a bit of study, knowing your lifestyle goals, and working with the process of elimination. You'll eventually find a number of areas that look attractive.

Another interesting point is that you really don't have to visit all the possible locations to get an idea of how they can influence you. Quite often you will meet people from different places that you like or dislike. It seems that people tend to help or hinder you, depending on your personal line that runs through the place they are from!

The simple steps are:

1. Know what you want. Define your needs.
2. Go through the process of elimination.
3. Keep in mind that the strength or weakness of a planet in the natal chart has a great deal to do with how it affects a location.
4. Check out all the Local Space indications, because they are just as significant. (Local Space steps are at the end of Chapter 2).
5. Do a relocation chart to check out the other aspects to the angles, i.e. Ascendant/Descendant, including the Anti-Vertex/Vertex.
6. Check the difference in the positions of Pluto, Venus and Moon lines.
7. Take note of the latitude; where paran crossings occur use only Medium Coeli/Imum Coeli and rise/set positions (see below).

8. Be sure to check planets on the geodetic map (see Chapter 7).
9. After the major indicators are understood, look and see if you still have the same sign on the Ascendant and Medium Coeli. Also take note of planets that have shifted into new House positions.
10. The half-sums or mid-points involving the angles will be changed.
11. If you use the Arabic Parts you should be aware that they will change when you move from the birth place. The most commonly used Arabic part is the "Part of Fortune." It is derived from adding the positions of Ascendant and the Moon and then subtracting the position of the Sun. (Add and subtract in signs-degrees-minutes, or in 360 degrees or minutes from 00 Aries.) The Part of Fortune will always remain in the same House because the Ascendant moves in proportion to the Sun and Moon positions. It can, however, make new aspects to the relocated angles and natal/birth planets.

The Latitude Influence of Parans

The use of "parans" is yet another important factor in locality astrology. Paran comes from the Greek *paranatellonta*, which means "rising side by side." Robert Hand defines parans as "simultaneous bodily transits of two or more bodies over the horizon or meridian circles of a given place at the *same* time."[3]

There seem to be seven types of possible parans on the mundane circle. By mundane circle I am referring to the right ascension degree on the meridian at the Medium Coeli and Imum Coeli and 90 degrees from these points (often called rise and set points). (The *oblique ascendant* is the intersection of the celestial equator and the horizon, whereas the standard Ascendant is the intersection of the ecliptic and the horizon. Parans *don't* seem to work with crossings of the Medium Coeli and the standard Ascendant/Descendant, only with Medium Coeli/Imum Coeli and rise/set crossings.

The seven types according to Hand are:

1. Two bodies rising together (conjunct the oblique ascendant).
2. One rises while the other sets (oblique ascendant opposition the oblique descendant).

3. One rises, the other culminates or anti-culminates (oblique ascendant square right ascension).
4. Two bodies set together (conjunct the oblique descendant).
5. One body sets, the other culminates or anti-culminates (oblique descendant square right ascension).
6. Two bodies culminate or anti-culminate together (conjunct the right ascension).
7. One culminates while the other anti-culminates (right ascension opposition right ascension).

When you look at your Astro*Carto*Graphy® map, paran types 2 and 7 will not be immediately noticed. Paran types 2 and 7 indicate that there is an opposition in the birth chart, so they would probably not remain hidden indefinitely.

Hand bases the strength of the parans on three very solid facts. First of all the only types of paran that can exist are when planets are *already* in close conjunction, square or opposition. Most astrologers would agree that these types of aspects already indicate a dynamic planetary relationship.

The second point is one that relates to the concept of diurnal rhythms. Without going into too much depth on this subject, diurnal rhythms are simply a four-fold division of a 24-hour cycle. The four points are the rising, upper culmination, setting and lower culmination. The way in which we measure a day takes into consideration the Sun/Earth relationship in this four-fold pattern, which is actually a 24-hour day, plus or minus four minutes. Everything within this cycle is measured in time; the rising and setting are 12 hours apart, and so are the upper and lower culminations. There are roughly 6 hours difference from a rise to an upper or a set to a lower, etc. The daily or diurnal rhythms are different each day, so when a person is born they have a particular diurnal pattern which is like a permanent imprint. Parans emerge when you place the conjunction, square and oppositions on the angles in the diurnal cycle.

The third and perhaps most important point is that when two planets are in an aspectual relationship, namely the conjunction, square or opposition, a latent paran situation already exists. It becomes actual when the planets hit the angles. (This can also take place with transits and progressions.) Most astrologers would agree that planets in hard aspect and on the angles indicate one of the most powerful arrangements of planets and angles possible.

We are reminded by Hand that the most interesting thing concerning parans is the fact that they are "latitude specific." Astrologers are familiar with the fact that the sidereal time in chart calculations gives them the degrees of right ascension (east or west), which is the Medium Coeli or Tenth House cusp. This zodiacal degree is then used as a reference point to find the appropriate latitude and ascending degree. The degrees on the Ascendant/Descendant change at different speeds—some move fast, others more slowly. In the Northern Hemisphere Leo takes the longest, Aquarius the shortest; in the Southern Hemisphere the reverse is true.

The implication of all this is that at any given moment of time a paran can be present at one latitude and not at another. If two planets are in conjunction or opposition you know that at some time during the day they will be on the angles, in paran. These times differ according to latitude. Looking at a Table of Houses would clearly show when the above aspects would hit the angles.* (These are the standard Ascendant/Descendant, and oblique or equatorial Ascendant.)

Indeed all the parans are powerful influences, yet two of the seven have a special feature of their own. These two are the paran squares, also called "crossings." Their uniqueness stems from a number of factors. The other five parans only involve planets in conjunction and opposition. Conjunctions and oppositions between inner planets as well as the inner and outer planets happen quite frequently, and then you have a potential paran. It becomes actual when the aspecting planets align with one of the angles; the paran is activated and a great amount of energy is released. The square parans are somewhat different in that the two planets involved may not be in an exact square, and therefore the paran will not happen until the square is exact. The conjunction and opposition paran will always hit one of the four angles within any 6-hour period (the actual time depends on the latitude).

The most important point that makes square parans (also called crossings) different from the other five is that they always involve two angles of a different axis—First and Seventh, with the Tenth and Fourth—and therefore are 90 degrees from one another; whereas

---

*Hand suggests that the right ascension Medium Coeli of the four angles can be used to find all the parans by the simple method of cross comparing the degrees. See pp. 75 and 76 of *Essays on Astrology.*

with the conjunction and opposition parans only one axis/angle is hit at a time. They are either on the right ascension Medium Coeli/right ascension Imum Coeli—Tenth/Fourth—south-north meridian, or on the right ascension/oblique ascendant—First/Seventh—easterly-westerly direction. The square paran always involves *both* major angle axes, making them far more significant than the others, because now the whole chart is involved by stimulating the two axes at once. This paran also has a much tighter orb than the others, which means it will be active for a shorter period of time and occur less frequently.

The two square parans are easily located on your astro-locality map, because they show up as an intersection of two lines, thus forming a cross, or X. Jim Lewis appropriately calls them "crossings."[4] These square parans or crossings can happen anywhere on the Earth's surface depending on your birth chart.

These paran squares are either actual paran squares or a technical/trimetric type that is created by the graphics alone. The actual one is when you really have a square between two or more planets in your birth chart. If you do not have squares in your chart you will never experience this type. The technical-trimetric type shows that when you have 360 degrees of the zodiac, they are proportioned across the surface of the sphere, which decreases in size as you move toward the poles. You will notice that there are a greater number of these crossings in the polar regions and this is a direct result of using the equator as a measurement. (By the way, in a Local Space chart, the horizon in the extreme latitudes still has distinct angles, which are the cardinal directions.)

In most cases, the best policy is to disregard these polar crossings above 70 degrees north latitude or below 70 degrees south latitude. It is not likely that you would live in these places, and with the energy they contain chances are that you wouldn't want to stay there long if you did happen to visit.

Every time you notice an ascending or descending *curved* line crossing a *straight* Medium Coeli or Imum Coeli line, you have located a powerful square paran. These crossings are the most potent places on Earth for any individual. A radius of at least 200 miles should be used.

Perhaps the most important feature of these crossings is the fact that they not only create a powerful force in a localized area, but they tend to ignite that particular latitude for the whole of the planet. This influence is not as strong as it is in the 200-mile radius of the actual location, but it is detectable planet-wide at the latitude of the crossing (Jim Lewis discovered this in his research).

These parans are not indicated on your map, so it is up to you to either draw them in or, at least, circle the important crossings, and list the latitudes. Naturally they are more noticeable when two, three, four or more of them fall within a few degrees of latitude.

Because crossings are not very overt except in the areas where they actually occur, their effects can go unnoticed. Let's say you have Jupiter on the Medium Coeli, and that this *straight* line runs down the East Coast of the United States on 75 degrees west longitude. The Jupiterian energy would be active all along this line. If there were no *curved* rise or set lines crossing it, why would you live in Boston but not New York, or Washington D.C. but not Baltimore? The answer (notwithstanding Local Space influences) is that a number of *curved* rise or set lines have intersected somewhere else on the planet and thus will cross the vertical Jupiter/Medium Coeli line.

The parans or crossings are, in fact, another way of determining the *exact* locations. Each of these crossings has a different meaning depending on the planets involved. In Chapter 3, two-planet combinations are briefly described. Most texts which explain planets in conjunctions (especially Jim Lewis's[5]) should prove quite helpful in understanding these important latitudinal influences.

A Johndro Relocation Technique

Johndro has put forth an alternative technique to the standard relocation chart. In his method only the planetary positions are shifted, *not* the angles. The shift made in right ascension is quite easy to calculate. Simply note the difference in longitude from the birth place to the new location. Add if the movement is east of your birth place; subtract if the movement is west. (In order to get the exact positions for all the planets it may be necessary to convert all of them to right ascension position first.)

If a planet is 20 degrees of Cancer and you moved 10 degrees to the west, then 10 degrees is subtracted, giving the new position of 10 Cancer; if the move was east then 00 Leo is the new position (20 Cancer plus 10 degrees). This method is especially helpful when the birth time is *unknown*, therefore making the angles method impossible to use. The new planetary positions (including the Nodes) are then compared with the birth/natal positions and angles.

This method represents a symbolic movement, not an actual one. In the standard method the angles of your chart are actually changing from one location to the next, just as the transits are actually happening. This symbolic movement is then similar to secondary progressions and solar arc directions, because they are not actually occurring in present time. However any seasoned astrologer who has seriously used progressions will tell you that they do indicate major trends and significant events in your life. Some astrologers regard them (when they are exact) as two or three times as strong as the strongest transit, i.e. long duration outer planet conjunctions and oppositions.

The Fixed Stars and the Geographic and Celestial Spheres

The fixed stars, Nodes of the planets, equators and centers of the local, galactic and super-galactic planes, pulsars, comets, meteors, black holes, and many other types of astronomical phenomena are being studied by astrologers. What they discover may turn out to be very useful, because each of these points can be plotted on a map at certain geographic locations. Some astrologers feel that one's personal myth can be discovered by locating the zenith over the birth latitude and longitude. Using Figure 17 on page 138 or Figure C on page 245, you can plot this for yourself. What star(s) is the zenith close to, and what constellation is it in? Each constellation corresponds to a myth or symbolic story. Most books list about 72 different Greek myths, but varied cultures have distinct or more detailed interpretations for various star patterns. In the future the author hopes to do more research in this area.

The fixed stars have been used by every developed culture in the timing of special calendar events. E. Johndro,[6] R. Ebertin,[7] V. Robson,[8] J. Rigor,[9] T. Landsheidt,[10] P. Sedgwick,[11] and others have seriously studied the fixed stars and other cosmic influences.

Philip Sedgwick's book *The Astrology of Deep Space* is the first major attempt to explain influences from deep space. Alice Bailey's *Esoteric Astrology* also tried to explain things, but I believe it is too abstract for most people. Reinhold Ebertin's work *The Fixed Stars* is the easiest to read. It is well researched, historical, and straightforward.

One of the best books on the subject is Michael and Margaret Erlewine's *Astrophysical Directions*.[12] Its emphasis is not on interpretation but on clearly describing the major coordinate systems used in astrology, and providing an outline of every type of astronomical phenomenon used by astrologers. In Appendix A, the Erlewines explain in their own words the sky (above) and the Earth (below) connection.

Composite Local Space Charts

Eventually the question comes up about the possibilities of using a composite Local Space chart. One of the immediate problems with this approach is finding two people who are in such circumstances where they really work as a unit. The bonds of love and marriage along with living together certainly bring people together, but I remain unconvinced that decisions are a compromise or shared agreement. Most decisions are made by one partner alone; sometimes it's a compromise, most often it is not.

The objects in the home seem to be divided evenly; there is his favorite chair, room, etc., and her favorite pillow, room, etc. Husband and wife may share the house payments or rent, the car, refrigerator and television, but their personal preference dictates that the rest of the house falls under the heading of sovereign territories.

I believe events in the home, community or while traveling tend to trigger each person's *own* planetary arrangements. I'm not ruling out the fact that the composite Local Space chart may actually work, but that it should only be looked at when the information in the two individual charts fails to work properly.

Astrologers have taken a composite of two people and found that transits and progressions seem to work, but these cycles are strictly related to timing. In locality astrology you are dividing space, not time. I'm not entirely sure that equal proportions of space will work, even though I've seen it apparently work on occassion. At any rate the area needs to be more fully investigated.

Transits and Progressions in the Locality Charts

In the examples section of this book, references have been made to the use of transits and progressions in locality work. Perhaps one of the most important points is that transits and progressions *must* stay within the particular system that you are focusing on. When the Local Space horizon circle is being used, all transits or progressed positions must be in azimuth and altitude. The Prime Vertical will show positions in amplitude and in 360 degrees starting from the east point: the ecliptic in zodiacal longitude, and the equator in right ascension. Most comprehensive computer programs will give you transiting positions in all of the four systems, but progressions only in the ecliptic system.

Progressions in azimuth sounds intriguing, and I have found it to work. You can take a progressed aspect position from the birth chart and convert it to azimuth and altitude. The planetary positions of solar arc directions or secondary progressions are exclusively measured along the ecliptic and compared to the ecliptic/zodiacal-longitude placements in the birth chart. I suppose you could convert the progressed positions back into azimuth and look for aspects to the natal Local Space chart. Remember that aspects in one system will *not* be the same in another.

Different systems really emphasize different attitudes, and orientations to trends and events. Although all of the major coordinate systems used in astrology intersect and therefore depend on one another, it is almost certain that confusion would arise if systems were randomly mixed. What is true for one is not necessarily true for the other. A trine on the ecliptic can easily be a square in azimuth or vice versa. The differences in equatorial right ascension and the ecliptic have also been sighted. This is another great area for research.

Locality Angles

I've known many astrologers, friends and clients who have experienced a major event but were unable to find the aspects that should have triggered it. When they have this trouble in pin-pointing the influence, the first thing that I suggest is to look at the relocated Ascendant and Medium Coeli degrees. Exact aspects to the locality angles by progressions and/or slow moving outer planets (especially conjunctions and oppositions) cannot be overlooked. Your relocated angles show the movement in space/place, and the longer you reside in a location the greater will be the influence of the new angles. The locality angle, in my opinion, will never override the birth place angles, but experience has shown that they have often run a close second.

For example, a person is born in Poland and is moved at 2 months of age to New York, and lives there for 87 years. Although the birth place angles may still work, it's almost a foregone conclusion (in this extreme example) that the New York angles will be equally valid.

Even the movement of a few hundred miles or less can rotate the chart and place a problem planet out of aspect to an angle, and sometimes bring a favorable planet-aspect into contact with the changed angles.

The Relevance of Country, State and City Charts

The country, state and city where you live has an inception or birth chart; for that matter, so does the company you work for, the car you drive, and the house you live in.

It may be next to impossible to find the time when your car rolled off the assembly line, however you can do a chart for when you signed the papers to buy it. The same holds true for your house. Corporation times are different and more challenging. The time the state rubber-stamped the incorporation papers can't be considered valid because it is only a formality. The actual opening of the doors of a business or the first meeting which produced a definite agreement seems to be more valid. Getting correct times for events certainly may take some effort, but so did birth times until the legal system unknowingly came to astrology's rescue by requiring birth times.

The supposed birth charts of collectives are always suspect, as anyone who has investigated the birth time of the United States will attest to. Even if you have an accurate chart of a city, state or country, it may not be able to give specifics. Even though we are a government of and by the people, these charts may only reveal what is going on in terms of the governmental structure.

In the case of the United States, the birth event was a Declaration of Independence, agreed upon July 2nd, and signed on July 4, 1776. However the government was not fully functioning until 1789. If astrologers can ever agree upon a United States chart, it may at least prove useful in describing the collective.

I have a strong hunch that the personal aspects in different localities as well as Local Space indications may show the influences at work without ever looking at a country, state or city chart. This does not rule out the fact that if you broke the laws of a country or state, or had some other direct dealings with the government, then perhaps these charts could give you some additional information.

The ability to get at specific information about an individual's interactions with an organized entity, be it political or social, can be done. However I think that astrolocality information is the first step. Suppose your chart and that of Australia, Texas or New York looked good in synastry and composite. Australia is a very large country, Texas a huge state and New York City a large and complex city. Exactly where you should be in each of these places can be obtained from astrolocality indicators, making it unnecessary to do a full investigation if you know that the personal influences are constructive. Any major positive influence will act as an intuitive guide. Circumstances will develop that will set you down in the appropriate location. This can happen without ever looking at city, state or country charts.

In the final analysis I think that these charts are important enough to look at when dealing with governments, etc., but are often too general when compared with astrolocality information.

Local Space Charts of Cities

The large cities of our present day and age are almost states or counties unto themselves, much like the city/states of the ancient world. In fact, it is my opinion that the charts of major cities within a state almost totally override the state charts. California is dominated by San Francisco and Los Angeles, Texas by Dallas and Houston, New York by New York City. Maybe the people outside the major metropolitan areas play down this fact, but it remains clear that the large cities have the majority of commerce, culture and votes!

In looking through Marc Penfield's[13] and Moon Moore's[14] books on city, state and country charts, I was struck with the idea of how perfect Local Space charts would be for cities and countries. Cities and countries are spread out over the surface of the land, and in this flat Earth context what could better represent planetary influences on the horizon/surface than Local Space charts?

I first began to look at cities that I was very familiar with, such as Denver and Chicago. The Denver chart* appears to be reasonably accurate (see Figure 23 on page 165). Neptune points north-northeast and south-southwest. (Remember Local Space lines travel in both directions, even though the planet will only be positioned in one direction.) The Neptune line to the north-northwest goes into the Rocky Mountain Arsenal, a very polluted area, and a place where nerve gas was once stored. Neptune to the south-southwest is an indicator of the difficult soil problem in that part of the metropolitan area. The Moon line is close to the same direction as Neptune (in the south-southwest) and runs through the largest lake within the Denver city limits. Also, a considerable amount of annexation took place in these directions. The north Node is almost due northeast (and southwest); it points to the airport, where people make connections. Uranus squares the Node, showing that it represents airport connec-

---

*Calculated for Nov. 1, 1858 at 9:55 A.M., LMT, from Joy Lynn Hill. Penfield's data of Nov. 22, 1858 at 11:35 A.M., LMT does not work.

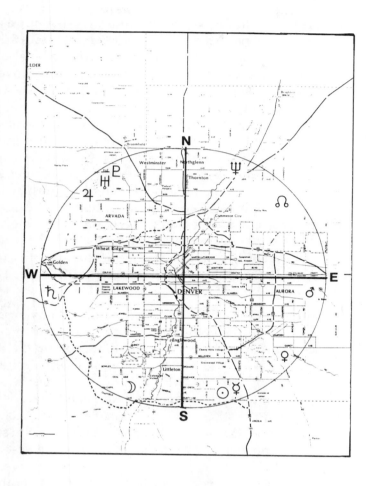

Fig. 23—Denver and the Local Space Horizon

tions. The Mars line in the Denver chart points in east-southeast and north-northwest directions. In the east-southeast area it passes through Lowery Air Force training center, and Buckley Air National Guard base. Saturn runs almost due east and west; the line crosses over the Federal Center and Fitzsimmons, a large army hospital; in West Denver it passes through the poorest side of town.

Four planets occupy the northwest and north-northwest along with the southeast and south-southeast. Jupiter to the northwest points to the old affluent sections and the Elich Gardens, an amusement park. Jupiter to the southeast shows the new affluent areas. Venus is in this area also, as an indicator that it is the most beautiful part of town. A close Uranus/Pluto conjunction line runs through the busy downtown area and into the Denver Technological Center to the southeast. Farther northeast is Rockey Flats, where there is a good deal of uranium (Uranus) pollution. The Sun/Mercury line runs in the south-southeast through the Denver University college area, where many young people live.

In the case of the Chicago chart,* I am not quite as convinced (see Figure 24, page 167). However there does seem to be a fair amount of accurate indications. The Jupiter/Uranus conjunction (to the north-northwest) intersects O'Hare Field, the nation's busiest airport. The Saturn line runs through the South Side, one of the largest impoverished areas in the country. The Mars line in its slightly east of south direction runs past the location of the once huge and infamous stockyards. Neptune in its southeast direction points to the greatest source of pollution, Gary, Indiana. The Moon in its south-southwest direction runs through the largest concentration of forest preserves. The Venus east-northeast line runs into the famous Art Institute, and the location of the 1933 World's Fair.

Using the planets on the horizon should work for countries as it does with cities. In my limited investigation into this area it appears to work. In the 5:10 P.M., 7/4/1776 United States chart, six of the ten planets point to the west. Showing the westward movement of people and influence, California is the most populous state. Washington D.C. has to be used as a central point, even though going south or east puts you into the Atlantic.

In the charts of other countries, such as Israel, the Local Space chart shows Mars, Saturn and Pluto to the northeast, which is the area

---

*August 17, 1803 at 1:15 P.M., from Penfield's *Horoscopes of the Western Hemisphere.*

Fig. 24—*Chicago and the Local Space Horizon*

167

of the Golan Heights and Syria, Israel's most formidable enemy. In the Local Space chart of Russia, the planets don't seem to reflect the dangers of invasions from the east; instead the Moon/Mars conjunction line to the southwest moves into China and Afghanistan!

This is yet another area for research, and in the future the author hopes to look at the charts of cities and countries and compare the various lines with major historical events.

Notes

1. Johndro, Edward, *The Stars,* and *The Earth in the Heavens.* New York: Samuel Weiser, 1970, reprinted.
2. Johndro, *The Stars,* p. 118.
3. Hand, Robert, *Essays on Astrology.* Gloucester, Massachusetts: Para Research, 1980, pp. 65 and 98.
4. Lewis, Jim, *Astro*Carto*Graphy,* San Francisco, CA: Jim Lewis, 1976.
5. ibid., Lewis.
6. ibid., Johndro, *The Stars.*
7. Ebertin, Reinhold, *Fixed Stars.* Aalen/Wuertt, Germany: Ebertin-Verlag, 1971.
8. Robson, Vivian, *The Fixed Stars and Constellations in Astrology.* Wellingborough, Northamptonshire, England: Aquarian Press Limited, 1979 (reprinted).
9. Rigor, Joseph, *The Power of Fixed Stars.* Hammond, Indiana: Astrology and Spiritual Publications, 1979.
10. ibid., Ebertin, pp. 84 and 85; Dr. Theodore Landscheidt, *Radio Waves and Structural Elements of the Fixed Stars,* 1965.
11. Sedgwick, Philip, *The Astrology of Deep Space.* Birmingham, MI: Seek-It Publications, 1984.
12. Erlewine, Michael, *Astrophysical Directions.* Ann Arbor, MI: Heart Center, 1977.
13. Penfield, Marc, *An Astrological Portrait of America and its Cities.* Seattle, WA: Vulcan Books, 1976.
14. Moore, Moon, *The Book of World Horoscopes.* Birmingham, MI: Seek-It Publications, 1980.

CHAPTER 7

GRID SYSTEMS

A planetary grid system is any series of lines laid out across the surface of the Earth in an attempt to measure some particular, pre-designated system of ideas, correlations or theories. Some grid systems have correspondences to geographical longitude and latitude, others do not. The idea of grid systems has been used on a smaller scale in Chinese urban planning, and in Arabian design. The theme of grids runs deep in human experience, whether seen in the creative lines of the "spider woman" of the tribes of the American southwest, in the "lines of the world" in Carlos Castaneda's Don Juan books, in the magic weaving of intersecting lines in the marriage/medicine baskets among other tribes, or in the tangle of world lines that Einstein referred to. The pattern is the same; it is a search for a system to make order out of chaos. It is a way of locating power points, healing sources, and vortexes of every sort. While carefully studying and following these apparently invisible lines we become like the Yogic-Hindu analogy of the wild geese, who navigate without a road map yet always find their way home!

Ptolemy's "Old World Grid"

One of the oldest grids was used by Ptolemy and perhaps also by many of his peers. It is quite simplistic, dividing the Earth into four basic quadrants, with a horizontal line running east and west at approximately 36 degrees north latitude, and a vertical north-south line placed at 37 degrees east longitude (see Figure 25 on page 173).

171

There is speculation that 35 E 15 also may have been used as an intersection; Jerusalem is located at this longitude. (The Egyptians used 31 N 30 and 30 E 06.) It is interesting to extend the east/west line into North America, where it seems to divide the Snow Belt from the Sun Belt as well as the old allegiances of the Confederacy and the Union of the American Civil War.

Ptolemy's grid produced four quarters: the northeast quadrant (encompassing northern Asia), the southeast (southern Asia), the northwest (Europe) and the southwest (Africa). Ptolemy also relates the four elements with the quadrants. The Fire signs are connected with the northwest-Europe; northeast-Asia (northern) with the Air signs; southeast-Asia (southern) with the Earth signs and southwest-Africa with the Water signs. Over a period of time, certain countries and kingdoms were assigned one of the three zodiacal signs within the particular element. When Morrison republished William Lilly's *Introduction to Astrology*, a section was included wherein Lilly listed five to eight countries after each sign of the zodiac. Llewellyn George followed suit by including an expanded list in the famous *A to Z Horoscope Maker and Delineator*.

Sepharial's Geodetic Equivalent

Another and more important astrological grid was popularized when Sepharial somehow came across it sometime prior to World War I. He called it the "Geodetic Equivalent" because it was in fact a correspondence of the twelve zodiac signs and geographic longitudes. 00 Aries was set at the meridian of Greenwich England, and the signs followed in the usual order eastward. Thus Pisces is west of the line and Aries is east (see Figures 26A, B and C on pages 174-6, "Geodetic Maps").

Why should we use Greenwich, England for the starting point? There are three good reasons; the first (and perhaps the best) is the opinion of many mundane astrologers that the geodetic system repeatedly works. Although I can't quote extensive statistical studies proving it, I can suggest that the reader experiment with it (see below).

Johndro offers a second and more technical explanation by reminding us that each time the Vernal Equinoctial point coincides with the backdrop of the stars (28,000+ years on the equator and 25,000+ years on the ecliptic), it is 33.5 degrees farther west. The distance on the ecliptic from the Great Pyramid to Greenwich is about 31.5

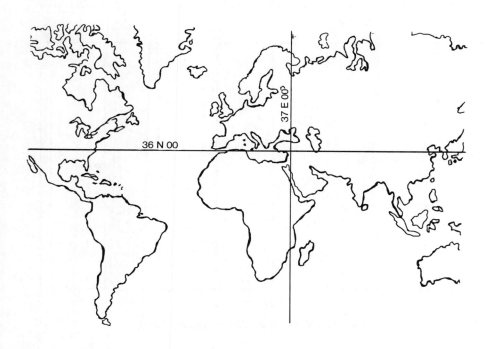

36 N 00

37 E 00

Fig. 25—*Ptolemy's Old World Grid*

173

Geodetic M.C.'s

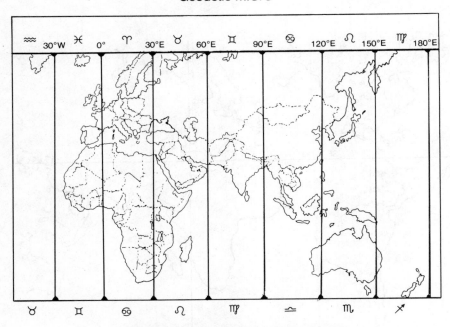

Geodetic Ascendants for Latitudes

Fig. 26A—*Geodetic Map of Europe, Africa and Asia*

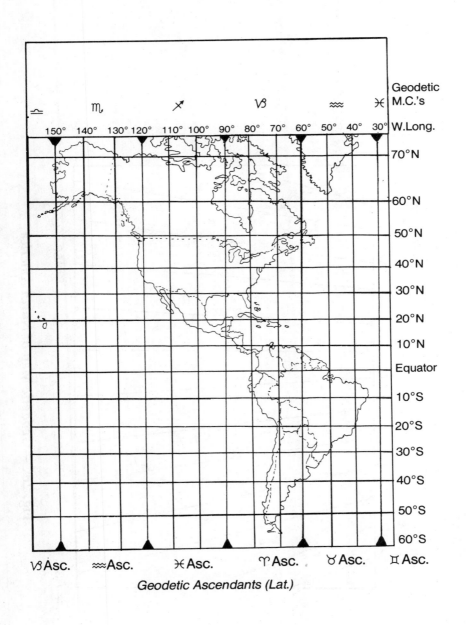

Fig. 26B—*Geodetic Map of the Americas*

175

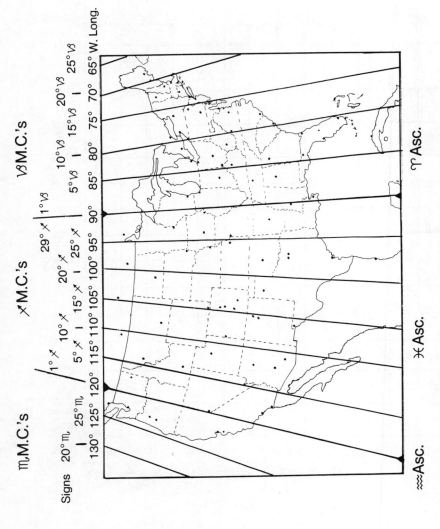

Fig. 26C—*Geodetic Map of North America*

Table 17
Geodetic Equivalents for Major World Cities

Town	Latitude	Longitude	Midheaven		Ascendant	
Amsterdam	52°22′ N	4°53′ E	Aries	4°53′	Leo	0°37′
Athens	37°56′ N	23°38′ E	Aries	23°38′	Leo	4°58′
Bangkok	14°0′ N	100°30′ E	Can.	10°30′	Libra	11°13′
Berlin	52°45′ N	13°24′ E	Aries	13°24′	Leo	6°11′
Brisbane	27°30′ S	153°0′ E	Virgo	3°0′	Sag.	18°30′
Brussels	50°52′ N	4°20′ E	Aries	4°20′	Can.	29°6′
Cairo	30°6′ N	31°26′ E	Tau.	1°26′	Leo	7°53′
Canberra	35°17′ S	149°18′ E	Leo	29°18′	Sag.	20°6′
Chicago	42°0′ N	88°0′ W	Cap.	2°0′	Aries	3°53′
Copenhagen	55°40′ N	12°30′ E	Aries	12°30′	Leo	7°50′
Hong Kong	22°0′ N	114°0′ E	Can.	24°0′	Libra	23°53′
Jerusalem	31°45′ N	35°14′ E	Tau.	5°14′	Leo	21°54′
Lisbon	38°45′ N	9°10′ W	Pisc.	20°50′	Can.	10°34′
Manila	14°30′ N	121°30′ E	Leo	1°30′	Scor.	2°41′
Mecca	21°0′ N	40°0′ E	Tau.	10°0′	Leo	11°58′
Melbourne	37°50′ S	144°59′ E	Leo	24°59′	Sag.	17°36′
Mexico	19°30′ N	99°0′ W	Sag.	21°0′	Pisc.	17°26′
Montreal	45°30′ N	73°38′ W	Cap.	16°22′	Tau.	3′0′
New Orleans	30°0′ N	90°0′ W	Cap.	0°0′	Aries	0°0′
New York	40°45′ N	74°0′ W	Cap.	16°0′	Aries	29°15′
Paris	48°50′ N	2°20′ E	Aries	2°20′	Can.	26°6′
Prague	50°5′ N	14°25′ E	Aries	14°25′	Leo	5°1″
Rio de Janeiro	22°55′ S	43°9′ W	Aqu.	16°51′	Tau.	14°50′
Rome	41°55′ N	13°0′ E	Aries	13°0′	Can.	29°13′
San Francisco	37°47′ N	122°25′ W	Scor.	27°35′	Aqu.	7°42′
Shanghai	31°30′ N	121°30′ E	Leo	1°30′	Libra	28°49′
Stockholm	59°20′ N	18°0′ E	Aries	18°0′	Leo	14°45′
Sydney	33°54′ S	151° 8′ E	Virgo	1°8′	Sag.	20°33′
Tokyo	35°43′ N	139°43′ E	Leo	19°43′	Scor.	12°55′
Toronto	45°38′ N	79°30′ W	Cap.	10°30′	Aries	20°53′
Vienna	48°15′ N	16°20′ E	Aries	16°20′	Leo	5°17′
Warsaw	52°13′ N	21°2′ E	Aries	21°2′	Leo	11°8′
Washington	38°53′ N	77°3′ E	Capr.	12°57′	Aries	23°9′
Wellington	41°16′ S	174°47′ E	Virgo	24°47′	Cap.	15°43′

degrees. Thus, there is a definite relationship between the Great Pyramid longitude (which is recognized by *all* grid researchers) and the Greenwich longitude.

The third theory is offered by Charles Jayne. He suggests that when you divide the Earth into two halves looking for the most-land/least-water and least-land/most-water hemispheres, you will discover two "poles." The pole of the most-land hemisphere, which he calls the "principle hemisphere," is at 47° north and about 1° west 30', very close to the Greenwich line. He doesn't mention the location of the pole for the most-water hemisphere, but I suspect that it is somewhere just east of New Zealand. Also see Cathie, p. 278.

The uses of the the geodetic map are many, but before we mention them, some details need to be added. While looking at the Geodetic map (see Figures 26A-C), notice that across the top are the zodiacal signs, and that each of the 360 degrees corresponds to a specific degree of geographic longitude. As you will notice, most of Europe is contained within Pisces, Aries and Taurus, as is Africa. The Middle East is Taurus and Gemini. Asia and most of Australia is under Cancer and Leo. Virgo covers extreme eastern Australia, New Zealand and the Siberian penninsula. Libra has western Alaska and Hawaii. The United States is under three signs: Scorpio, Sagittarius and Capricorn. South America is divided in half; the western half is all Capricorn and the eastern is Aquarius. Greenland is mostly Aquarius (see Table 18, page 179).

Each degree of the zodiac and each degree of longitude are connected. Each one of these degrees also represents a Midheaven or Medium Coeli for a particular area. Let's say you are living at 75 degrees west longitude, which is geodetically 15 degrees of Capricorn. You know that 15 Capricorn is the geodetic Medium Coeli. To get the Ascendant you open a Table of Houses and find the correct latitude north or south. The Medium Coelis are fairly uniform: 4 minutes=1 degree, and a degree = 60 miles at the equator and about 50 miles at 40 degrees north or south. The Ascendants will vary according to latitude. In Figure 26C on page 176 you can see that Aries is the most common Ascendant. Notice also the different degrees of Capricorn on the Medium Coeli. In mundane work, the oblique/equatorial Ascendant is considered (the Ascendant at 0 degrees latitude).

Table 18

United States Geodetic Coordinates for Each Degree

° W Long.	° Capricorn MC		° W. Long.	° Sagittarius MC
67	23		91	29
68	22		92	28
69	21		93	27
70	20		94	26
71	19		95	25
72	18		96	24
73	17		97	23
74	16		98	22
75	15		99	21
76	14		100	20
77	13		101	19
78	12		102	18
79	11		103	17
80	10		104	16
81	09		105	15
82	08		106	14
83	07		107	13
84	06		108	12
85	05		109	11
86	04		110	10
87	03		111	09
88	02		112	08
89	01		113	07
90	00		114	06
			115	05
			116	04
			117	03
			118	02
			119	01
			120	00

° W Long.	° Scorpio MC
121	29
122	28
123	27
124	26
125	25

The United States is comprised of three different longitudinal sections and signs (see Table 18 or Figure 26C). From 90 degrees west longitude (the center of Central Standard Time) all the way into the Atlantic lies territory under the earthy sign of Capricorn. This is where the country was established and where much of the establishment, including the government, still operates. The natural boundary is the Mississippi River, which is close to 90 degrees west longitude. Beyond 90 degrees west you leave the conventional, somewhat boring, yet organized part of the country. Think about the wide open wheat fields out west, the adventuresome Rocky Mountains, and the colorful southwest; it's all under Sagittarius. Scorpio begins at 120 west longitude just west of Santa Barbara, California; the line runs through central Oregon and Washington states. We are now away from the dryness and optimism of Sagittarius, and into the Water/emotion of Scorpio. . . the ocean, fog, and also the emotional extremes. I'm sure you've heard the old story about how the United States is on a little slant and anything (anybody) that "gets a little loose" slides to the West Coast; even though people tend to go to extremes there, it does have the deep transforming and regenerative qualities of Pluto/Scorpio. By the way, Juneau, Anchorage and Fairbanks, the three principal cities of Alaska, are within the Scorpio longitudes.

The longitudes do *not* change as you go south of the equator, since they are continuous north-south lines running from pole to pole. The Ascendants *will* vary according to the latitudes. Be sure to check the equatorial Ascendant (00 latitude—the oblique Ascendant always 90 degrees from the Medium Coeli).

The general theory of how this grid works is quite simple, at least on its surface. When a *natal* or *transiting* planet is conjunct or in opposition to the Medium Coeli, Imum Coeli or any of the ascending/descending points, then at that locality on Earth an event corresponding to the nature of the particular planet(s) will take place. So place your natal planets on the geodetic map and see if there are any correspondences; be sure to use the opposite degree, i.e. 10° ♈—10° ♎, or 20° ♏— ♉, etc.

There are a number of different arrangements of transiting planets that can take place on the geodetic grid. The most obvious and perhaps the most powerful is when the slow planets—Jupiter and Saturn—or the slowest transits—Uranus, Neptune and Pluto—conjunct a longitude Medium Coeli degree. This happens all the time, and if a planet is at 10 Capricorn, it is also at 10 Cancer, its opposite on the grid.

Remember that the planets are not really overhead at a particular location, but are symbolically there due to the overlay of the zodiacal signs on planetary longitude.

The transits of Jupiter through Pluto are used as major indicators because of their slower motion. The faster moving planets are basically used to determine the exact day when an event may occur.

The most powerful arrangement is when one or more slower transits conjunct the Medium Coeli/longitude, and at approximately the same time two or more planets are conjunct the latitude—Ascendant/Descendant axis. Another powerful position is when there is only one planet on each angle, i.e. longitude/Medium Coeli and latitude/Ascendant, or two planets only on one angle, i.e., transiting parans. Even when one slower planet is on the Medium Coeli, very strong events may occur. The squares and trines to the angles may also work, but it seems that the effects are weak, unless at the same time a slower transit is conjunct the Medium Coeli or Ascendant. Denver, Colorado is at 15 Sagittarius geodetically (3 Pisces Ascendant), so when Uranus was moving toward the center of Sagittarius, I decided to observe firsthand if Uranus/Sagittarius/Ninth House events would take place. The correspondences and/or rulerships *all* fit into the Uranus/Sagittarius/Ninth House categories. When Uranus was within 1 degree of orb, i.e. 14 to 16 Sagittarius in September and October of 1985, the following events occurred:

1. The building of a new convention center in the unused RAIL YARDS in Denver was defeated.

2. The "SPACE Command Center" in Colorado Springs was approved.

3. United, Continental and Frontier AIRLINES pledged millions for the new airport.

4. The Denver BRONCOS won and lost two key games (the team happens to have Uranus on the Medium Coeli).

5. The LIGHT-RAIL rapid transit was defeated (delayed) in Denver.

6. "Storage Tech," a major HIGH-TECH company located north of Denver, made a financial turnaround.

7. Denver became the CABLE TV capital of the United States when five companies began to merge through buyouts.

8. The first of the MX WARHEADS were installed at Warren Air Force Base just east of Cheyenne, Wyoming (100 miles due north of Denver).

9. Colorado became the first state to make it mandatory to report AIDS.

Later, in December of 1985, when Saturn squared the 3 Pisces Ascendant of Denver, many wells were found to be contaminated just north of the city.

Denver, being at the mid-point of Sagittarius, should be a very Sagittarian and Ninth House place. Here are some current statistics that prove this point: highest and driest major city, 130+ consecutive sellouts for the Denver Broncos, most cars per capita of any U.S. city, greatest number of personal computers per capita of any U.S. city, highest educational level of any U.S. city, and fourth busiest and most economical airport in the United States. I should add that it is the sunniest city in the U.S. However, when the winds are calm, stagnant air inversion develops, and then Denver can have the worst air pollution in the country (this happens about 6 to 10 days a year). Is this the reason that people in Denver consume more vitamins than people in any other city in the United States? Denver is also within 4 hours of air travel from any city of 1 million people or more in North America. It's also the only place in North America where satellite transmissions to both Europe and Asia will arrive in one bounce.

A Johndro Geodetic Technique

Johndro offered a technique using the geodetic grid, calling it the "Birth Locality Chart" or the BLMC for short. Although this technique can be used by anyone, it is especially designed for *unknown* birth times. The longitude of your birthplace is converted into a certain degree in a sign according to the astrological geodetic layout (see Figure 29). You add to this the actual amount in degrees that your birth Sun is from 00 Aries; the result is your BLMC. Then you look at any Table of Houses for the BL Ascendant, Vertex, and other House cusps for the latitude in question. Example: For someone born with the Sun at 10 Aquarius at 100 west longitude, which is 20 Sagittarius geodetically:

$$
\begin{array}{rr}
20 \text{ Sagittarius} = & 250 \\
10 \text{ Aquarius} = & +310 \\
\hline
& 560 \\
& -360 \\
\hline
& 200
\end{array}
$$

200 degrees = 20 Libra BLMC.

Another way of putting this is:

Step 1. Find the distance of the natal/birth Sun from 00 Aries.
Step 2. Add this to the birthplace geodetic Medium Coeli.
Step 3. This gives the BLMC.

A Zodiac Latitude Grid

The overlay of the signs in the geodetic longitude grid is a very helpful mundane astrological tool. While thinking along these lines in the early seventies, I came across an idea about a latitude grid which corresponds to the signs. It really has nothing to do with planets in declination or latitude, nor does it attempt to replace the Ascendants derived from the geodetic grid. I haven't completely tested this theory, but I think it's important enough to merit an explanation here.

There are 90 degrees of latitude both north and south of the equator, and thus we have two very distinct hemispheres, with different weather and geomagnetic patterns.* Instead of the twelve signs stretching from the north pole to the south pole, there are two sets of zodiacal signs. Each set begins at the equator and reaches to 90 degrees north and/or 90 degrees south latitude (see Table 19).

Naturally, the Earth signs should start at the equator, since it is the center of the Earth, which has an actual equatorial bulge. Next are the Fire signs representing the heat exchange regions. They actually begin 1 degree below the Tropic of Cancer in the north and 1 degree above the Tropic of Capricorn in the south. These points represent the northernmost and southernmost points, where the vertical rays of the Sun reach the Earth; it also measures the extremes of the ecliptic above and below the equator. Following Fire are the Air signs, indicative of the temperate zone, and of the jet stream wind patterns. The Water signs come last, ending at the polar regions, where massive lakes and the great polar ice caps are located. The signs follow in the usual fixed, mutable, cardinal qualities, and the order of elements in the zodiac.

The Chart of the World

Another astrological grid of ancient origin has been called "The Chart of the World." The information was reprinted in 1928 by Manly P. Hall, who quotes in the *Third Book of Mathesis* by Julius Firmicus

---

*Some astrologers feel that this distinctiveness points to the theory that it is only the Piscean Age in the Northern Hemisphere, while in the Southern Hemisphere, it is the age of Virgo, the opposite sign.

Table 19

Correspondence of Latitudes and Zodiacal Signs

Northern Latitudes

CANCER	82.30 to 90.00 N
PISCES	75.00 to 82.30 N
SCORPIO	67.30 to 75.00 N
LIBRA	60.00 to 67.30 N
GEMINI	52.30 to 60.00 N
AQUARIUS	45.00 to 52.30 N
ARIES	37.30 to 45.00 N
SAGITTARIUS	30.00 to 37.30 N
LEO	22.30 to 30.00 N
CAPRICORN	15.00 to 22.30 N
VIRGO	7.30 to 15.00 N
TAURUS	00 to 7.30 N

00------------------------*equator*------------------------00

Southern Latitudes

TAURUS	00 to 7.30 S
VIRGO	7.30 to 15.00 S
CAPRICORN	15.00 to 22.30 S
LEO	22.30 to 30.00 S
SAGITTARIUS	30.00 to 37.30 S
ARIES	37.30 to 45.00 S
AQUARIUS	45.00 to 52.30 S
GEMINI	52.30 to 60.00 S
LIBRA	60.00 to 67.30 S
SCORPIO	67.30 to 75.00 S
PISCES	75.00 to 82.30 S
CANCER	82.30 to 90.00 S

Maternus concerning the positions of the heavenly bodies at the time of the establishment of the inferior universe: "According to Aesculapius, therefore, and Anubius, to whom especially the divinity Mercury committed the secrets of the astrological science, the geniture of the world is as follows: They constituted the Sun in the 15th part (degree) of Leo, the Moon in the 15th part of Cancer, Saturn in the 15th part of Capricorn, Jupiter in the 15th part of Sagittarius, Mars in the 15th part of Scorpio, Venus in the 15th part of Libra, Mercury in the 15th part of Virgo, and the horoscope in the 15th part of Cancer."[3] (Ascendant or Medium Coeli?) There is really nothing new about the placement of certain planets in certain signs; it is known by all astrologers as rulership, a planet-sign correspondence. However, there are two interesting points concerning this ancient world chart. The first: why did they make the Ascendant 15 degrees Cancer? One answer may be that it puts the Moon conjunct the Ascendant. This makes sense, as Cancer and the Fourth House have to do with land, the forces of nature and beginnings, etc. The other point of interest is the choosing of the middle 15th degree of the signs. Does this have some implication for the geodetic map? Although there is no reference made to any geodetic sectors, it seems obvious to me that when you look at the beginning and ending of the signs on the geodetic grid, as well as the middle of the signs, there is a surprising number of major world cities (see Table 17).

Note the mid-sign positions in Europe: the mid-Aries point runs very close to Berlin, Prague and Rome. In the United States there are two mid-sign areas. The first is fairly obvious because it runs down the densely populated East Coast. The "megalopolis," as it is called, runs from Boston in the north to Washington, D.C. in the south. New York, Newark, Philadelphia, Baltimore, Providence, Washington D.C. and many other large cities are all near 75 degrees west longitude or the 15 Capricorn-geodetic. The world chart places Saturn here, thus making it a place of great importance. The mid-sign location for Sagittarius is 105 degrees west longitude. Those who have never lived along the front range of the Rockies may not think it a significant area, but if we add up the placement of strategic government and military facilities, it should be apparent that 105 W. longitude is an area of major importance. It starts in Canada at early-warning sites; farther south is the first line of missile sites in central Montana. Continuing south we can locate Warren Air Force Base (where many of the MX missiles are) outside of Cheyenne, Wyoming; entering Colorado, we can begin a

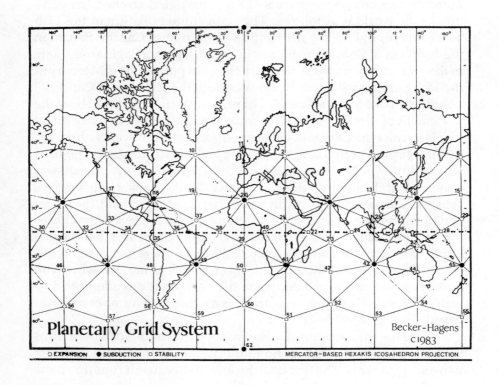

Within the figure:

Planetary Grid System

Becker-Hagens
c 1983

○ EXPANSION   ● SUBDUCTION   □ STABILITY

MERCATOR–BASED HEXAKIS ICOSAHEDRON PROJECTION

Fig. 27—The Planetary Grid System

186

long list of places: Rocky Flats Nuclear Weapons Plant, Rocky Mountain Arsenal, National Geophysical Data Center, National Earthquake Center, National Oceanic and Atmospheric Research Center, The Federal Center, North American Defense Command (the war White House), Space Command Center, Air Force Academy, Falcon Field, Fort Carson. In New Mexico: Los Alamos, a large research center, and White Sands Missile Range! I really don't have a fast answer as to why all the government and military operations should fall under a Jupiter/Sagittarius Ninth House line except that it all has to do with the long-distance travel of aircraft and missiles as well as world-wide communications. It developed rapidly after the Los Alamos nuclear test area in 1942 and NORAD (1952) were chosen because they are remote, yet centrally located.

Other Major and Minor Grids

There are many types of grids which seemingly have no astrological connections. Yet, it is possible that some relationship may be found in the future between astrological and non-astrological grids.

The best place to start is with the work of William Becker and Bethe Hagens.[4] Bill is a professor of industrial design and Bethe is a professor of anthropology. Bethe teaches at Governor's State University in Park Forest, Illinois; William Becker teaches at the University of Illinois in Chicago. This husband-and-wife team has done exhaustive research of all kinds on grids and accompanying theories, from Buckminster Fuller to the "American Society of Dowsers." What they have come up with is a planetary grid which they call "The Unified Vector Geometry Polyhedron Sphere," or UVG for short. Over the years, the bits and pieces have fallen together, and the UVG grid is the result (see Table 20, Figure 27 on previous page, and Figure 28 on pages 188 and 189).

Becker and Hagens were inspired by Christopher Bird (an independent researcher of the "unknown"). He revealed a Russian model which was really an improved-upon version of a ten-Node grid system first proposed by Ivan Sanderson, founder of "The Society for the Investigation of the Unexplained."* The Russians felt that their icosahedron grid corresponded with seats of "ancient" civilizations, fault lines, extremes of atmospheric pressure and streaks on the lithosphere which appeared on photos from space!

---

*It should be mentioned that at the same time of the Russian research (early 1960's) Bruce Cathie, an independent researcher in New Zealand, had discovered part of the world grid.

Fig. 28
The Unified Vector Geometry (UVG) polyhedron spheres

The UVG coordinates also fit quite well with many of the other proposed Earth grids as well as appearing to complement known "ley lines" in England and elsewhere. These same lines are called the dragon paths in the Chinese Feng Shui system.

The UVG grid is really a composite of five very ancient types of geometric shapes. These five regular Platonic solids start with the simple 6-sided cube; around and within the cube a series of triangles can be imagined and drawn. A composite of the last three geometric patterns, the octahedron, dodecahedron and icosahedron, produces the UVG polyhedron (a hexalic icosahedron when projected on Earth), with 120 triangles and 62 major grid points, which are connecting vertexes of the various circles or equators. Within each of the 120 triangles on the Earth there are 16 lines, with 45 intersecting points producing 62 minor grid triangulations (see Figure 30). These 120 identical triangles are all composed of 30-, 60- and 90-degree angles, producing a grand total of 4,862 major and minor points on the Earth's surface (see Table 19 for approximate locations).[4]

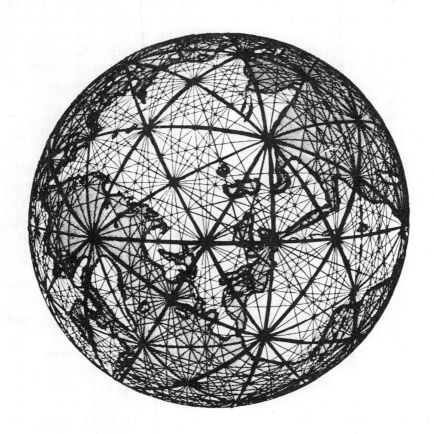

Looking at Figure 31, page 196 (Europe), it can be seen that the starting point is near the "Great Pyramid" of Egypt. Becker and Hagens choose their starting point in the Mediterranean, at the midpoint between the two outlets of the Nile between Masabb Rashid and Masabb Dumyat (31 N 42 latitude and 31 E 09 longitude).

There is some controversy as to where the major grid point #1 should start. Robert Temple in *The Sirius Mystery*[5] uses 31 N 30 latitude and 31 E 14 longitude. He bases this on what he calls the "Behdet Egyptian Geodetic Scheme." Behdet was a town on the Egyptian coast that was a major center and the pre-dynastic (before 3200 B.C.) capital of Egypt.

On the astrological geodetic grid, the longitude 30 E 00 is the end of Aries and the beginning of Taurus. With 31 E being used in the above grids, it is the equivalent of one Taurus and some minutes. (The latitude grid 30 N 00 to 37 N 37 encompasses the sign of Sagittarius.) There are many comparisons that can be made between the various grids, but how to accurately interpret the various meanings could prove to be quite a challenge.

The well-researched Glastonbury, Stonehenge and Avebury minor grids (but major ley lines) are contained in one of the larger European triangles. Compare the lines with Figure 29, page 191.

Becker and Hagens have also pinpointed the minor points within the three major triangles which cover the United States (see Figure 30, pages 194-5). The sacred power points that are reconfirmed are too numerous to name. See if these lines match the locations of ancient ruins, unusual formations or other anomalies in your area.

In their investigations, Becker and Hagens found a number of incomplete grids and maps that tend to confirm the (non-sacred) UVG master grid. In Figure 33, page 198, you'll see the famous "Piri Reis Map"[6] (with part of the UVG superimposed over it). It is over 400 years old and was analyzed by the U.S. Navy. The Navy said that it had correct circular grid projections!

In Figure 35, page 201, other comparisons were shown with the UVG grid and two different maps. Churchwood's "Oahspe" book, map, and another from the Lemurian Fellowship of Ramona California,[6] are superimposed with a UVG grid.

Still another map or grid by Ivan Sanderson marks what he calls "The Twelve Devil's Graveyards" around the world (Fig. 34, page 200). Its vortexes come very close to the UVG coordinates (see Figure 27, p. 186).

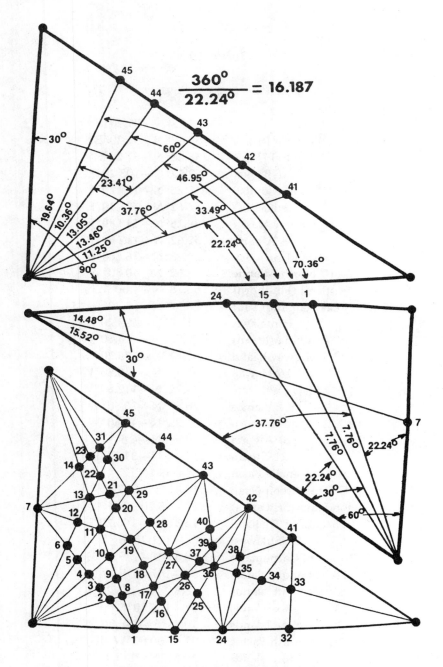

$$\frac{360^{\circ}}{22.24^{\circ}} = 16.187$$

Fig. 29—*Unified Vector Geometry*
Basic Triangle

191

Table 20

The Planetary Grid System

1/Egypt	31.72°N—31.20°E
2/Western Russia	52.62°N—31.20°E
3/Central USSR	58.28°N—67.20°E
4/Lake Baykal	52.62°N—103.20°E
5/Sea of Okhotsk	58.28°N—139.20°E
6/Bering Sea (Aleutian Is.)	52.62°N—175.20°E
7/Gulf of Alaska	58.28°N—148.80°E
8/Alberta	52.62°N—112.80°W
9/Hudson's Bay	58.28°N—76.80°W
10/North Atlantic	52.62°N—40.80°W
11/Scotland (Findhorn)	58.28°N—4.80°W
12/Karachi (Pakistan, Indus R.)	26.57°N—67.20°E
13/Himalayas	31.72°N—103.20°E
14/Iwo Jima (Japan)	26.57°N—148.80°W
15/Midway Island	31.72°N—175.20°E
16/Hawaii	26.57°N—148.80°W
17/Baja California	31.72°N—112.80°W
18/Bahamas	26.57°N—76.80°W
19/Mid-Atlantic North	31.72°N—40.80°W
20/Algeria	26.57°N—4.80°W
21/Sudan	10.81°N—31.20°E
22/Somalia Basin	0°—49.20°E
23/Chagos Archipelago	10.81°S—67.20°S
24/Ceylon Plain (Sri Lanka)	0°—85.20°E
25/Gulf of Thailand	10.81°N—103.20°E
26/Sulawesi	0°—121.20°E
27/Gulf of Carpentaria	10.81°S—139.20°E
28/Solomon Islands	0°—157.20°E
29/Marshall Islands	10.81°N—175.20°E
30/Phoenix Islands	0°—166.80°E
31/Caroline Islands	10.81°S—148.80°W
32/Mid-South Pacific	0°—130.80°W
33/Clipperton Islands	10.81°N—112.80°W
34/Galapagos Islands	0°—94.80°W
35/Peru	10.81°S—76.80°W
36/Amazon	0°—58.80°W

37/Guiana Basin	10.81°N—40.80°W
38/Romanche Gap	0°—22.80°W
39/Ascension Island	10.81°S—4.80°W
40/Gabon	0°—13.20°E
41/South Africa	26.57°S—31.20°E
42/Indian Ocean Ridge	31.72°S—67.20°E
43/Wharton Basin	26.57°S—103.20°E
44/South Australia	31.72°S—139.20°E
45/Loyalty Islands	26.57°S—175.20°E
46/South Pacific	36.72°S—148.80°W
47/Easter Island	26.57°S—112.80°W
48/Nazca Plate	31.72°S—76.80°W
49/Rio de Janeiro	26.57°S—40.80°W
50/Atlantic Ridge	31.72°S—4.80°W
51/Atlantic-Indian Ocean Basin	58.28°S—31.20°E
52/McDonald Is. (Indian Ocean)	52.62°S—67.20°E
53/South Indian Basin	58.28°S—103.20°E
54/Kangaroo Fracture	52.62°S—148.80°W
55/Emerald Basin	58.28°S—175.20°E
56/Udintsev Fracture	52.62°S—148.80°W
57/Albatross Cordillera	58.28°S—112.80°W
58/South American Tip	52.62°S—76.80°W
59/East Scotia Basin	58.28°S—40.80°W
60/South Atlantic Ridge	52.62°S—4.80°W
61/North Pole	90.00°N
62/South Pole	90.00°S

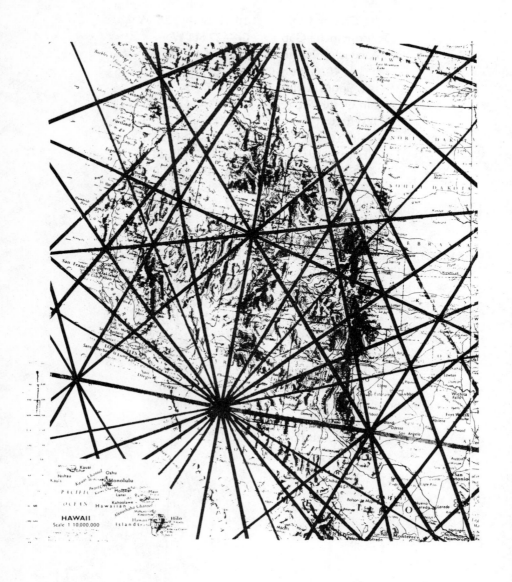

Fig. 30—*The United States and UVG Geometry*

194

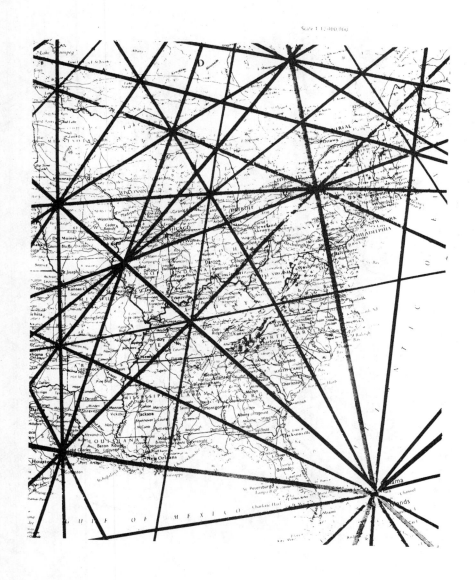

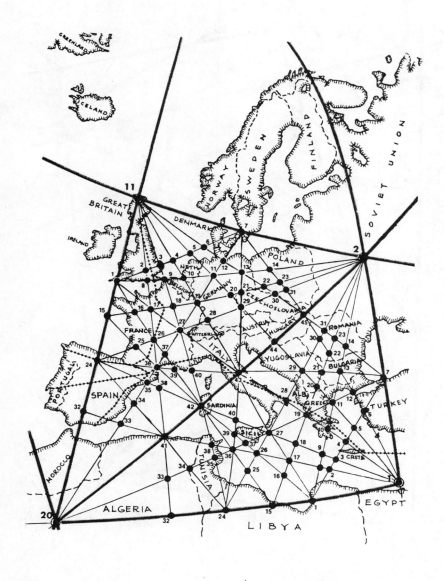

Fig. 31

Unified Vector Geometry applied to the map of Europe.

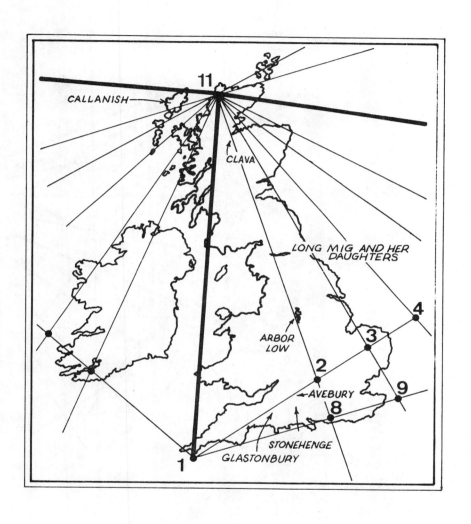

Fig. 32

*Unobstructed minor grid energy lines focus into
a Basic Triangle corner in the British Isles, which have probably
the largest clustering of megaliths in northern Europe.*

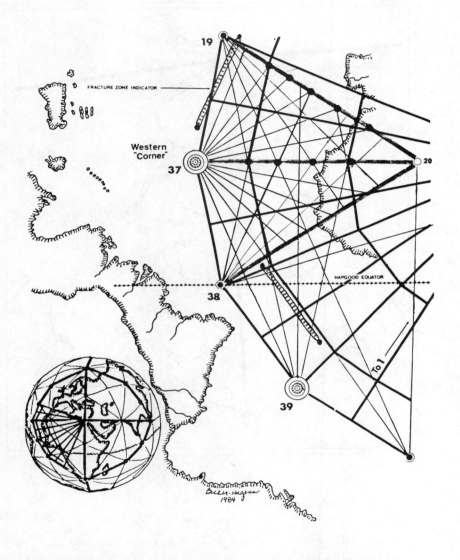

Fig. 33—*The Expanded Cartography of Admiral Piri Reis*

198

Bruce Cathie's investigations have shown that UFO sightings and other strange phenomena correspond to the UVG grid.[7] Cathie uses a system of exact harmonic numbers, which he feels is a key source of literal and symbolic knowledge. Cathie independently came up with many of the same major points that are on the UVG grid (see Figures 36 A and B, pages 204-205, and Appendix D for more figures and explanations). Cathie has also shown harmonic connections between Greenwich, the Vatican and the Great Pyramid.

Ancient Grids

Jose Arguelles, in his book *Earth Ascending,*[8] presents 50 different grids based on what he calls the laws governing whole systems. The book has an excellent introduction on geomancy and global historical trends. Arguelles uses what he calls the "Psi Bank," which is a code used to access knowledge as part of his "Holonomic Equation." The psi bank is also a binary code that can be used to store and retrieve all manner of information. By using the psi bank and many other theories and placing them on the geographic sphere, I discovered three examples that I felt were most relevant (see Appendix B).

Temple's Mid-Eastern Oracle Grid

Robert Temple developed a grid in his book *The Sirius Mystery,*[9] and named it "The Eastern and Western Oracle Octaves" (see Figure 38, page 207 and Table 20). The oracle centers start at Behdet, 31 N 30. For every degree of latitude north there is another center, and each of these is connected with a planet as well as with various centers both east and west, tree codes, and divine births.

Behdet, Egypt at 31 N 30 is really part of the larger Egyptian geodetic-grid system (see Figure 37, page 206). In this figure the north, south, east and west boundaries of the ancient grid are outlines. These boundaries are *not* considered speculation by modern authorities because there is ample evidence in writing and actual stone markers to show that they were agreed upon and used thousands of years ago.

The agreements were not unanimous. The greatest Pharaoh, Ahkenaten, wanted to set up a new capital of Egypt. The new city was to replace Thebes, and its location was 27 N 45, midway between the southern and northern boundaries of 24 N 00 and 31 N 30 respectively. The longitude would have been off center (31 E 14), at 30 E 50

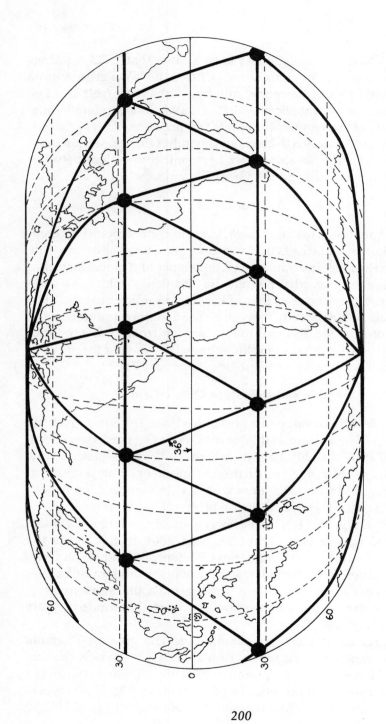

Fig. 34

The Twelve Devil's Graveyards of Ivan Sanderson

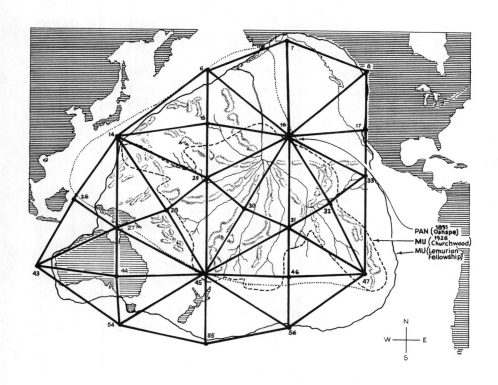

Fig. 35
Base map adapted from Lemurian Fellowship.

to put it on the Nile River, which was not only considered sacred, but was also the main source of food, water and transportation. This city of Aten would have been the new geodetic center or navel of Egypt, as it was called. It was never completed due to political opposition and the death of Ahkenaten. Yet the Egyptian coordinates were used as the zero meridian in the ancient world just as we use Greenwich today. Many other countries located their capitals and shrines at regular intervals from these points, e.g. Nimrod, Sardis, Persepolis, An-Yang, etc.

As we have learnt, Behdet and the Great Pyramid are still used in the UVG and others. Researchers seem to agree on the longitude of 31 E 14, but what latitude to use: Behdet/31 N 30, Great Pyramid/30 N 06 or Aten/27 N 45, is still open to question. (Cathie uses 31 E 09 and 29 N 58; see Appendix D).

Harleston and the Pyramids of Mesoamerica

In *Mysteries of the Mexican Pyramids,*[10] Peter Tompkins quotes extensively from the research of Hugh Harleston. Harleston spent many years studying the great pyramids of Mexico. He felt that the Sun pyramid and others of Teotihuacan were examples of a "four-dimensional, advanced computer with the request to display an ideal architectural design that would incorporate major universal constant, geodetic, atomic, astrophysical and other cosmic information in the minimum number of structures, all of which had to conform to the right-angle, Cartesian coordinates on an optimum scale model of the Earth."[11]

Harleston discovered many extraordinary facts about the dimensions of the pyramids, which exhibit a basic grid system. Harleston took the four-faced tetrahedron (which is like the four-faced Sun Pyramid he was studying) and placed the apex of it at the South Pole (see Figure 39B, page 210). The base of this equilateral triangle closely matched the latitude at the Sun Pyramid of 19 N 47. The tetrahedron and the sphere with a diameter of 12 is a unique pairing, because with a radius of 6 the ratio of the area is 2 to 1, an occurrence possible only once.[12] We are reminded that the tetrahedron is the shape of the carbon atom, the basic building block of living organisms (See Figure 40, page 212, and Figure B, page 287, and especially Appendix F.)

Livio Stecchini's Egyptian and Ziggurat Grids

Peter Tompkins in his first book on world pyramids, *Secrets of the Great Pyramids*,[13] asked the specialist Livio Stecchini to look into the geodetic and measurement systems of ancient Egypt. What Stecchini produced was an incredibly detailed, comprehensive system. He systematically pieced together the dimensions, measurements and historical references, creating an odyssey of discovery and wonder.

The Egyptian geodetic system was no mere abstraction, but like the Great Pyramid, it was based on exact measurements. Even the natural length of the Nile river measured out as one-third of the latitude of the Earth, as it started at the equator and ended at 30 N 06. The Great Pyramid lies at 30 N 00, a difference of 6'; the Egyptians favored 6' because it was one-tenth of a degree of latitude. This was how they measured latitude in 6' "Belts," as they called them. Later the Greeks would call them "zones."

In studying the ecliptic they noticed that Mercury (the Egyptian god of measurement and travel) would deviate more than any of the other planets—to 7 degrees north or south of the ecliptic. They therefore determined that the ecliptic was a total of 14 degrees wide, and called it the "great highway." As measured by Mercury, half the highway was 7 degrees; the Egyptians related the number 7 to the seven known planets and also to their geodetic grid. Seven degrees added to the southernmost boundary of Egypt gave them the northernmost boundary: 24 N 06 + 7 = 31 N 06, and in turn 31 N 06 was 6/7 of a degree of longitude at the equator (refer to Figure 39A, page 210 and Figures C and D, pages 288-289).

When Ahkenaten started his geodetic revolution, his intent was to restore once and for all the *true* geodetic center of Egypt. It has been stated that this new center was located at 27 N 45 and 30 E 50 on the Nile and one degree off the central longitude. The Egyptian grid ended at 55 N 30. The latitude was 2 x 27 N 30, or 55 N 30. This latitude of 55 N 30 was also significant, as it marks the spot where the distance of a degree of latitude equals that of a degree of longitude measured at the equator. The exact latitude where this takes place is 55 N 12; this was taken into consideration when the ancient Egyptians later revised the geodetic navel to 27 N 33 x 2, or 55 N 12. In these northern latitudes the river Dnieper in Russia was used as a systematic counterpart to the Nile.

It is interesting to note that Delphi, the geodetic navel of ancient Greece, is at 38 N 28; this is the Sun latitude according to Temples'

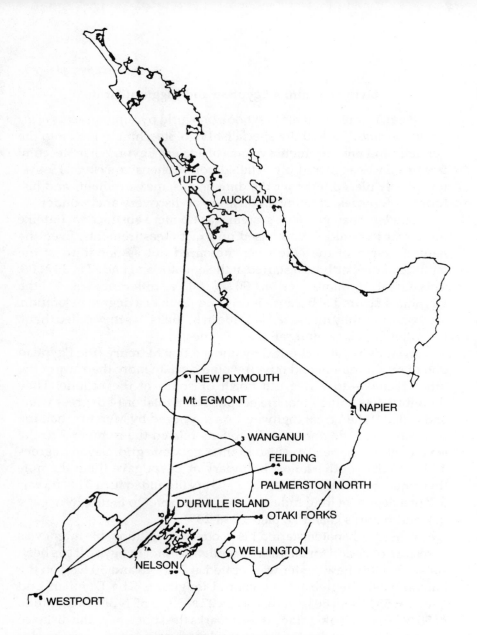

Fig. 36A—New Zealand

Showing section of first trackline discovered of world grid system. This map was originally published in my first book, Harmonic 33, *in 1968. The trackline extends from the position of a UFO sighted in the Kaipara Harbor, Auckland, to a position at D'Urville Island where two large UFOs were seen to disppear in a flash of light.*

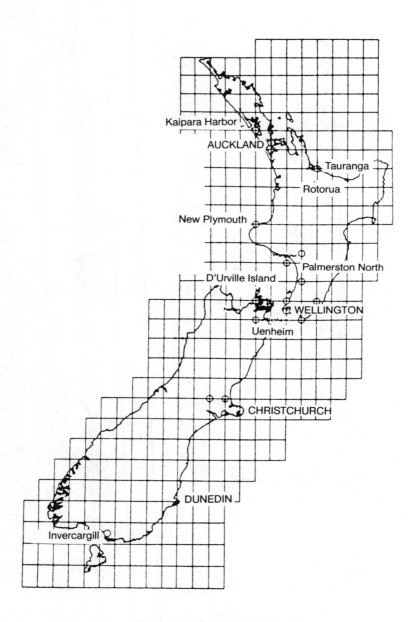

Fig. 36B—*New Zealand*

Original grid map produced in 1965. The map shows a section of the grid over the New Zealand area. The small circles are positions of UFO activity. The grid lines are spaced at thirty minutes of arc. Note the frequency of sightings occuring at grid intersections.

205

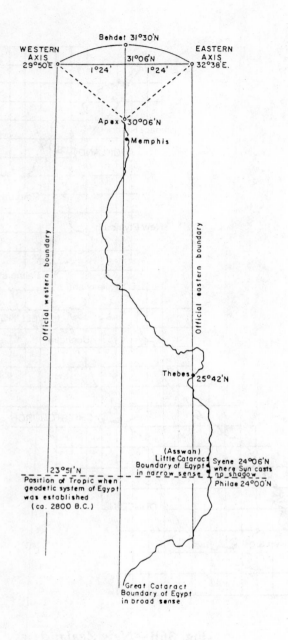

Fig. 37—*The Sirius Mystery*

206

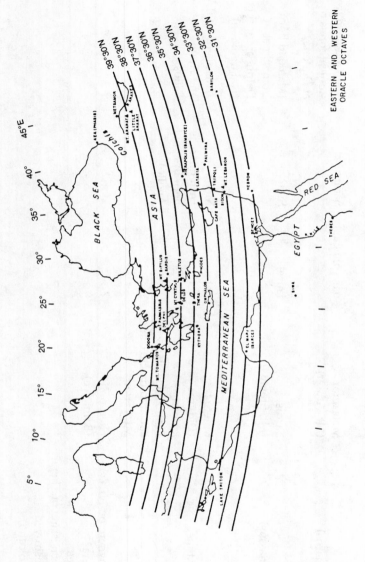

Fig. 38—The Oracle Octaves (with latitudes)

The latitudinal bands—such as those that criss-cross the omphalos stones—graphically demonstrate the oracle octaves descending from Dodona to Behdet and from Mount Ararat to Hebron.

207

Table 21
Chart of the Oracle Octaves

	W. Center	E. Center	Tree-Code	'Planet'-Code	Divine Births
8.	Dodona (Mt. Tomaros)	Metsamor (Mt. Ararat)	oak (phegus)	Saturn?	Mankind born from stones (bones of Earth) at Dodona
7.	Delphi (Mt. Parnassus)	Sardis (Mt. Sipylus)	laurel	Sun?	(Mankind born from stones at Delphi according to rival tradition)
6.	Delos (Mt. Cynthus)	Miletus (Didyma, also known as Branchidae, its associated oracle center) Mt. Latmus	palm	Moon (Artemis was born first, not Apollo)	Artemis (Diana) and Apollo born on Delos
5.	a. Somewhere on NE coast of Cythera? b. Rhodes c. Thera on island of Thera? (If so, destroyed by the volcano)	Hierapolis (Bambyce)	?	Mars?	?

4.	Omphalos (Thenae) near Knossos on Crete	willow	Jupiter	Zeus (Jupiter) was born on Crete
3.	Somewhere on south coast of Cyprus? (associated with Paphos? Akrotiri?) Cape Gata?	cypress (the word cypress is derived from Cyprus)	Venus	Aphrodite (Venus) born at Cyprus
2.	Lake Tritonis (also known as Lake Triton) in Libya/Tunisia	cedar	Mercury? (seb in Egyptian means both 'cedar' and 'the planet Mercury')	Athena (Pallas) born at Lake Tritonis
	Sidon (Mt. Lebanon)			
1.	El Marj (Barce) Libya	?	?	?
	Babylon			
0.	Behdet	wild acacia	Earth?	—
	Hebron			

Note: At one degree of latitude north of Dodona and Ararat is the mystery center of the Cabeiroi on the island of Samothrace.

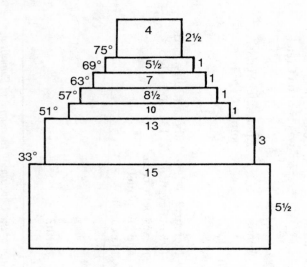

Fig. 39A—*The Ziggurat of Babylon*

The ziggurat of Babylon, says Stecchini, would have been perfect trigonometrically if the height of the first three steps had been as originally conceived: 30, 48 and 55½ degrees. But the Babylonians raised the first step to 33°, the approximate parallel of Babylon.

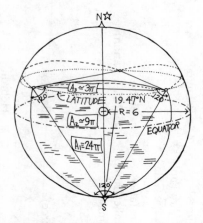

Fig. 39B—*Harleston's Sphere*

Harleston finds it significant that if you stand a tetrahedron on its nose at the South Pole it will form three triangles above the equator, splitting world into four equilateral great-circle triangles which will exactly divide into areas of 1/3 above and 2/3 below the equator.

grid. Dodona, a Greek sister center, was approximately 1 degree north at 39 N 32, and this corresponded to Saturn in Temples' grid system. The significance of these two places is further clarified when it was discovered that the length of these latitudes is equal in scale to the passage of a minute and/or second of sidereal time on the equator.[14]

The ancient Egyptians were great adherents to what they called "Maet," or cosmic order/measure, and their geodetic system is only a part of a much more profound cosmology.

The Babylonians also had a geodetic system, although it is less well-known than the Egyptians'. The Babylonians built "ziggurats," stepped pyramids whose corners pointed in the four directions. The seven steps were called the "House of Seven Bonds of Heaven and Earth," and they were painted in certain planetary colors. The steps/degrees of latitude can be seen in Figure 39A, page 210; each of the seven steps represented a specific latitude, and each had a key number assigned to it. In turn, each rectangular face was in proportion to the increased shrinking of longitude while moving north toward the pole. The latitudes were 6 degrees apart; Stecchini says that this was done so that an easily remembered cosine could be obtained by dividing its length by 2/3. Also, each latitude could be found by multiplying the height of each step by 6, e.g. 6 x 5.5 = 33N.

The Andes Lines

The whole continent of South America has much to tell us about the planetary grid, as well as grid systems in general. In the Nazca area of Peru there are hundreds of ancient lines that criss-cross the desert floor (see Figures 41, page 213). These seem to be a miniature grid system or what looks like an enlarged local space chart. The lines have some astrological/astronomical purposes, but it seems the major reason for them was for ancestral worship. As the Indians say: "They point to the Gods," i.e. the powers and forces of the Earth and in space. These incredibly straight lines have yet to be connected with the larger planetary grids.

Skinner's Isometric Grid of Chinese Rural Markets

Skinner's hexagon structures (Figures 42A and B, pages 214-5), which connect major and minor Chinese cities and towns, are not a simple flight of imagination but are based on extensive integration of past research and deep understanding of Chinese economics and social structure.[15]

Skinner says that each town is connected with six neighboring towns and that a standard marketing area includes about 18 towns. Each town has six major paths that radiate from it. Skinner sees these paths as an arterial system of social and economic energy—a kind of Ch'i of commerce.

It seems very probable that many other ancient civilizations had their own grid systems. There are many mysteries yet to be discovered. The grids that are known seem to directly or indirectly validate certain other grid systems. All the particular grids are apparently part of some grand puzzle that is only now beginning to take shape and reveal its hidden meaning.

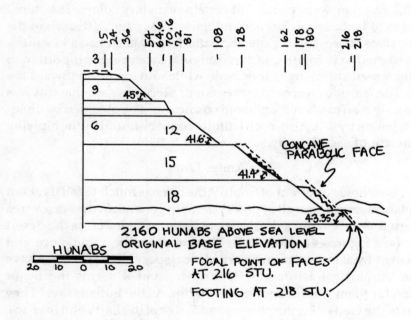

Fig. 40

Conversion of the Sun Pyramid's metric measurements to hunabs is shown by Harleston's theoretical reconstruction. The solid lines indicate the restoration by Batres in 1906 to 1910, and by the Mexican Institute of Anthropology and History in 1963 to 1964. The dotted lines use the Citadel logic and are based on refilling almost exactly the parts left off. The mathematically sequenced lengths of the pyramidal bodies follow a series of increasing sums. The individual heights and also the elevations above sea level are factors of the number 3 (see page 287).

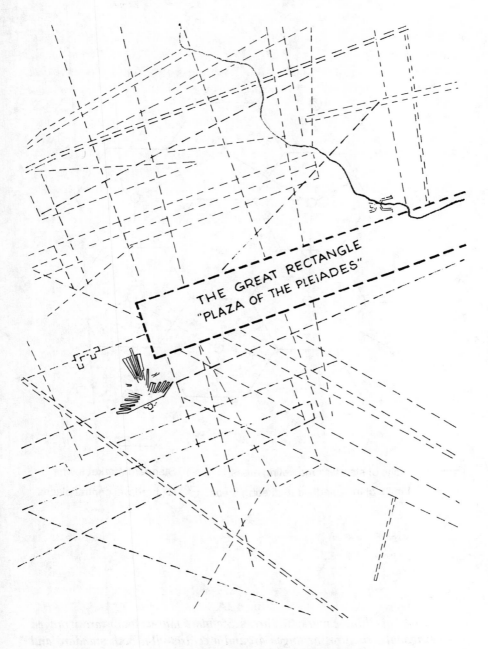

THE GREAT RECTANGLE
"PLAZA OF THE PLEIADES"

Fig. 41—Nazca Lines of Peru

213

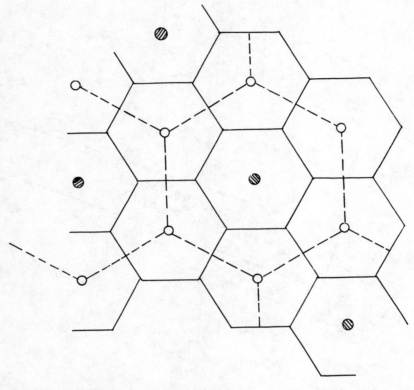

—— Limits of standard marketing areas	○ Standard market towns
- - - - Limits of intermediate marketing areas	◉ Higher-level central places

Fig. 42A

Model of Chinese marketing areas. Standard market towns are arranged as hexagonal structures arranged around a central city. Both standard and intermediate marketing areas are indicated.

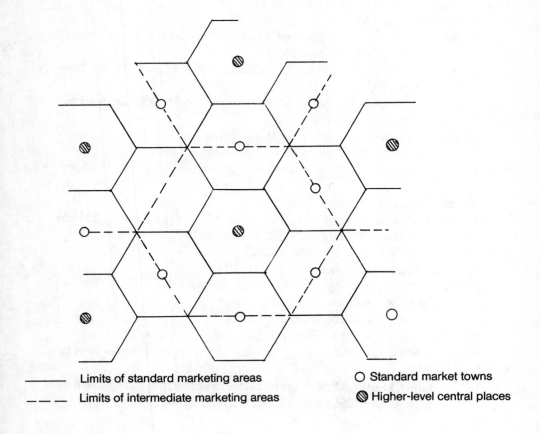

Limits of standard marketing areas   ○ Standard market towns
Limits of intermediate marketing areas   ◉ Higher-level central places

Fig. 42B
Marketing areas with interconnecting roads indicated.

215

Notes

1. Sepharial, *Geodetic Equivalents*. Tempe, AZ: AFA, 1970, reprint.
2. Manly P. Hall, *The Secret Teachings of all Ages*. Los Angeles: Philosophical Research Society, 1977.
3. ibid., Hall, p. LVI
4. Bill Becker and Bethe Hagens, *The Planetary Grid: A New Synthesis* in *Pursuit*, 2nd Quarter 1984.
   Also see: Christopher Bird, *The Planetary Grid* in *New Age Journal*, May 1975, pp. 36-41.
5. Robert Temple, *The Sirius Mystery*. New York: St. Martin Press, 1975, Chapter 5.
6. Becker-Hagens, *Pursuit*, op. cit. pp. 56 and 57.
7. Bruce Cathie, *Bridge to Infinity*, Adventures Unlimited.
8. Jose Arguelles, *Earth Ascending*, Boulder Co: Shambala, 1984, pp. 55, 85, 93.
9. ibid., Temple, pp. 124, 146, 149.
10. Peter Tompkins, *Mysteries of the Mexican Pyramids*, New York: Harper & Row, 1976, pp. 279-281, 251, 252.
11. ibid., Tompkins-Harleston, p. 263.
12. ibid., Tompkins-Harleston, p. 279-281.
13. Peter Tompkins, *Secrets of the Great Pyramid*. New York: Harper and Row, 1971, pp. 183-189.
14. ibid., Tompkins-Stecchini, appendix.
15. ibid., Tompkins-Stecchini, pp. 184-188.
16. Tony Morrison, *Pathways to the Gods*. New York: Harper & Row, 1978.
17. William Skinner, *Marketing and Social Structure in Rural China, Journal of Asian Studies Vol. 23, No. 1, Nov. 1964.*

CHAPTER 8

HOROSCOPE EXAMPLES

Carlos Castaneda

The elusive and mysterious teacher Carlos Castaneda, author of *The Teachings of Don Juan, The Eagle's Gift* and six other books on the Toltec magical system, is a source of excellent material for relocational astrology (see Bibliography on page 238).

The life experiences of Carlos are rich with supernatural, magical and bizarre episodes which catapulted him into separate realities unknown to most people. His books are incredibly entertaining, and at the same time filled with lucid insights on the nature of life.

One of the main reasons for his sustained popularity is his natal Jupiter within one degree of the Tenth House cusp in his natal chart (see Figure 43A, page 218). His writing ability stems from two sources: his Mercury in Sagittarius in the Eighth House gives him literary flair in writing about the mysterious side of life; also, Mercury is quincunx (150°) Pluto in the Third House of writing, indicating the right amount of stress to drive him to express his writing ability. (The inconjunct or quincunx is known as an irritant which leads to fulfillment.) Jupiter conjunct the Medium Coeli is also Jupiter in the northerly direction. It is not southern, because his place of birth is in Peru, which is below the equator. The northerly direction is one of mystery and adversity (see Figure 15), but with Jupiter there one would receive guidance and protection from various forms of destructive energy. One would be made aware of certain laws that could act as shields for the mental and domestic well-being of the person.

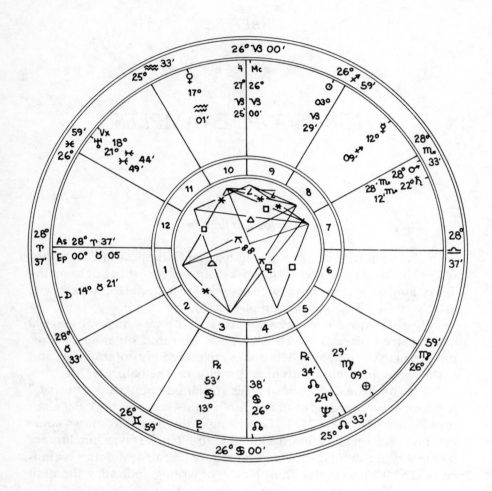

Fig. 43A—*Carlos Castaneda*

From Jansky, Astrological Review 73/74, 1:51 p.m. EST; *rectification by*
Steve Cozzi.

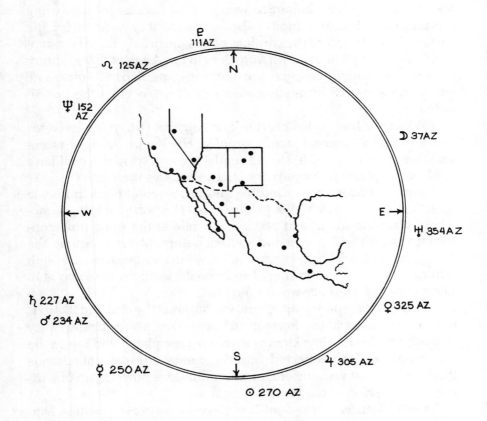

Fig. 43B

A Local Space chart for Don Juan's Sonoran home.

—Examples in this section start at 0 degrees azimuth at due east.

219

Although Carlos doesn't talk much about his early life, we can assume that Jupiter's influence was present because of his strong philosophical direction. Jupiter also points the way north, being the closest planet to any of the cardinal points, including the Ascendant and Descendant. The azimuth from Peru to Los Angeles (a temporary home) is not within 10 degrees of any planet; perhaps this means he left South America from somewhere in Brazil, a move he has alluded to.

When we look at his chart in Los Angeles (where he lived for many years), a different picture unfolds. His Venus (in right ascension) is in very close sextile to the Tenth House cusp, which could in a mild way enhance his popularity. Uranus squares the Tenth cusp (2° orb) and produces very unsettling and erratic conditions in his life direction. Pluto trines his First House cusp (1.8° orb), helping somewhat by adding depth and resiliency, while at the same time contributing to his withdrawn and solitary nature. Mercury square the Ascendant (12' orb) again shows the need to communicate through writing. However, the writing of eight books would seem to point to more than just Mercury square the First.

In the Local Space map, Uranus is conjunct the east and it also is the closest planet to the horizon (6° orb). This makes Uranus very powerful in this locality. Uranus is an Air-type planet and it is in the east, which is also connected with the mental Air element. Uranus therefore is most responsible for the continuous outpouring of writing over a period of ten years.

Carlos learned the ancient Toltec system from two teachers, Don Juan and Don Jenero. Most of his learning experiences took place in two locations in Mexico: the Sonoran desert in northern Mexico, and around Oaxaca in southern Mexico. From careful research I have been able to find the approximate location of Don Juan's house in Sonora (Figure 43B). Looking at the Local Space map for Carlos in Los Angeles, and plotting the azimuth to Sonora, we find that Carlos had to travel on his Venus line. This Venus line has extra importance, as it is within two degrees of the azimuth of the Winter Solstice azimuth degree. Therefore traveling on this Venus line involves matters of the heart, but in a serious way. The Winter Solstice point always brings a Capricorn/Saturn influence to the planets that are within three or four degrees of it. What in fact happened is that Carlos formed a stable relationship with Don Juan, one that continuously brought him back for more teaching, even though Don Juan frequently subjected him to unexplainable and life-threatening encounters with unknown forces. Carlos had to discipline the desires of his heart, and bring into balance his life's direction. Love is what brought him back, love of the path, and of his teacher. Don Juan had told him on many occasions that you must follow a path with heart and no other.

In the Sonoran desert, his Uranus is six degrees away from the east, much weaker than in Los Angeles, where it was almost exact. However, the Sun here is a little less than eight degrees from the south. Considering the leadership qualities of Don Juan in his never-ending assaults on the ego of Carlos, this may point to the possibility of error in the birth time, which would make the Sun closer to the south. The direction south is the place of self-realization, and this is what eventually happened to the self-image (Sun) of Carlos. It was redefined and merged with the real self within (south). Uranus trines his First cusp there, causing sudden and positive personality changes. The Node also trines the Ascendant, showing the success of personal associations.

The latitude of the central Sonora location is 29 north; the altitude (especially in the Prime Vertical) becomes increasingly more important as you get below 30 degrees north latitude (or above 30 degrees south). Venus happened to be the lowest planet to the horizon at that location. The most sacred planet in Mesoamerica, Venus was to have an added meaning for Carlos.

Don Juan asks Carlos to search in his heart (Venus) and find out why he wants to learn the Toltec path of knowledge. Carlos asks Don Juan if he will at least accept his desire to learn. Don Juan says that he would if Carlos can find his "spot," that he has a spot of his own, and that he knows where the right one is for Carlos. But Carlos must find it for himself to prove his intent to learn. Don Juan explains that the spot is a direction that can vary from place to place, and that a person will feel strong and happy when facing in that direction. The spot also wards off fatigue and offers protection from enemies.

Don Juan does not give any hints to Carlos on how to find the spot, but he encourages him to experiment. Carlos then goes through a series of body positions while facing in different directions. After marking different directions in his mind and with his shoes and jacket, at about 3:00 A.M. he thinks he has found the spot. Don Juan informs him that it is not the one. Finally at about 5:15 A.M. he notices a bluish-green light in a southeasterly direction. After he falls asleep on that spot, Don Juan informs him that the spot to the southeast is in fact his spot. Looking at the Local Space chart for Carlos at the location of Don Juan's house in Sonora, it can be seen that Venus is in the southeast (325 azimuth), with Jupiter at 305 degrees of azimuth, more towards the south.

Jupiter and Venus, the great benefics (as they have been called), should give the strength and protection that Don Juan had mentioned. Also, at this time of day, transiting Venus was in the east-southeast.

Don Juan also said that there was a bad or enemy spot and that Carlos had found it as well. Although the exact direction is not given, I believe it to be in the southwest, because Mars and Saturn are in that location for Carlos (Saturn at azimuth 227, Mars at azimuth 234).

There have been many critics of Castaneda's works. Most of the criticism centers around how much was fact and how much was fiction. If Carlos was only fictionalizing, how could he have guessed at the right location for his spot?

Albert Einstein

Although there is no way of verifying the accuracy of this chart with solid evidence, nor with personal statements, the fact remains that the chart does tend to prove itself from a Local Space point of view. Einstein was born in Ulm, Germany (southwest of Berlin) on March 14, 1879, at 11:30 SM LMT. He had Jupiter sesquiquadrate (135°), the First within a 45' orb, and Mars semi-square (45°) the Tenth House cusp (56' orb). These are not very powerful aspects, yet they are close in orb. Jupiter adds positivity to Einstein's outlook; Mars gives an added push toward his direction (see Figure 44A, facing page).

In Berlin, he still has the Mars aspect plus a sesquiquadrate of Uranus to the First House (41' orb) and a square of Venus to the Ascendant (1° 23' orb). Jupiter is not in aspect with the Ascendant here, and so it doesn't neutralize the other adverse aspects. The three aspects in Berlin taken by themselves would not be considered difficult, however when the minor aspects pile up in a certain locality they begin to reinforce each other. Mars is about 8 degrees above the horizon in Berlin, closer than any other planet. This of course would tend to aggravate the Mars First House aspect along with indirectly feeding the discord of the other aspects. So Berlin for Einstein was an unsettling (Uranus), unpleasant (Venus), and potentially violent (Mars) place.

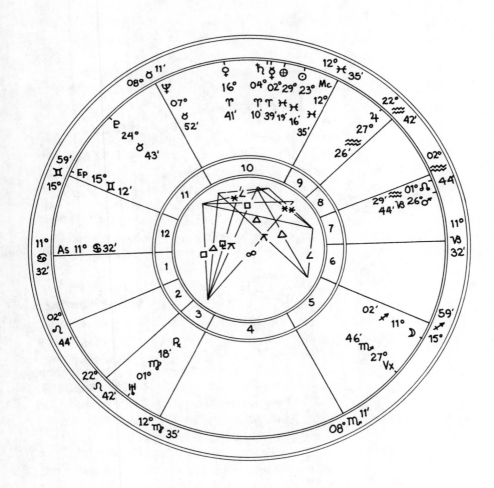

Fig. 44A—Albert Einstein

From German birth registry

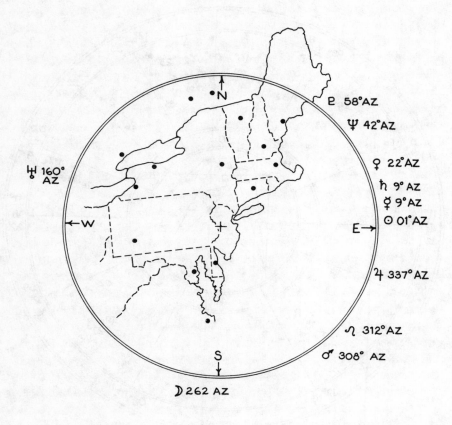

Fig. 44B

A Local Space chart for Albert Einstein's Princeton home.

Perhaps if this discord were not present, he may have delayed his permanent exit from Germany, and a delay could have cost him his life, as it did so many others. Projecting the azimuth to New York, we find that he traveled on his Neptune line. This is a very tricky as well as mystical line. It has been mentioned that it has to do with new realities and with refinement. These two words are especially descriptive in Einstein's case, since he refined his formulas at Princeton, and changed mankind's concepts by opening up new realities in physics. One other point is that if he appeared to be what he really was (a Jew escaping the country with secrets of the universe), he may never have been able to leave Germany. In his case the illusionary quality of Neptune offered him an advantage.

In Princeton, New Jersey, Einstein had the Moon square the First (1.5° orb), a minor aspect which indicates that the public and publicity (Moon) would be somewhat of a disturbance to his outlook. The major influence is the Sun, which is conjunct the east (38' orb) and is also one of the three planets that are close to the horizon. The brilliance of his individuality really was able to shine forth, and of course, his popularity was world-wide. The Sun in the east is in its natural place, where it rises, and this placement gave Einstein great vitality and confidence. The Sun is 4.7 degrees below the horizon, with Uranus at 4.5 below, and Jupiter 6.1 above; this is a remarkably successful combination. Uranus represents his new ideas in physics; the Sun, his individual creativity; and Jupiter, the functioning of the abstract mind and the overall success of everything he attempted.

Venus is conjunct the Summer Solstice, making his personal life very sensitive and touchy, but at the same time productive. We could say that he put his heart into his work and had many powerful social encounters. Venus allowed him expression of feelings, and he came across as warm, making him somewhat atypical of most scientists.

Mark Twain

Mark Twain was born in Florida, Missouri (November 30, 1835, at 4:45 A.M. LMT, according to Huggins in *Astrology* magazine, January 1970). He had only two weak aspects in that locality. The Moon trined the Tenth House cusp, but was 1 degree 45' from exact (see Figure 45A, page 226). This aspect may have given him some intuitive impression about his direction in life. Since Mercury was also in aspect to the Tenth, making a square (1° 23'), this may have given him

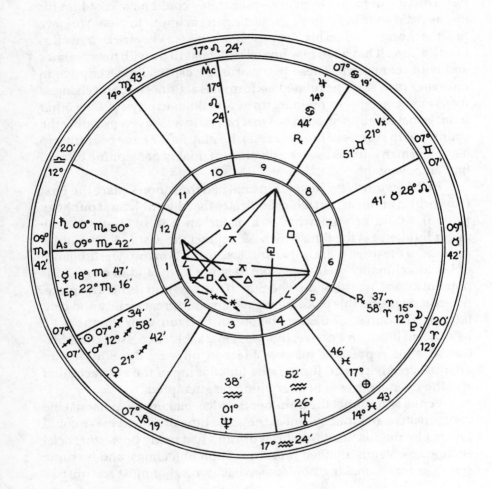

Fig. 45A—Mark Twain

From Mark Edmond Jones, Sabean Symbols, 1953

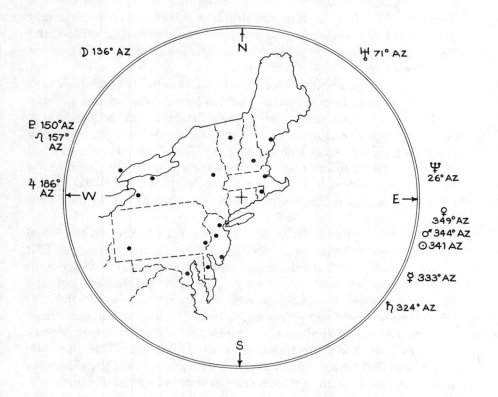

Fig. 45B
A Local Space chart for Mark Twain's Hartford home.

227

ideas about writing as a career, but did not necessarily provide a chance for self-expression. He grew up in Hannibal on the Mississippi River, which is about 35 miles northeast of Florida; this is also the direction of Twain's Neptune azimuth line. Pure fiction comes straight from an active imagination, so it was no wonder that he created the fascinating stories about young boys like Huck Finn growing up on the Mississippi.

Interestingly enough, Mark Twain did not find his real destiny in that area. One of the reasons may be that Saturn was 8 degrees above the horizon and in the east. Mercury was 7 degrees below the horizon, also in the east. This combination can produce deep thinking, especially since both planets were in the east, the place of Air. The real expression of his talent did not happen; they were not close enough to the horizon. In addition, he experienced the delaying influence common with Saturn. (Both Saturn and Mercury were in the Local Space Twelfth House).

A helpful placement in that location was Jupiter in the Local Space Seventh House in opposition to the Summer Solstice. This showed that practical education and material wealth along with spiritual growth would come through good relationships, and perhaps by traveling west. Twain did go west; his major trip was to San Francisco after he spent some time in Nevada. The azimuth in that direction showed an unusually large combination of five lines: Sun, Venus, Mercury, Mars and Pluto. Since he traveled on so many lines, it can be safely said that he left for a variety of reasons. Among the planetary lines, Mars was the closest to the azimuth direction from Hannibal to San Francisco. Definite action had to be taken to cause a deeper (Pluto), mental (Mercury), social and financial (Venus), and individualistic (Transpluto) reality to break forth .

His San Francisco locality chart is filled with activity. The most powerful influence is the Moon; it is only 23' above the horizon and also conjunct the west (3° orb). Involvement with others on deeper levels is present, and strong emotions also play a big role. Many women entered his life at this time; it could have been too much of a good thing, which could have caused too much change and dependency.

Jupiter was 6.5 degrees from the South, not a close aspect, but one that could moderately improve his professional life. Three other positive factors entered into the picture: Jupiter square the Ascendant (1° orb), Mercury sextile the Medium Coeli (1° orb), Mars sextile the

First (2° orb) and lastly Mercury conjunct the east in a 5.2° orb. The question arises with all this Jupiter influence (a Jupiter square is not usually considered negative) and Mercury influence: Why didn't he stay in San Francisco? The answer lies in the remaining two aspects. Saturn is only 20' from an exact conjunction in the east, so it is more powerful than Mercury, which is over five degrees from the east. As I have indicated in Chapter 3, "There is very little that is sociable, warm or friendly about this place." (Taken out of context, this may sound a bit harsh, because Saturn does have a constructive influence in making us more practical, responsible and realistic.) The other spoiler here is Pluto conjunct the Seventh (2° orb), a place where petty tyrants can play on your weaknesses. Undoubtedly, Mark Twain learned many important lessons there, but the close aspects of Saturn and Pluto eventually outweighed the Moon, Mercury and Jupiter aspects.

His next major move was to Buffalo, New York. He would have to travel on his Jupiter line to get there. This is an indicator of success, and a time in his life when things were on the increase.

In Buffalo, he had Mercury conjunct the First (1° orb), a good place to start writing, which is exactly what he did. Buffalo was not destined to be his home for long, and there are some definite reasons why. Uranus was 3 degrees from the north, i.e. conjunct the Fourth House cusp. This is a very disruptive and disturbing influence, especially with career and home matters. Another uncomfortable aspect was Saturn 1 degree from the Winter Solstice. This influence can be great for control and concentration, but it is also depressing and restricting—definitely not in the style of Mark Twain.

Hartford, Connecticut was the place where he had his most productive years of writing. To get there, he travelled a short distance on an assortment of lines, making the move difficult to interpret.

In Hartford, Uranus is away from the Fourth House cusp and Saturn is 3 degrees from the Winter Solstice, lessening its impact. Mercury is away from the Ascendant, but is still the closest planet to the horizon (as it was in Buffalo). Mercury this strong would certainly cause a person with writing talent to express it. The mild Saturn influence gave him just enough discipline to get the job done. An added factor is that the Sun is square the Medium Coeli (1° orb) here; this shows Twain's popularity, prominence and individual creativity.

Mark Twain made a number of trips to London. In so doing he travelled on his Neptune line, the same line that triggered his imagination when he travelled to Hannibal. No doubt his trips to England gave him plenty of ideas for his book *A Connecticut Yankee in King Arthur's Court.*

Benito Mussolini

A number of years ago I came across a statement in a book I was reading which aroused my first interest in Local Space Astrology, and locality astrology in general. It was the Wilhelm Wulff book *The Zodiac and the Swastika.* Although I knew next to nothing about Local Space Astrology at the time, he related a story that really stimulated my curiosity.

Wulff was one of many German astrologers who was forced to work for the Third Reich during World War II. He was in Rome when Mussolini was kidnapped under orders of certain German officers. The German High Command in Italy wanted him back right away but had no idea where he had been taken. They demanded that Wulff use astrology to find Mussolini.

Wulff stated that he used the East Indian technique that locates missing persons! I had never heard of any such astrological technique. Wulff's calculations showed that Mussolini was 75 miles southeast of Rome. There was only one possible location and that was the island of Ponza, and it was here that Mussolini was found. Years later, when I used my own calculations, I came up with 76.5 miles south-southeast of Rome. I thought I had erred, because it put the point out in the ocean, but when I looked at the map I found the small island of Ponza (see Appendix G).

In Rome, Mussolini had Neptune opposition the Summer Solstice point. (He was born July 29, 1883, at Dovia la Pre, Italy, at 2:00 P.M. LMT, according to Gauquelin—see Figure 46A). This point tends to sensitize, nurture and cause growth. Therefore his Neptune was more active than normal in this location. Neptune in political affairs has a lot to do with spies, propaganda, false pretenses, etc. Neptune opposed his Ascendant at his birthplace north of Rome. He was obviously quite proficient in deceiving the public, as well as projecting the country's problems on chosen scapegoats. The practice of deception and projection have long been known to be sinister skills of Neptune.

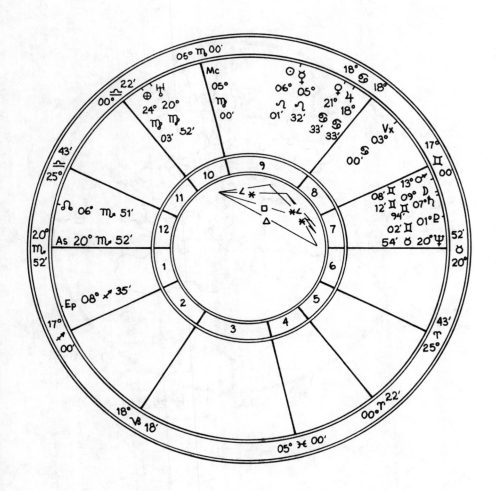

Fig. 46A—*Benito Mussolini*

From M. Gauquelin #1745, Vol. 5

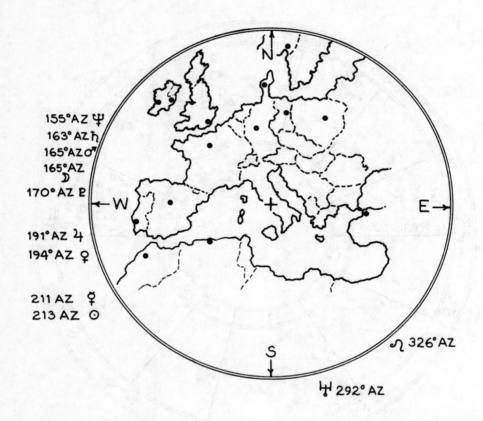

155°AZ Ψ
163° AZ ♄
165°AZ ♂
165°AZ ☽
170°AZ ♭

191°AZ ♃
194°AZ ♀

211 AZ ☿
213 AZ ☉

♌ 326° AZ

♅ 292° AZ

Fig. 46B
Mussolini's Rome Local Space chart.

Napoleon I of France

Napoleon's home and the seat of his power was in Paris. (Born August 15, 1769, Ajaccio, Corsica, at 11:52 A.M. LMT, corrected time, see Figure 47A). It is here that he was most successful and influential, and for good reason—the Sun was within 4 degrees of the south and it may have been near magnetic north. This of course is a position of prominence, power and leadership. Also Jupiter and Uranus were both close to the horizon (Jupiter 6° below it, and Uranus 4° above it). Jupiter and Uranus working together can bring about sudden success in the areas of money, influence and technical knowledge. Most people would agree that Napoleon acquired fame and wealth in a spontaneous manner, yet where did his technical abilities lay? Besides being open to progressive thought, his chief technical talents were expressed in the military. He was brilliant and innovative when it came to the use of artillery. The types of cannons he used and the proper positioning of them was often decisive in winning battles. In addition Pluto was conjunct the Summer Solstice degree, thus the power of death and transformation was geared towards growth.

His natal Moon squared the Ascendant in Paris, within less than a half-degree orb. Although this is not a powerful aspect, it does indicate that the public (Moon) was periodically disturbing and fickle toward him and his views (Ascendant). Paris, therefore, was a successful (Jupiter), revolutionary (Uranus), intellectual (Mercury) and emotional (Moon) place for him.

Two major events stand out in Napoleon's military and political career: the disastrous Russian campaign and the defeat at Waterloo. The planets closest to the azimuth connecting Paris and Moscow were Saturn and the Moon. Saturn is the planet that is the closest (to the azimuth degree) and therefore its influence should be considered dominant. Had Napoleon known about this, he may have altered his plans, because with Saturn you should expect delays and limitations. The interesting fact is that Napoleon won all the battles, but lost the war!

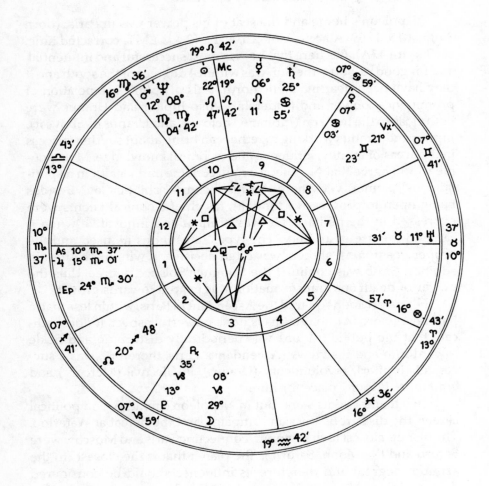

Fig. 47A-Napoleon I of France

From Weynn's Astrology, *June 1944, and from P. J. Swift, English astrologer
published in 1812; rectification by Steve Cozzi.*

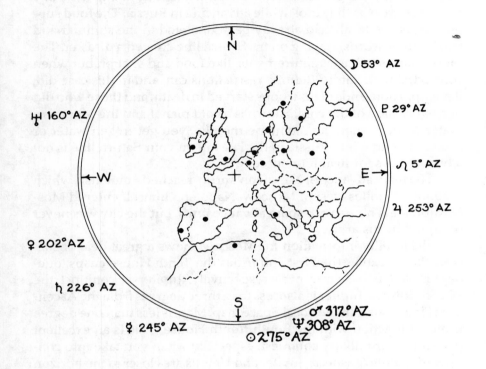

Fig. 47B
Napoleon's Paris Local Space chart.

Local Space astrology reveals two important factors that contributed to the great loss of life and his subsequent defeat. First of all, Napoleon and his generals made a fatal mistake in taking the same route in retreat as they took while advancing in Russia. The food supplies from the locals had already been depleted in the summer and fall. In other words, staying on his Saturn line created a disaster. The Moon relates to basic requirements, like food and shelter, but when connected with Saturn definite restrictions can, and in this case did, develop. Thousands of his troops starved to death, and those who did not starve died of the cold. Saturn is a cold planet and the Moon is a Water planet; when you combine the two, you get frozen water or snow. Marching into Russia in the late fall on your Saturn line is not advantageous for health or success.

The main advance of Napoleon's army reached Smolensk, which is about 190 miles west of Moscow. Napoleon himself entered Moscow for a few hours with some advance units, but the city was never occupied by his army.

His locality information for Moscow shows a great deal of success. Pluto sextiles the First and trines the Tenth House cusps, one-degree and two-degree orbs respectively. Jupiter is conjunct the Winter Solstice. Jupiter is also less than three degrees from the Ascendant First House. In the Local Space map, Mars is less than one degree from conjunction with the South/Tenth House. This is an excellent placement for military conquest, especially when you take into consideration Pluto's aspects. Jupiter and Uranus are closer to the horizon than in Paris (Uranus is 5.5° below and Jupiter is 3° above).

Napoleon's case is an excellent example of how traveling on certain lines over a prolonged period of time can affect the outcome of events. His army had been traveling on the Saturn/Moon lines for over six months, so even though he won the majority of battles, he lost the war. His army did not have the physical strength nor supplies to make it through the Russian winter.

Historically the loss at Waterloo ranks about equal with the Russian defeats. Napoleon's last major battle was fought here about 10 miles southeast of Brussels, Belgium. At the beginning of the battle (11:30 A.M. on June 18, 1815) the Moon was in the northeast (azimuth 14). This placement may not have been very significant, except for the fact that it was conjunct Napoleon's Moon opposing Saturn for that locality. The Moon, in the case of a military battle, would show where an army may be vulnerable to attack. History tells us that the turning point of the battle took place when the French front lines were pierced in the northeast (Moon). The battle was over at around 8:00 P.M. At this time the conjunction of Mars and Pluto was in the northeast, right on top of Napoleon's Moon! He failed to realize how weak the northeast part of his lines were, and for the second time his Moon/Saturn opposition worked against him.

Notes

All chart information in this chapter is taken from *The American Book of Charts*, Lois Rodden, Astro-Computing Services, San Diego, 1980.

For references to Local Space material throughout his extensive series of books, the following works by Carlos Castaneda should prove helpful:

1. *The Teachings of Don Juan.* New York: Pocket Books, 1968. Pages 29-34 (finding spot), 113, 154, 162, 165, 171, 193, 202, 228.
2. *A Separate Reality.* New York: Pocket Books, 1971. Pages 228-231.
3. *Journey to Ixtlan.* New York: Pocket Books, 1972. Pages 48, 106, 144, 151, 155, 163, 166, 193, 201, 252.
4. *Tales of Power.* New York: Pocket Books, 1974. Pages 59, 220, 232, 233.
5. *Second Ring of Power.* New York: Pocket Books, 1977. Pages 14, 26, 31, 32, 35, 36, 40, 62, 78, 252, 313.
6. *The Eagle's Gift.* New York: Pocket Books. Pages 67, 104, 174, 189, 196, 242, 249.
7. *The Fire Within.* New York: Pocket Books, 1983. Indirect references throughout the text.
8. *The Power of Silence.* New York: Pocket Books, 1987. Indirect references throughout the text.

APPENDICES

Michael and Margaret Erlewine

I. The Celestial Sphere

From *The Astrology of Local Space,* published by
The Heart Center, 1977.

T he Celestial Sphere is an exact projection of the Geographic
Sphere, and this fact allows for some very interesting astrological considerations. Coordinates on the celestial equatorial sphere are measured in right ascension (similar to zodiac longitude) and declination,
a little later on. For now, we will investigate the relation between the
latitude factor (declination) in the equatorial system and geographic
latitude. Each place and city on this Earth is located at a specific
latitude somewhere between the equator and the poles. Ann Arbor,
Michigan (where we live) is located at 42° latitude, north of the
equator. There is a circle of 42° latitude that stretches across the USA
and on around the Earth. Thus there are other cities on the globe that
also are located at 42° north geographic latitude. You may want to
look and see what cities share your same latitude—either above or
below the equator.

Now the interesting fact about the relation between geographic
latitude and declination in the equatorial sphere is that there exists a
circle of stars on the celestial sphere, located at a declination that
matches the geographic latitude of your home. The stars on this circle
are the only ones that ever pass over your town, and each parallel of
geographic latitude on the Earth has a matching parallel of declination
on the celestial sphere. The diagram on the next page will illustrate
this fact. Ann Arbor is located at point *a* on the rotating Earth. Star *a* is
directly overhead at what is called the zenith. As the Earth turns,

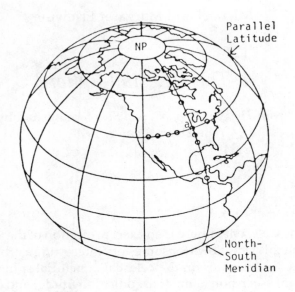

Figure A

*Cities located along the north/south meridian
and parallel of latitude.*

it will carry Ann Arbor to point *b* and on around in a circle until point *a*
is reached once again. There is also another circle of stars that pass
exactly under Ann Arbor—at a declination circle of -42° (42 degrees
south declination). Every city on Earth could be described in terms of
the kinds of stars and other objects that make up the declination circles that equal the circle of geographic latitude at which they are
located. You may want to look up the degree of declination in this list
that is the same as your geographic latitude to see what kind of points
and stars circle over your head each year and each day.

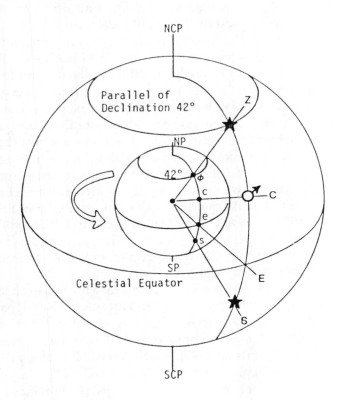

Figure B

What we have done for the declination factor on the celestial sphere we could also do for the right ascension or longitude equivalent in this coordinate system. Right ascension is similar to zodiac longitude in that it is measured from 0 ° to 360°, *but* it is measured along the equator and not along the ecliptic or zodiac. We shall return to the difference between these two systems later on. Right now, we will investigate the relationship between right ascension and the geographic meridian that runs from the North Pole through your birthplace and on to the South Pole.

Figure B on the previous page shows the Earth on which we have drawn both parallels of geographic latitude and north/south geographic meridians of longitude. Point *a* illustrates a city located somewhere in the Midwest. The finder lists in *Astrophysical Directions* (or in an atlas), arranged by geographic longitude and latitude, will allow you to look up other cities located along the parallel of latitude where you are, and also cities located along the north/south geographic meridian that passes through your location. We have illustrated this with small circles in the diagram that represent other cities located along these two directions on the globe. We have seen how there is a circle of stars on the celestial sphere that equals the circle of geographic latitude for any spot on Earth. We can do the same for the geographic longitude factor. In fact we do this each time we cast a natal chart and locate the Local Sidereal Time (LST) or right ascension of the Mid-Heaven (RAMC). We stop the Earth's motion and hold it still to see what part of the heavens is overhead our birthplace; another way of saying this is we determine in what direction of the heavenly sphere the Earth was pointed or oriented.

Once we have found the LST or RAMC for a birth, we can look up the equivalent Mid-Heaven (MC), Ascendant and House cusps in any Table of Houses. We can also look up the direction of the heavens "out there" or overhead on star maps. Your LST may be expressed in Hours-Minutes-Seconds (H-M-S), which you will find along the edge of these maps, or in Degrees-Minutes-Seconds (D-M-S) of arc (rather than time), and these too are given on the maps. (H-M-S may be converted to D-M-S by simply multiplying by 15, and D-M-S may be converted to H-M-S by dividing by 15). Look up your RAMC or LST on the equatorial star maps and locate the right ascension meridian that was overhead at your birth and the direction in space to which your birth location was pointed or oriented. ALL stars and points along the line of right ascension running from top to bottom on this map were in line with the geographic meridian for your birth. The diagram (Figure C on the facing page) will illustrate this: (1) Ann Arbor is located along the 42nd parallel of latitude, (2) The north/south geographic meridian (o, c, e, s) passes through Ann Arbor at o, (3) This meridian equals point Z, C, E and S when projected on the celestial sphere, (4) All points located along this celestial meridian will be aligned and in conjunction with the north/south geographic meridian for Ann Arbor, (5) Only star Z is *also* conjunct by declination=latitude for Ann Arbor, (6) The planet Mars (at C) would be overhead and to the south of Ann

even the galactic and supergalactic planes—correspond symbolically to the various different dimensions or levels of our consciousness—as they exist now, in mutual interpenetration. These levels can be sorted out; and as astrologers we may learn to read these different levels as separate, yet related and whole dimensions of our experience.

Let me rephrase all of this. Our Universe, and therefore our Life, can be described or expressed in astrological terms using any one of several fundamental planes of reference: ecliptic, horizon, etc. These different planes and their respective coordinate systems are like different languages (or algebras), in that they each can express the same moment in time, the same planets—in fact, each can express the entire universe; and yet each orders these same objects and data *in a different way* so as to bring out and raise a particular dimension of reality above the general threshold of our life and awareness. Since our life and consciousness appear to flow through at least several quite distinct levels, it is our conviction that the most sensible method by which to express or map these different levels is through such fundamental orderings, or reference planes. Our almost exclusive concern for the plane of the Earth's orbit—the ecliptic or zodiac and the relation of all activity to this plane—results in a loss of contrast and dimensionality that the use of these alternative coordinate systems provide.

There are at least two basic factors to consider when examining these various coordinate systems; and they are summed up in the familiar axiom: "As above, so below; yet after another manner." The first factor is an indication that the various coordinate systems may be ordered to form a hierarchy in terms of a progressive "inclusivity," or greater comprehensiveness. In other words, the Galactic coordinate system includes the Heliocentric, which *includes* the Geocentric, which *includes* the Horizon, and so forth. This represents the "As above, so below" portion of the phrase; and this "wheels within wheels within wheels" concept is well understood, and a popular one through which to express the various dimensions of consciousness. In other words, a large frame of reference or coordinate system somehow involves information of a larger or more *meta*-physical kind when considered in relation to a more particular or less inclusive system.

The second factor to be illustrated in the phrase "As above, so below: *yet after another manner,*" while of equal importance, is less well understood. The great reference places and their respective systems of coordinates are not only inclusive of one another (that is, larger and smaller in relation to each other), but they are also *inclined* at different angles or attitudes to one another. In other words, learning to use and understand the nature of a more inclusive system, such as the Ecliptic or Zodiac system, in relation to the Equatorial or "Right Sphere" system, is *not only* a matter of ordering the information along a different plane (taking a larger view or picture); it *also* involves a fundamental *change in attitude*, or inclination. This shift in attitude, or reorientation of attitude, is an important concept for astrologers to consider and to absorb.

Let me present an analogy which might relate to interpreting these various planes in our everyday life. We are becoming ever more aware on a social level of the Cosmic or transpersonal perspective as being associated with the idea of Expansion, with a more Whole-View; yet we have not understood on this same broad social level that such a change in scale or scope may also involve a basic change in attitude: a fundamental change in approach to life. We can no longer be inclined in directions we once were; and this must amount to a radical change—that is, change at "root" level—in our activity! Furthermore, a basic misunderstanding as to what is involved in spiritual growth has resulted from an attempt to view such growth exclusively as some kind of "enlargement;" one wistfully looks forward to growing beyond the particular terms of his everyday existence. This is a result of ignorance of the *change in attitude*—the change in point of view, or vantage point—that accompanies true spiritual development: a change very difficult to imagine or assess for one not aware that such change is a natural and expected part of any deeper initiation.

So much for metaphysics. Much of my own research here in Ann Arbor has revolved around these various coordinate systems and the dimensions of life they describe. In particular, I have been concerned with the inclinations or attitudes of one system to another. I like to tell myself that the reason for this interest may be due to the fact that I was born with such a "bad" attitude towards some facets of life in this world, that vast changes in attitude on my part have been necessary simply for my survival. Let me repeat: these different coordinate systems are great Languages or Orderings of our total reality, and each one raises to our attention its characteristic gestalt of whole dimension of life.

To my knowledge, L. Edward Johndro was the first modern astrologer to make a life-long concern the articulation of the difference between whole coordinate systems (Ecliptic and Equator).

And in my opinion, a final assessment of Johndro's work may not deal so much in terms of his technical genius alone as with the scope and comprehension of his vision; and in particular, that focus of it relating to the essential differences between events as interpreted on the ecliptic or on the equator. In recent years, this research has been carried on and developed further by Charles Jayne, Theodor Landscheidt and others. Our research at the Heart Center School of Astrology has centered on the difference and relationship between the Geocentric and Heliocentric ecliptic systems and, in recent years, on questions of cosmic structure; in particular on an attempt to assess the meaning of the Galactic and Supergalactic planes as they stand in relation to one another, and to the zodiac. With these ideas in mind, we are ready to examine a most particular and fascinating system of coordinates: that of the Horizon. There is no intention here to document or "prove" the validity of this system in this very preliminary research. Our purpose is to present the impression we have formed regarding the dimension of our life we have found to be mapped in the chart of Local Space; and to provide those interested with the means to calculate such charts. We would very much appreciate feedback and comments from those of you who investigate this very interesting dimension.

In simple terms the Local Space (LS) chart is a map of the 360° of horizon surrounding an event such as a birth. . . much as we might look around us toward the east, west, north and south. In this coordinate system, the fundamental plane to which all else is referred is the horizon of the observer; and the position of the various planets *as they appear* from this location are projected onto the horizon using the coordinates "azimuth" and "altitude." Azimuth is the equivalent of zodiac longitude in this system and is measured for our purposes, from the east direction, through the North and on around in a counterclockwise direction, in the same way that we measure the traditional signs and houses. Altitude, analogous to ecliptic latitude, is measured above and below the horizon to the poles from 0° to 90°. It is worth the emphasis of repetition to stress that, from the standpoint of the Local Space chart, *the horizon is the whole azimuth circle* as it ranges around the wheel of the chart—not simply the line described by House cusps I and VII, as our astrological habituations tempt us to think. This, then, gives a sort of "flat earth" perspective, as it were, the visible horizon being much like a "Magical Circle." And as tradition teaches us regarding the nature of the Magical Circle: the Circle is realized to be the equator of a sphere which extends above and below the plane of the local horizon (apparent or rational horizon cuts the infinite sphere in coincident circles). Here is a map, in space, of an event from a topocentric perspective, or local center; and this, an astrology of Local Space.

Before we dive into the techniques useful in this new dimension of Local Space, here is our impression of "what it is all about": the general feeling of what portion of life is captured through this coordinate system. The most remarkable factor, and the key concept you may need in order to appreciate the particular quality of the Local Space chart, is that *every* object in the universe—whether Celestial or Mundane—has an equal and valid position in this chart. Not only the planets and stars, but on an equal basis, cities, countries and even the local water tower or the neighbor's house can be represented. All that concerns us here is the direction of any object in space—not the distance. In other words, the Celestial Sphere and the Mundane or Geographic Sphere exist side by side and are interchangeable! A star is a city is a neighbor. We can walk towards, write letters to, or get up and move into—for instance—our Seventh House. Even more startling, we can travel into our natal planets, since they also represent a direction on the globe in the chart of Local Space. Here, in a hopeless intermingling of various planes of reference and of objects, a strange and, I must confess, somewhat magical view of our world begins to emerge: one in which every city and friend becomes a radiating center of influence. Here for the first time the long history of Magic, witchcraft and sorcery take on a practical reality, where local deities and preferred directions become the rule, and we are thrust forever beyond the threshold of the just "slightly remarkable." The psychedelic character in Local Space charts is unmistakeable and appears to be intrinsic to the system. The world seems to appear as a kind of grand talisman and vast ritual ground through this perspective. The closest popular image of a similar nature in the modern consciousness is the remarkable world of Don Juan as generated by the author Carlos Castaneda. Here is no "subtle plane," but a personal landscape painted in bold and clear strokes, a world where the modern man is learning to move across the face of the Earth in an endless adjustment and tuning of his radix—of his self. Individuals driven in particular directions on a checkerboard world, unable to resist travelling to a goal that is no particular place on Earth as much as it is a direction within them: the direction of a force, or of a planet: "There! where Power hovers," to use Don Juan's expression. In a word, here is perhaps the most vulgar system, where the obvious is enthroned and the subtle unnecessary. Here then are some specific approaches we have found to be most useful in examining these charts.

Once you have mastered the mathematics involved in erecting these charts (programs that calculate Local Space charts are available from Matrix Software for most popular name computers) involved in erecting these charts, and have laid them out on 360° wheels similar to those pictured herein, a probable series of questions you want to investigate may arise. Let us consider some of them.

Compare the planets in the Local Space chart with your geocentric natal chart. As you will soon note, the individual aspects between two planets can be very different in the two kinds of charts; *also*, the larger Whole Chart Patterns may indicate a different quality. A planet may achieve great focus in the Local Space chart that is not brought out in the Geo chart; and yet you may have intuited and sensed the added importance of this planet or principle in the make-up of the individual involved, and yet had no physical basis for your intuition.

The single most important use of Local Space in the astrologer/client relationship in our experience has been in locality shifts. One of the most frequent questions asked the astrologer during a reading is: where would be a good place for me to live? I have made use of the quite valid and useful traditional technique of adjusting the RAMC of the radix to the new locality and coming up with a new Ascendant and so forth. The radix positions then are read in terms of these new angles. Local Space is by nature suited to express both celestial and geographic positions on one map or chart. Its special nature introduces several concepts not encountered in other techniques.

Radix Local Space Charts

Aside from the planetary aspects, there are two primary indicators of strong or high focus in the radix Local Space chart: (1) a planet is on or near the horizon (it has low altitude); and (2) a planet is conjunct to one of the four angles of cardinal directions. It is worth noting which of the planets is closest to the horizon, even if not conjunct. We use standard orbs for azimuth—although we haven't arrived at any "final rules" in this respect. It is also worth noting which planet is the most elevated (has the greatest altitude). And parallels and contraparallels need investigation. The nature of parallel/contraparallel, as far as interpretation is concerned, may be somewhat different here since they do not describe coincident arcs (as time passes), as do parallels in declination.

We are now ready to examine a technique that gets to the heart of what these charts are all about. At this point we have in front of us our radix Local Space chart, with the various planets plotted on it. As we mentioned earlier, we can also plot the positions of cities and places on the Earth on this map; so, our next project then will be to translate all of the important cities in our lives into their equivalent positions on our radix map of Local Space. We should be sure to include not only the places we ourselves have lived in or visited, but also the cities that we have always thought that we might like to visit—that bring a warm feeling to mind, and so forth; the positions of cities where friends and not-so-friendlies live, where there are business relationships, etc. We then examine these places in terms of their position (or direction) on the LS chart with these thoughts in mind: Are these cities in aspect? In particular by conjunction or opposition? Are they in alignment with planets in the chart? In what quadrants and houses do these cities fall? and are any on the angles? We have found that individuals tend to move towards cities that are also in the direction of planets that represents the particular kind of energy they may require at that time. An individual, for instance, needing to invoke the key to success, often obtained through Jupiter, may make one or several moves in that direction. Although its concept is so simple as to be almost embarrassing, this technique has shown itself to be of great value. In any case, its value seems to be *substantial* rather than hypothetical. Next to, for example, some of the cumbersome and ultra-traditional place rulerships, proposed national birth charts, etc.—most of them very arbitrary, the complex and confusing juggling of all these factors seem a rather specious approach to the locality problem, and their results rather tentative. The LS chart, at least, can show a concrete, measurable reaction of the individual, even in the same locality, as much as their LS charts vary from one another, and whatever may be the intrinsic character of a place—and places undoubtedly have this, as a selection of people could react very differently to it from the point of view of each one's own make-up. Moreover, each one could react differently at times, under different astrological conditions. Although the mathematics involved in this system may seem a bit complex, the application of its technique is simple and direct; and this does much to recommend it.

Locality Shifts in Local Space

After the basic information in the radix chart has been taken in, we may want to construct secondary charts for the various localities where the individual has lived or travelled. These charts are equivalent to ones cast for this locality at the time of birth, as if one were born there. This involves a transformation of the radix planet's position, as well as a shift around the angles of these positions. Aside from the initial direction from the radix of the locality shift, there are other factors to note.

Through a shift in locality, a planet (or even a city) may be brought into (or away from) the horizon. We have found that a planet achieves high focus when on the horizon, in terms of its activity within the individual. In other words, we can adjust and tune our radix—and ourselves—through locality shifts, much as we might tune a musical instrument. Another objective that might be accomplished by a locality shift is to bring a yet farther away city to high focus—say, to an angle, or in aspect to a planet—allowing a *second* locality shift to be made in its direction. This alters or modifies the psychic interaction of person and place by altering the direction of approach to it. The effect achieved would be quite other than that invoked by approaching it directly. Some of the magical quality of the dimension can be seen in the checkerboard-like world concept that emerges, where individuals not only move in relation to a planetary energy they require but are ever adjusting and jockeying into position to achieve the most resonant move. Aside from the focus achieved through the angles and planets, we may compare aspects and Whole Chart Patterns with the radix LS chart, considering changes in altitude, and so forth. Another point of interest which has proven very useful in our work is examining the aspects that the planetary positions in the Local Space locality shift make to the radix LS chart; in particular by bringing one planet to a conjunction with another. As Charles Jayne has pointed out to me, this amounts to progression of the chart through space, rather than time (a very elegant concept)—for those of us, perhaps, who find it hard to wait! We have found that both the conjunction and oppositions (the alignments), as formed by this progression in space, are most significant.

There you have the fundamental ideas with which we have worked thus far. The usefulness of these charts in the astrologer/client relationship should be clear. We have used these charts in our practice with success, and have found that many people are concerned with where they might live in order to bring the Self into some resonant and satisfying focus. Perhaps modern man is developing an intuitive sense for self-adjustment and focus through locality shifts—something that ancient man did very little of. It appears that one can enrich and complement various qualities of the radix through location adjustment—bringing our needed energies to one place and time, moving elsewhere for another life episode at another time. What we will need before this technique could ever achieve widespread use is a set of easy tables of azimuth and altitude to be designed and made available to astrologers, thus doing away with the somewhat complicated trigonometry. I hope some of you will brave the necessary calculations and take advantage of this opportunity to explore the astrology of Local Space.

III. Local Space

From the 1978 edition of the Circle Books Astrological Calendar

I want to relate to you a powerful new way (new to me) of coming to know ourselves through astrology. It involves another kind of map or chart of our birth moment: a map of the space surrounding the birthplace; and this form of topo-centric astrology we call the astrology of Local Space (LS). First I should tell you how I happened on to this fascinating approach.

I was involved in an attempt at understanding the many different House systems that astrologers use, trying to "decide" which, of all of them, might be the best for my purposes. For several years, I had not used any house system at all, but only the four angles of the chart, in a kind of protest or disgust at the lack of agreement among astrologers concerning systems of house division. It seemed rather strange to me that there were so many competing house systems. For many years of my astrological practice, I lacked the necessary mathematical background to decide for myself which of the many house systems made "sense" to me. I could only read about the merits of each house system and take the word of "those who knew." I came to use the Campanus system of houses because many of those astrologers that I respected most used this system. In recent years, I had been learning enough spherical trigonometry on my pocket calculator to make my first attempt at solving the mystery of House division.

I have always been a slow learner; so I had to sit down with an equatorial star-map of the constellations and attempt to draw out graphically the various ways of dividing space and time—in hope of being enlightened as to which house system had the most going for it. Of course, I wanted to draw out the House systems using my own natal chart. This was kind of complex, for I had to calculate, using spherical trigonometry, the 360 degrees of my radix horizon and plot this curving line on the star map (see illustration, page 256-7). All house systems agree on the validity of the horizon, and so I felt this was the place to start. This proved to be a most worthwhile exercise. I soon became aware that regardless of which House system was used, what was of interest to astrologers was not the horizon in its own right,

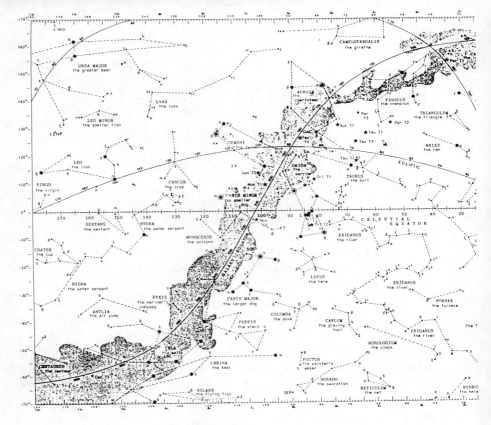

Figure D

but just those few places where it crossed or intersected our beloved Zodiac or ecliptic. In other words, House systems are concerned with different ways of sending meaningful lines to intersect the zodiac; and these intersecting points are then the cusps, or sensitive points, for that individual—a kind of astrologers' acupuncture points.

Laying these House systems out on a map helped me—a great deal—to understand what in fact the various House systems were. But I yearned for some simpler way to deal with it all. I reached a point where I took the problem into my own hands and said, "OK Michael, let's suspend judgment on which of all these House systems is best and do something very simple, although perhaps unsophisticated, that will make sense to you." I started off by making the center of our House system the place where one is born, and I put the pole of the system overhead—the pole of the birthplace—and instead of using more complex methods of division, I divided the surrounding space into a simple pie of twelve divisions radiating out from the birthplace. This was represented on the Earth (geographically) and through space (astronomically). This, then, would be my very own House sys-

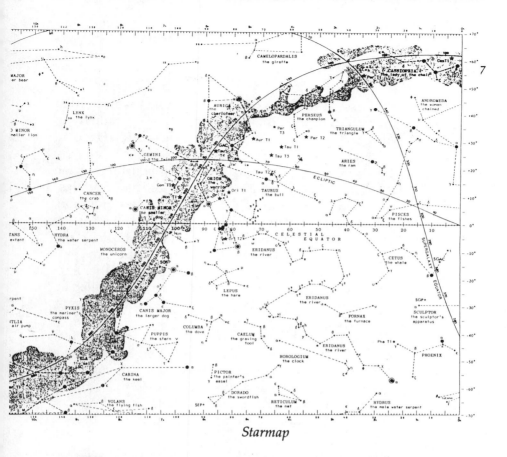

Starmap

tem! The points where the twelve radiating lines intersected the Zodiac place would be the House cusps or sensitive points in this system. I was, at this point, as "bad" as the other astrologers who had developed their own systems. I did find that, although this method of House division was quite radical compared to the more familiar systems, the particular cusp degrees of the zodiac had already proved significant and were already "favorite" and previously noted points along the zodiac. My friend and fellow astrologer James Coats promptly termed this the Radiant House System, since the cusps radiated out from a central place on Earth. I had, in my own way, stumbled upon what I found out was already known as the Horizontal House System, which, along with the Campanus System represents one of two obvious and complementary ways to divide the space surrounding a birth into equal parts. The astrologer L. Edward Johndro calls the Campanus System "the Ferris wheel," and the Radiant or Horizontal System "the merry-go-round." Astrologer Charles Jayne has been pointing out the need to investigate this Horizontal System of Houses for many years.

I was still interested in those twelve little points where these radiating lines intersected the old familiar zodiac. Then something very important began to occur to me. I began to see that the Horizon System was a complete system in itself, just as the zodiac is, stretching a full 360 degrees around the heavens. Instead of considering the horizon as a necessary means to get at and define these zodiacal pressure points, I began to follow on the star map the line of my radix horizon through the heavens to the point where it intersected the plane or line of the Zodiac on this map. This point was, of course, my Ascendant and 7+ degrees of Sagittarius. But my eyes kept going past the Ascendant, following my horizon until it intersected another line: that of the plane of our galaxy; at which point the first shock rolled in. My horizon intersected the galactic plane constellation Cygnus, the Swan.

At this point, I must relate a more personal story to make clear what was happening. Over the past years, I had been assembling a book containing stellar points and planes: *Astrophysical Directions,* and in the process I had to calculate and plot quite a few maps of the heavens. In this way, I came to know and develop a sense of the major constellations in a much more intimate way than ever before. Throughout this work, I noted a "fixation" on a couple of constellations in particular. Above them all, I revered the constellation Cygnus; and on repeated occasions, for no reason I could determine, I felt such deep identification with this constellation and what it seemed to signify that tears came to my eyes. Now I find that Cygnus was one of the two constellations where my own particular horizon crossed the great plane of our galaxy—a kind of galactic Descendant and Ascendant; the other being the constellation Vela, the Sails, another constellation to which I had always been very sensitive. Well, I had to laugh at this point. What, I said to myself, if the entire 360 degrees of the horizon of my birth is as sensitive as the Node where it crosses the Zodiac, the Ascendant. What if there are other basic planes of importance to us, besides the Zodiac, to which we respond? Did I have a galactic and supergalactic Ascendant and new sets of constellations or "signs" to come to know?

At this point, I must shrink a long, and to me, beautiful story and simply say that this discovery was the first of a great many such mini-enlightenments I was to have. I searched through my collection of horoscopes to see how my friends and acquaintances were oriented. I was discovering the strength and power of the local horizon. I had accepted and used the Ascendant and Vertex and other sensitive ecliptic points in my work, but always with the accent on the zodiac. I had never stopped to think that in each case it took another plane to bring these Nodes or points of intersection into existence—in this case, it was the plane of the horizon. And yet I had, in a subconscious way, used the horizon in all my work. I could now see that each individual had a kind of unique orientation or attitude to the whole cosmos and that in the horizon we had a plane capable of revealing much more about oneself than just those sensitive points which relate to the Zodiac.

At any rate, I began to explore the whole of the heavens from *my* point of view. For a time, I forgot the Zodiac and instead began to inquire, and thus to learn a great deal about my own attitude and orientation to my birth event, to my life. Somewhere during this time, another idea occurred to me that proved to be most compelling: the horizon also traced a path on maps of the Earth, as well as the heavens. I had calculated by this time a complete chart of the planets' positions in the Horizon System using the system's equivalent to Zodiac longitude and latitude called—azimuth and altitude. How, I wondered, would the directions of the planets in my horizon chart relate to directions and cities on this Earth? I soon developed the trigonometry needed to answer these questions—quite a prodigious undertaking for me—and thus began a real "magical mystery tour" through my life history. Although I have lived in several different places, the one major move in my life has been from Lancaster, Pennsylvania (my birthplace) to Ann Arbor, Michigan. Of course, what I wanted to know was, what direction was Ann Arbor from Lancaster? That is, what degree did Ann Arbor occupy on my radix or birth horizon?

And here rolled in the second great shock wave. Ann Arbor was right in the direction of my natal Jupiter position on the Local Space chart—within two degrees. In other words, a move to Ann Arbor was a move in the direction of my natal Jupiter. Jupiter rules my Ascendant and its position above the Seventh House cusp had made it very prominent in any analysis of my chart. At any rate, I wondered at such a coincidence and set out to answer some of the other questions that now began to pop up in my mind. What about the other places I had lived, or to which I had travelled or thought of travelling to? The history of my travel came before my mind. . . some places of joy and learning, others of sorrow and pain. I plotted the directions and calculated the charts for all of these places, and what I found through reading these charts was overwhelming; it marked my initial surrender to what now appears to be—for me—a major discovery in my astrological life: that of Local Space. I erected different Local Space charts. These amounted to maps of the space surrounding each place as if I had been born there, rather than at Lancaster. The story of my life and self, interpreted and confirmed through my reading of these Local Space charts, was moving—to say the least.

Let me cite an example of the sort of thing I found. I am well known to my friends as being a homebody. It is very difficult for anything to induce me to leave Ann Arbor. At one point in my life, however, I sold everything I owned. My wife and I moved north to go into the green plant business, to manage our own greenhouses. I actually left Ann Arbor and moved away! It so happened that we were a couple of years ahead of our time in offering fine greenhouse plants to people; the demand for these plants and the plant store craze did not appear until later. We lost everything in this venture. On the material or investment plane, it was a disaster. Now, in my Local Space chart I have triple conjunction of the Moon, Uranus and Saturn to the same degree; in anybody's astrology, this has accounted for quite a strong focus. The move into the greenhouse business was a move precisely—to the degree—into (or towards) this triple conjunction! I had actually *moved into* my Moon-Uranus-Saturn conjunction! It was as if we had gone there to wrestle and come to terms with my Saturn (or with Satan, you might say)—and come out the wiser for it. For this experience, as hard as it was, ended many more superficial fears on my part concerning loss. We lost what to us at the time was everything, and still our life went on.

What had impressed me through this voyage of discovery was the potency of the *entire* horizon, and of more than just a couple of its points; and the fact that somehow the orientation of an individual to the cosmos made a difference, or was reflected in behavior and activity at the supramundane level. It took me quite a while to "develop the faith," or to let myself believe that God was so thorough in his/her influence as to be all-pervading down to the finest details. It was a while later before I could entertain with grace the idea that this same orientation or attitude was reflected *as much upon the map of the Earth* as upon the map of the heavens. Another way of putting this (and this is, to me, the beauty of Local Space astrology), is that Heaven and Earth are interchangeable, or are in the last analysis one living entity—a single whole. This is made ever so clear in the LS chart, where every object in the universe, celestial and mundane, has an equal and valid position. Not only the planets and the stars, but on an equal basis, cities, countries, and even the local water tower or friends' houses can be represented. All that concerns us is the direction in space: the orientation, not the distance. In Local Space the Heavens and Earth, the Celestial and Mundane (or Geographic) spheres exist side by side and are interchangeable.

In drawing this year's article to a close, I would like to share a few experiences and thoughts with you concerning some of the structure in space beyond the Zodiac and how it can be of value in individual development and growth. Let me relate a personal story as to how I first got interested in the deeper regions of space. Our research, as some of you will know, has centered on the difference and relationship between the geocentric and heliocentric ecliptic systems. My interest in the space surrounding our solar system was minimal. I was put off by the billions of stellar objects out there and, on a more basic level, by the ideas of Coldness and Blackness I had been programmed to associate with outer space. Distant space somehow represented the epitome of "otherness" and "foreignness" to me. I was embarrassed, in terms of astrological usage, by all of the books I had read on the fixed stars, with the exception of L.E. Johndro's book *The Stars.* How was I to determine the significance of these billions of stars and use them in my practice, when I had enough difficulty, as it was, using the nine planets?

And then the unexpected happened. I had a dream. It was not an ordinary dream but one of those dreams that are more real than waking consciousness—that take months to understand and absorb. In my dream an "astrologer" appeared to me whose eyes were filled with light. There were rays or stalks of light coming out of his eyes. This strange being said but one word: "LOOK!" and with his arm turned and pointed to the night sky. I looked. The sky was filled with brilliant points of light. The stars and all of this starry material was clustered together to form the great glowing arch of the Milky Way or galactic plane. It was wondrous beyond description and in that instant my heart went out from me and filled this bright space. Never again have I had the feeling of being here on Earth, warm and trembling before the Cold and Black of space. I became the space and light and reversed my polarity or attitude. I was a living representative of this mother galaxy. I was the spaceman!

From that night forward I began to venture beyond the zodiac in an inquiry as to the nature and structure of this universe. Here, in brief

262 / *Planets in Locality*

form, is what I found for myself: We are nodes or information aggregates. The Universe is in intimate contact with itself through us. The manyfold nature of the cosmic events is represented through our self and lives. There is not only a correlation between these seemingly remote cosmic events and our person, but an identity as well. Information coming from the Galactic Center, carried by electromagnetic and gravitational radiation from every last star and cosmic plane and event passes through us at all times. We are, in some way, a node or information complex caught in a matrix or web of manifestation.

The overpowering idea that occurs when we make some acquaintance with the universe and its structure is that there is no difference between out there and in here. We are out there! Our world and our self and relationships are a perfect reflection of what is and what is happening out there. Not an analogy, but an identity. Black holes, supernovae, quasars and the like are not remote cosmic events, but this identical story is represented, reflected, lived and acted out each day in our lives.

Information circulates through the universe and our identity or sense of our self is this very process of circulation. Identity is not a substance, but a relationship, in fact, a circulation and a process of communion or communication. Not only is there a connection between our life and that of our galaxy and universe, but *we are* the connection. A study of the structure of the universe, at any level, is a study of ourselves. In summary, the idea that I am elaborating here is: Astrology is not only a symbolic system of psychological discussion. The symbol is also, in fact, real. If we say it is an analogy, then the analogy is complete down to the limits of any specific example we might choose.

We are all time and space travellers. There are no better words that I know of than these of Emerson: "All inquiry into antiquity is the desire to do away with this wild, savage and preposterous There or Then, and introduce in its place the Here and the Now. Belzoni [an archaeologist] digs and measures in the mummy-pits and pyramids of Thebes until he can see the end of the difference between the monstrous work and himself. When he has satisfied himself, in general and in detail, that it was made by such a person as he, so armed and so motivated, and to ends which he, himself, should also have worked, the problem is solved; his thought lives along the whole line of temples and sphinxes and catacombs, passes through them all with satisfaction, and they live again to the mind, or are now."—*Essay on History*.

APPENDIX B

Jose Arguelles

The Holonomic Model of Knowledge

from Earth Ascending, *originally published by Shambhala Publications*

W hile the biological primacy of shamanic vision and geomantic knowledge remains constant, thus accounting for the AC current and the ongoing capacity for renewed insight in human history, its *prehistorical* primacy gives birth to the process of history itself. In this sense history is understood as the diversification of knowledge. Yet diversification into different fields does not necessarily mean loss of unity. In fact, this is virtually impossible. A basic holonomic axiom states: "If it works, it is related to everything else that works." The notion that there are different fields of knowledge that are unrelated to each other is fundamentally the result of a loss of sacred view.

At the core of the "holonomic model of knowledge" (Figure A) is shamanism, representing the primordial undifferentiated synthesis of knowledge and experience. From shamanism arises the mother science as well as the mother of the sciences: geomancy, the science that investigates the relation between man, heaven above, and Earth below. Given the three hieratic coordinates contained within this definition of geomancy, knowledge can be understood as three mutually evolving and intersecting fields: heavenly sciences, Earthly sciences, and human or biophysic sciences. Seen as a whole, the three fields of knowledge and their "celestial" and "terrestrial" subsets comprise the science of unity or holonomy itself.

All knowledge is strung along the thread or plumbline of transcendant insight, which corresponds to the mystic column or axis of

263

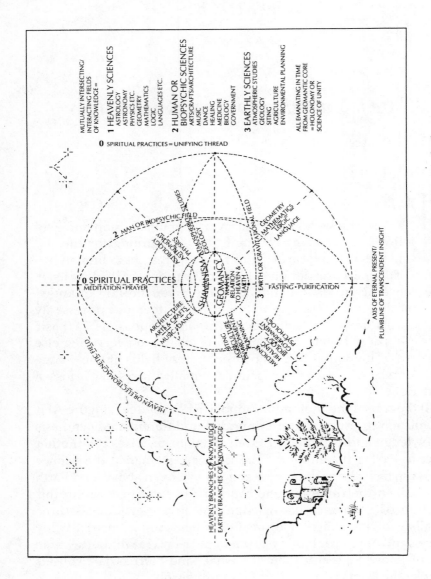

Figure A—*The Holonomic Model of Knowledge*

the eternal present. This plumbline provides the ground for the development of contemplative spiritual practices: meditation, prayer, vision-seeking, fasting, and ritual exercises. When there is a community recognizing the necessity to continue to develop such practices, usually within the context of a religious or spiritual belief system, then the result is a unity of vision. Knowledge in all its diversity is then viewed as so many facets of a single sacred prism. It is only when the plumbline of transcendant insight is "cut" that the center no longer holds, and knowledge is splintered into a Tower of Babel of specialized fields. This occurs when there is a loss of sacred view, as exemplified by the present stage of civilization.

Thus far we have seen how the natural flow of the seasons, in conjunction with the geomagnetic structure of the Earth and the electromagnetic fields of the heavens, describes both the psycho-cultural field of civilization and the basic structure of the psi bank (Figure B). We have also seen how the progression of civilization (history) through the hieratic and posthieratic stages is an organic co-creation of the basic matrix pattern of the psi bank.

In its essentials, the psi bank consists of four longitudinal holonomic memory plates, equatorially divided into eight seasonal memory plates. This gives us the basic overall design. It should be recalled that the psi bank warp (Figure B) consists of a fourfold longitudinal pattern as well, corresponding to the pattern/image at which we have now arrived through following the course of history. We then see that the geochronological flow of civilization, running laterally as it does, provides the basic woof thread to the psi bank.

Further articulation is provided to the psi bank when we divide each of the eight seasonal memory plates into three parts each, for a total of twenty-four sections of *psionic nimboid membranes.* Nimboid refers to precipitation-bearing phenomena, like clouds. The nimboid membrane divisions, occurring at the thirty- and sixty-degree latitudes north and south, correspond in atmospheric studies to the *tropopauses.*

The function of the tropopause is the generation of jet streams responsible for dramatic alterations in weather patterns. North and south of the sixty-degree latitudes lie the arctic and antarctic zones, just as the areas between the thirty-degree latitudes are the generally tropical zones. Between the tropopauses lie the temperate zones. In atmospheric studies these zones acquire the term "leaves."

The term "psionic nimboid membrane" has the following mean-

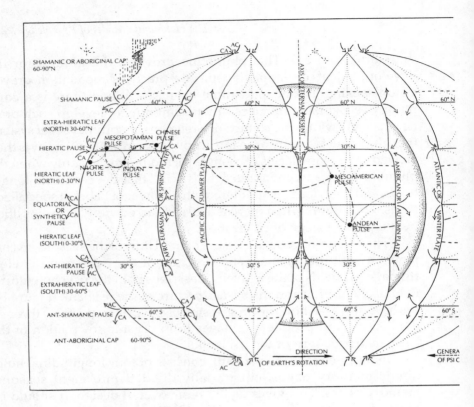

The following labels appear within the figure:

SHAMANIC OR ABORIGINAL CAP 60-90°N

SHAMANIC PAUSE

EXTRA-HIERATIC LEAF (NORTH) 30-60°N

HIERATIC PAUSE

MESOPOTAMIAN PULSE

CHINESE PULSE

NILOTIC PULSE

INDIAN PULSE

HIERATIC LEAF (NORTH) 0-30°N

EQUATORIAL OR SYNTHETIC PAUSE

HIERATIC LEAF (SOUTH) 0-30°S

ANT-HIERATIC PAUSE

EXTRAHIERATIC LEAF (SOUTH) 30-60°S

ANT-SHAMANIC PAUSE

ANT-ABORIGINAL CAP 60-90°S

MESOAMERICAN PULSE

ANDEAN PULSE

AXIS OF ETERNAL PRESENT

PACIFIC OR SUMMER PLATE

AFRO-EURASIAN OR SPRING PLATE

AMERICAN OR AUTUMN PLATE

ATLANTIC OR WINTER PLATE

60° N · 30° N · 30° S · 60° S

DIRECTION OF EARTH'S ROTATION

GENERA OF PSI C

Figure B

ing: high saturation, psi information-bearing, biopsychic "weather" patterns. Encoded in these membranes are the fundamental genetic memory patterns of the total holonomic recollection process—those patterns responsible, for instance, for the identical coding of *I Ching* and DNA.

In our discussion of the atmospheric correspondance, we may speak of *psychopauses,* and of hieratic and shamanic/aboriginal leaves. Just as the jet streams cause dramatic shifts in the weather pattern of the lower atmosphere, so the *psychopauses* may be viewed as the zones where major psychoatmospheric weather fronts are generated. These are of two kinds: the shamanic or aboriginal, and the hieratic, i.e. either of the AC (shamanic) or CA (hieratic) currents. The leaves or *psionic membranes,* in addition to possessing information storage which can be biopsychically precipitated (hence the term "nimboid")

266

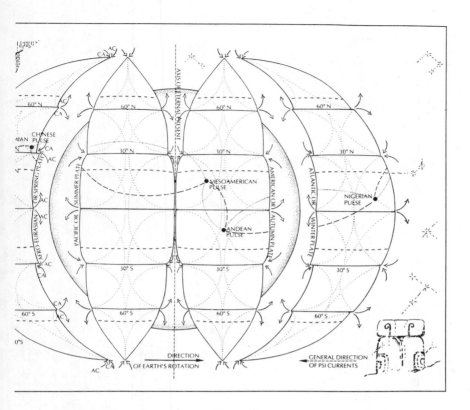

The Psi Bank showing the four quadrants, eight seasonal memory plates, and twenty-four psionic nimboid membranes.

represent general characteristics that moderate and control psychocultural conditions.

There is not necessarily a one-to-one correspondence between psionic membrane and geography. Rather, we can speak of directions or tendencies of AC and CA currents. The AC tendency is to flow from the direction of the magnetic pole toward the equator; the CA tendency is to flow the opposite way. Thus it can be seen that in the twenty-four-part structure of the psionic membranes, eight of the leaves are polar or aboriginal/shamanic, eight are purely hieratic or equatorial. The remaining eight, the extrahieratic leaves, signify the temperate zones of psychocultural development, i.e. zones where the essential crossover polarity of AC/CA currents operates.

The "geomatic flowchart" (Figure C) corresponds to the primary geomantic perception, heaven above, Earth below, and man in be-

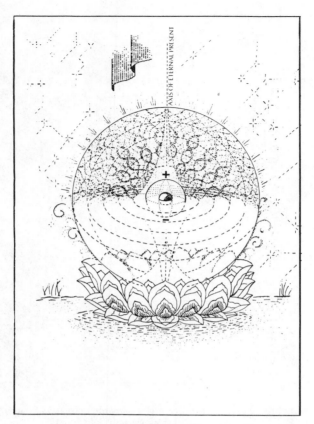

Figure C
Geomantic Flow Chart

tween. As we have seen, these three designations correspond respectively to the electromagnetic, gravitational, and biopsychic fields of the primary resonant field model. The geomantic flowchart emphasizes this three-part relationship as an organismic cycle revolving about the central axis which divides the model into two halves: man and weather.

As the two volatile variables between heaven and Earth, man and the weather comprise a unique binary relationship, the mutual interaction of which has long been a recognized foundation of all systems of geomancy. More generally, the weather or left-hand side of the geomantic flowchart represents the total spectrum of the phenomenal world known to man, the so-called subjective world of mind. The totality of these two halves, with all of their mutual correspondences, comprises the binary structure of nature and the holonomic model of knowing.

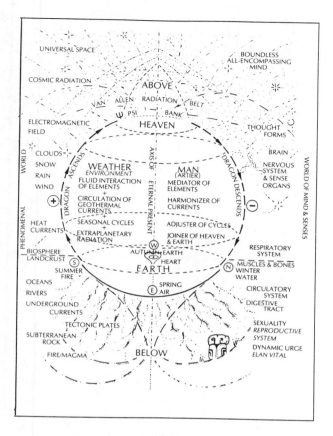

Figure D

Model of Evolved Psi Rings

The model (Figure D) of a holonomic topocosm with evolved psi bank rings depicts a consciously harmonized planetary field structure, the primal model of which is represented by the geomantic flowchart. The horizontal rings represent the motions of the planet in time—the gravitational field—while the vertical rings correspond to the cumulative articulations of the different psychocultural stages in the planet's evolution toward a consciously harmonized condition. The lotus, from which emerges this "planet with noosphere," to use de Chardin's phrase, is the age-old symbol of purity and awakened intelligence.

APPENDIX C

Steve Cozzi

Banishing Rituals

When you move into a new apartment or home, your first impulse is to clean it. So you clean the carpet, walls, kitchen cabinets, bathrooms, etc. Removing the dirt left by the former occupants is a very important ritual; however, removal of the physical dirt completes only half of the cleaning.

The simple fact is that people pollute both physically and psychically, half of which we see, half of which we don't. The unseen pollution is often more harmful. People create a lot of discordant energy when certain emotions are aroused. Hatred, jealousy, greed and other violent feelings are able to literally make the air crackle with energy. People also discharge sexual energy in all kinds of ways, and in different places. The energy contained in the sexual fluids has the most powerful properties for good or ill. Not every place will have psychic pollution. Also realize that you are banishing your own pollution as well.

Getting rid of this emotional/psychic pollution is the real purpose of a banishing ritual. When you move into a new house, I would suggest that to help with the general cleaning, you should also steam some onion and garlic in an open pan. In the evening some good quality incense can be burnt. Some people suggest a "bad vibe floor wash," which is composed of 1 oz. creosote, ¼ cup ammonia and a tablespoon of sea salt.

Another old remedy is the use of eggs. Eggs have a thin upper shell at the smaller end. Because the thin (membrane) shell top is

271

semipermeable, it has the ability to suck bad energy into its protein substance. You can put an egg wherever you suspect discordant energy to be. Always put the egg with the small or hollow top up. When you get rid of the egg, don't break it. (When it is eventually broken it will be with other garbage, and away from you.)

Another use for the egg is in treating a psychic attack* by someone or something. In this case you should write your name on the side of an egg with a pencil (not a pen). Put this egg as close to your head as possible when you are asleep. Use a new egg every night.

Banishing Ritual #1

This ritual should be more than adequate for removing negative energy in most situations. On a clean sheet of white paper, draw a pyramid-type triangle. The base should be larger than the sides. Place this paper on the ground in the center of the home or in the place that has the concentration of negative energy. The apex or top point of the triangle should face due north. Place a new white candle just in front of the apex of the triangle. Then place a stick of incense in front of the candle. Be sure and light them both just before you begin.

Now stand at the base of the triangle (facing north) with your arms extended outward. At this time if you feel it will be helpful, you can chant a divine name or mantra, e.g., OM, Amen, etc. Then place your awareness at the center of your forehead, and say with a loud and commanding voice, "All imbalanced forces and entities DEPART from this house and property NOW!" Turn clockwise to the east and repeat the same, then to the south and west, ending with the north for the final (fifth) time. Allow the incense to burn out. The candle can stay lit until the incense is gone.

Banishing Ritual #2

This ritual is called "Circle of Fire." It is not a typical banishing ritual because it prevents discordant energy from re-entering rather than just banishing. It is a short-term solution when a person is under severe psychic attack by human forces.

Face east. Use a divine name or mantra to help center yourself. Place your awareness at the center of your forehead. Then imagine

---

* There are a number of symptoms and each person will react somewhat differently. The most common are flu-like symptoms without having the flu; a dull pain in back of the head, unexplained irritability, intense butterflies in the stomach, unusual and disturbing dream symbols and states.

a large cross-handled sword in your right hand. See yourself twice your height and filled with great power. Picture a steady, pale-gold flame jetting out from the point of the sword. Begin to draw a circle around you on the floor moving in a clockwise direction. If you feel it may be helpful, ask the Archangel of each direction to protect you (see Table 13 on pages 120-121). Remember you start out facing east, then you draw the circle to the south, then west, then north and back to east again. This ritual, if performed at sunrise, will last till sundown. If performed at sundown, it will last till dawn.

Banishing Ritual #3

This ritual is designed to banish all elementals and non-human entities. Begin by drawing the five-pointed star or pentagram. Face whatever direction the imbalance force is emitting from. If you are unsure, face north. Extending your right arm outward, use the middle (Saturn) finger of your right hand to point. Extending the arm outward, start at your left hip level and draw a line of light up over your head level. Then draw the line down at an angle to your right hip level, now up to your left shoulder level, continue with the straight line over to your right shoulder level. Then draw the final line down to the left hip. You now have drawn the five-pointed star in front of you, and the way it was drawn will banish.

There are other ways of protecting yourself with the public or in the company of questionable people. Adding more garlic to your diet or taking garlic pills will keep your psychic centers closed. Silk is a great psychic insulator, i.e. thought forms can't penetrate it. Don't be surprised if you gain weight when you are subjected to prolonged psychic disturbances, as fat is a great protector/insulator.

Some people imagine that they are enclosed in glass, or better yet in a mirror, so that things are reflected back to their source. Keeping the body clean externally and internally through washing, meditation, fasting and wholesome living is a must. The medulla center at the back of the head is a very sensitive area, sometimes referred to as the psychic door or antenna. Putting the tongue to the roof of the mouth will close off this center, also the right hand placed there will help. A mild stomach and anal contraction is very helpful in uplifting your spinal energy and keeping the centers closed.

Bruce Cathie

Geographical Harmonics

from Bridge to Infinity
Quark Enterprises Ltd.

I nitially I believed that the Great Pyramid in Egypt had a connection in some way with the mathematical puzzle, and my first
efforts at solving the problem were centered round this area. I carried
out my calculations using the pyramid as a geometric focal point and
found that I was able to establish a series of harmonics which were
compatible with those found in the main body of my work. One particular set of harmonics was associated with a scientific establishment
in Cairo which indicated to me that research was possibly being con-
ducted in the same areas that I was interested in. The positioning of
this geometric pattern formed a direct relationship with the Greenwich longitude. This suggested to me that the line was not arbitrary,
but I felt that more evidence was required to prove the point beyond
doubt. In the end I decided to put the whole thing aside and let the
matter simmer for awhile. I had found in the past that a fresh look at a
problem often helped to find the required answers. A year went by
before I had another attempt at it.

The key to the geometric problem proved to be centered around
the city of Rome. I had spent several weeks feeding coordinates into
the computer relating to various religious centers, and places where
religious manifestations had occurred, in the hope of discovering a
connection with the natural laws of mathematics. The results I obtained
were quite startling.

It slowly became evident that the geometric placing of the Vatican
City could be of extreme importance. A careful analysis of the latitude

and longitude values within this small area was required to discover some rather interesting harmonics.

The geometric focal point of interest proved to be: latitude 41° 54' 22.68" north/longitude 12° 27' 08" east.

It took some time to solve the significance of the latitude position, but eventually I discovered that the difference in displacement of latitude, measured in minutes of arc, from the equator and the north geographic pole created an easily recognized harmonic value, as follows:

Latitude displacement
    from the North Pole   = 2885.622 minutes of arc.
Latitude displacement
    from the equator   = 2514.378 minutes of arc.
The difference   =   371.244 minutes of arc.

The resulting harmonic of 371244 is the reciprocal of the value 2693645 obtained from a unified harmonic equation.

The great circle displacement of the focal point from Greenwich longitude, calculated at the Vatican latitude, was seen to be:

555.5555 minutes of arc.

which is equal to:

69.44444 x 8 (one harmonic octave).

The harmonic 694444 repeating being the reciprocal of the speed of light, in free space; 144000 minutes of arc per grid second, relative to the Earth's surface.

The direct great circle distance between the focal point and Greenwich proved to be:

767.6 minutes of arc.

which is equal to:

12.7933 degrees.

If this value is subtracted from 360° in order to ascertain the great circle distance between the two points measured the long way round, then we have:

347.2066 degrees

which is half harmonic of:

694.4 (again the reciprocal harmonic of the speed of light)

The area of the cross-sectional segment of the Earth bounded by the focal point, the north geographic pole and the Earth's center, is equal to:

1377.783014 square degrees, in relation to the Earth's surface.

The square root of the reciprocal of this figure presents a harmonic of:

2694

All of these mathematical relationships will be regarded as pure chance, but I would like to add one more just to extend the laws of probability a little further.

The great circle displacement of the focal point in Rome and the longitude passing through the Great Pyramid complex at Cairo, calculated at Vatican latitude, is equal to:

833.3333 minutes of arc.

The square of this number is equal to:

694444.4 (the speed of light reciprocal)

Other interlocking harmonics were found to be associated with several of these points but I believe that those demonstrated will be sufficient to indicate the amazing coincidences which connect them directly with my own research.

It appears that the longitudes passing through both Greenwich and Rome have an important mathematical significance, but further research will be necessary to substantiate the theory. Maybe the required answers could be found within the ancient manuscripts held in the Vatican libraries.

The latitude of Greenwich has been listed with slight variations:

In 1776 = 51° 28' 40"
In 1834 = 51° 28' 39"
In 1856 = 51° 28' 38.2"

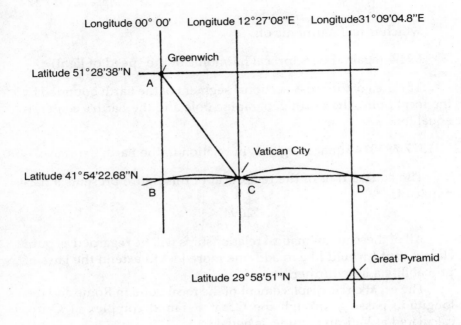

Distance A—C = 767.6 minutes of arc = 12.7933 degrees
360 deg. minus 12.7933 deg. equals 347.2 deg.
This is equal to a half harmonic of 694.4

Distance B—C = 555.555 minutes of arc.
This value divided by 8, or one octave, is equal to
69.4444.

Distance C—D = 833.333 minutes of arc.
The square of this number is equal to 694444.

Not to scale

Fig. A
Showing the relationship of Greenwich with the
Vatican City in Rome and the Great Pyramid in Egypt.

C, D, E, F = Corner aerial positions of grid polar square. Similar to aerial discovered by the survey ship Eltanin.

J—K = Polar axis.

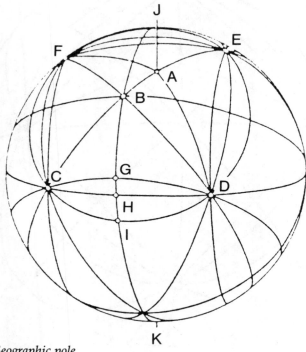

A = Geographic pole
B = Grid pole

Distance C—G—D = 3600 minutes of arc.
Distance C—H—D = 3418.6069.
Distance C—I—D = 3643.2 minutes of arc.

(3600 — 3418.6069) = 181.39308
(181.39308 x 4) = 725.57233
725.57233 = 26.93645 = 2693645 harmonic.

Fig. B

Showing relationship of grid structure to the geographic poles. Each of the two grids has a similar pattern, the interaction of which sets up a third resultant grid. The poles of the three grids are positioned at three different latitudes and longitudes.

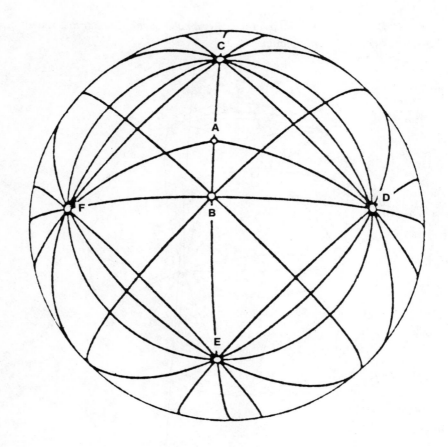

A = Geographic pole
B = Grid pole

C, D, E, F = Corner aerial positions of grid polar square
B—C, B—D, B—E, B—F = 2545.584412 minutes of arc

A—B Grid "A" = 1054.4 minutes of arc
A—B Grid "B" = 694.4 minutes of arc
A—B Grid "C" = 864 minutes of arc (resultant grid)

Fig. C

Showing the relationship of a grid polar square to the geographic pole. Each grid has a similar pattern. The pole of each grid is set at a different latitude and longitude.

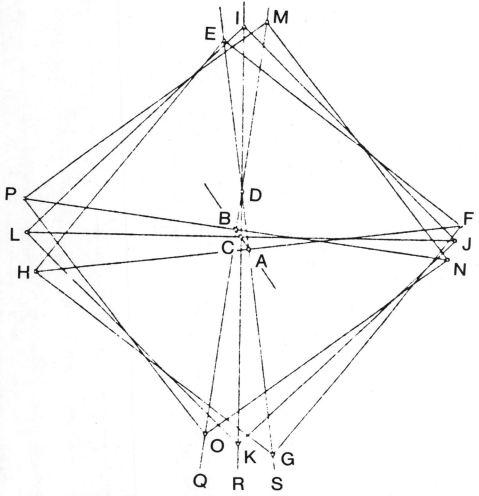

A: Grid pole "A": 1054.4 minutes of arc from geographic pole.

B: Grid pole "B": 694.4 minutes of arc from geographic pole.

C: Grid pole "C": 864 minutes of arc from geographic pole.

D: North geographic pole

E, F, G, H: Polar square "A"

I, J, K, L: Polar square "C"

M, N, O, P: Polar square "B"

Q: Longitude 105 degrees west

R: Longitude 97.5 degrees west

S: Longitude 90 degrees west

Fig. D

Showing the relationship of grid polar squares A, B, C. The polar squares are orientated in reciprocal positions around both the north and south geographic poles.

Steve Cozzi

Matrix Software and Local Space Charts

Where can I get a Local Space and other locality calculations done?

If you have an IBM-type computer, I would suggest looking into Matrix Software's M-95 AstroMap program. There are three versions: a screen only, one which does printed reports and data, and the professional version. The professional version will do all of the above plus it will print high resolution graphic maps with various continents of the Earth in the background and the local space planetary lines in the foreground. It gives all the aspects to the angles, and it will generate a circular Local Space chart (planets in azimuth). There are also plans to list the latitudes of all paran/crossings.

Instructions for producing a flat non-graphic Local Space chart on the Matrix Software's M-65:

1. Enter chart data as usual, but put in the latitude and longitude for the new location. Don't change the time zone from the birthplace location.
2. BEFORE you post the chart, select "#6 Houses," then select "Aries," for Aries Houses.
3. Post the chart.
4. Select "Same." This will keep you with the same chart.
5. Select "#8 Local spc."
6. Select "#4 Local spc." This will give you a Local Space chart.
7. Select "Output," select "Printwheel," select #3 (usually).

8. Turn the chart form upside down at the top (I.C.), write North at bottom (M.C.), write South, to the left (Dsc.) write West, and to the right (Asc.) write East.

9. The vertex should read 00 Libra; disregard the signs completely because now the planets are in azimuth, and your chart is like a compass, 360 degrees around you.

10. You can also select "Prime Vert" or "Azimuth." In the Prime Vertical chart, do steps 7 and 8 but remember the planets are now 180 above and 180 below you on the east/west Prime Vertical circle.

11. An Azimuth chart will start 00 at north and count clockwise, i.e. east=90, etc.

For Blue Star, enter Astro-Maps Programs following Menu.

Instructions for producing a flat, non-graphic Local Space chart on Astrolabe's NOVA (version II) for IBM:

1. Cast Natal Chart.
2. Select "Inmundo"—B.
3. Select "Local Space."
4. Same as #8, Matrix instructions.
5. Same as #9, Matrix instructions.
6. Same as #10, Matrix instructions.

Also explore Nova's Paran Selections.

Other sources:

Astro*Carto*Graphy®
P.O. Box 959, El Cerrito CA 94530

Astro Computing Services
P.O. Box 16430, San Diego, CA 92216-0430

Astrolabe
Box 28, Orleans, MA 02653

APPENDIX F

Peter Tompkins

Secrets of the Pyramids

[Professor Hugh] Harleston finds it significant that if you stand a tetrahedron on its nose at the South Pole it will form three triangles above the equator, splitting the world into four equilateral great-circle triangles which will exactly divide into areas of 1/3 above and 2/3 below the equator (see Figure A, p. 286).

A Teotihuacan sphere whose diameter is 12 will give an area of 144 π, a quarter of which is an easily reckoned 36π, and so forth. Again all the numbers run in a 3, 6, 9, 12, 24 series, unique with a sphere of diameter 12.

The tetrahedron, simplest of the five Platonic solids, is a perfect pyramid, a geometrical figure that represents the smallest number of points that will form a solid in three-dimensional space. It is constructed by uniting four identical equilateral triangles at their edges to form a body with four nodes, four faces, and six edges.

Harleston points out that the abstract properties of such a six-edged tetrahedron involve functions of 3, 6, thirds, square roots, and the number 1.06, all emphasized by the Teotihuacan displays.

When he inserts the tetrahedron into a sphere of diameter 12 some extraordinary relationships develop. When the diameter of the circle is 12 (and therefore its radius 6), the ratio of the area of the sphere to the tetrahedron is 2 to 1. This is the only case in which this significant correlation occurs.

The four points at which the great circles meet form the nodes of a tetrahedron inscribed in a sphere (see Figure A below). This apparently casual relation showed on closer inspection that an extraordinary and unique relation exists between a tetrahedron and a sphere whose diameter is twelve, one from which cosmic data ensues.

Oddly, or coincidentally, the relation between a tetrahedron and a sphere constitutes the thrust of the work of Buckminster Fuller, who, in his book *Synergetics*, maintains that the tetrahedron gives the basic mathematical blueprint for the universe.[1]

Noting that the lower portion of the fourth level was slightly convex and that it formed a triangle with an angle of almost 19.69 degrees to the vertical, it struck Harleston that this was also the latitude of Teotihuacan. This meant that when the sun crossed the pyramid at the equinox its rays would fall onto the north face of the fourth body at the same angle of 19.69 degrees to the vertical.[2]

To observe what would actually happen at the equinox, Harleston noted that the phenomenon in fact took place two days after the equinox. As the shadow did not wipe on the actual day, it meant the angle of the slope was 19.5 instead of 19.7, which could have been an error in reconstruction, or the angle was intended to convey some other meaning. However, observing the west face of the pyramid at the equinox, Harleston was able to witness a unique effect. As the sun crossed the zenith at 12:35' 30" (local noon at the longitude of Teotihuacan), the lower west part of the fourth face of the pyramid, which is in shadow during the morning, became illuminated as the

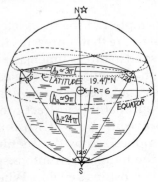

Figure A

sun's rays moved from south to north. The whole effect occurred in 66.6 seconds, a phenomenon which makes the Sun Pyramid a perennial clock, still transmitting its silent message, exactly as does the south corner of the Castillo at Chichen Itza, each equinoctal day of the year. All these structures would have had to be designed by architects aware of the considerable astronomical and geodetic data required to achieve such effects—*before* the buildings were begun.

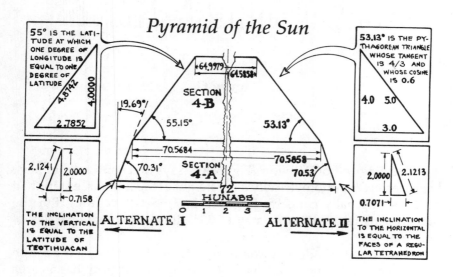

Figure B
Mathematical reconstruction of the Pyramid of the Sun
by Professor Hugh Harleston Jr.

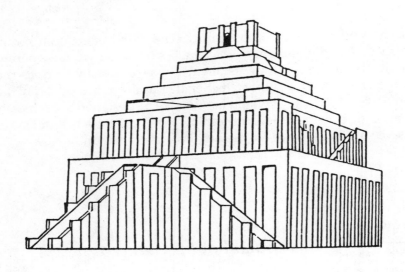

Figure C

The ziggurat of Babylon (Figure C), says Stecchini, would have been perfect trigonometrically if the height of the first three steps had been as originally conceived: 30, 48 and 55-1/2 degrees. But the Babylonians raised the first step to 33°, the approximate parallel of Babylon.

The cuneiform description of the ziggurat, known as the Smith tablet, specifically indicates that *each* level of the ziggurat has an area corresponding to standard units of land surface. Particularly important in Mesopotamian land surveying was the square with a side of 60 double cubits—the surface of the third step.

The slope angles at various heights also give important angles, such as $\sqrt{5}-1$, which is also incorporated into the Great Pyramid. Such triangles, and the number $\sqrt{5}-1$ (in common practice taken as the magic series 1-2-3) were fundamental in the operations of land surveying.

The third, fourth and fifth steps of the ziggurat make triangles with sides related to the Pythagorean 3-4-5 triangle.

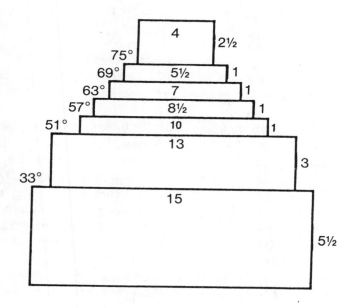

Figure D

In the original design, says Stecchini, the first step of the ziggurat was intended to represent the thirtieth parallel, but in Mesopotamia it was raised to 33° (Figure D), the approximate latitude of Babylon. Thereafter the Babylonians made each step rise in units of 6° of latitude. This made it possible for them to obtain an easily remembered cosine value for each step by simply dividing its length by two-thirds.

As the Babylonians liked to count by sixes, with a hexagesimal and sexagesimal system, the steps of the ziggurat rose in multiples of 6°. Further to simplify their accounting, the degree of parallel represented by each step could be obtained by multiplying the height of each step by 6; e.g., 6 x 5½ (first step) = 33°.

The system gave the Babylonians an extremely simple way of remembering the trigonometric value of each parallel.

Notes to Appendix F

The following remarks were contained in a letter written by Professor Hugh Harleston to the author dated May 22, 1988, in reference to the information conveyed by Peter Tompkins in this Appendix.

1.—"I had seven meetings with R. Bucky Fuller between 1976 and 1982. In 1976, during the first meeting, I explained to Fuller that the Teotihuacan unit of measure appeared to be 1.059463 m. Fuller instantly replied that this was the 12th root of the number "2," which it is. I then showed Fuller that in 1974, 1½ years *before* seeing his Synergetics I (in 1976), I had derived a relationship at Teotihuacan as the square root of 162 (base of the "Moon" pyramid) divided by 12. This is the relationship of the apothem of a regular tetrahedron of height 12, to its own height. The side of the tetrahedron is $\sqrt{216}$ and its triangle's height (apothem) is $\sqrt{162}$. The answer is 1.060660172, a number *not to be confused with:* $\sqrt{2} = 1.059463094$. *Both numbers were known to me and to Fuller.*

". . .I firmly believe that the Mayans knew the difference also; that they knew the values of the universal tetrahedron of height "12"; that they knew the square roots of 6x6x6 = 216, base of the "Sun" pyramid; and the square root of 3x6x9 = 162, base of the "Moon" pyramid; all names at Teotihuacan are FALSE, in Aztec, and should be renamed in MAYAN.

"The dimensional information of Teotihuacan also gives numbers: 6, 8, 12, 72, 96—the parameters of the tetrahedron inside a sphere of "6" radius. The entire Mayan system points toward facile handling of integral number geometry and chronology, because the long-term counts also follow these same numbers, which the Mayans used along with our modern system of 10, 100, 1000, 100000 and 1,000,000. To wit: tun = 360; katun = 7,200; nictekatun = 144,000; oxlahkatun = 1,872,000. I have isolated dimensions of 6, 60, 600, 6000; 72, 720, 7200; 8, 80, 800 and so on."

2.—". . . The angle was *not* almost the latitude angle; it was practically identical with the inclination of the faces of the regular tetrahedron: 19.4712°, and suggests it was deliberate by the Mayan designers of Teotihuacan. In 1984 I published that the "Teotihuacanos" were Mayans. In 1986, the Mayans were excavated in two tombs in the Citadel, to the north and south of the pyramid (falsely named "Quetzalcoatl" in Aztec/Nahuatl language, that was not used in Teotihuacan, since the Aztecs arrived when all had crumbled—no earlier than the 11th century).

APPENDIX G

Steve Cozzi

Formula for Calculating Mileage Distance on Planetary Lines

1. The first step is to ascertain exactly what planetary line(s) are the closest in connecting one place to another. If two or more planets are within a ten-degree orb in azimuth, then both should be used, although one of them is likely to be closer to the mark. There are two ways of doing this. The first is to look closely at your Local Space graphic printout (M-95) of the USA and/or world. Observe how the lines connect your present location with the places that you plan for travel or relocation. This program also allows you to start from any location and determine the planetary lines to any other location. First find latitude and longitude of the destination, and the program will give you the correct azimuth. Using this azimuth and comparing it with the azimuth of the planet(s) of your present location, you can quickly see which planet (if any) comes closest in azimuth degrees (use both directions).

2. The above program is helpful if you know your route and destination. What if you are speculating on traveling in a certain direction or to a large geographical region? For example, if you traveled on your Pluto line, how many miles would you travel? and what about your Neptune line or a close Mercury/Uranus conjunction? It is true that most people travel on different lines around their community every day, but when long-distance travel is planned, then the planetary lines pointing in different directions take on a different meaning. To take a trip northeast along your Saturn line from your home to the gas station is one thing, but when a longer trip is planned, the journey's dis-

tance would be longer. Therefore when using the formula or the basic mileage we can get a good idea of "important places" on the planetary lines.

3. Next we must look at the Local Space chart to find all conjunctions, trines, sextiles or inconjuncts (no other aspects have proved to be valid).* If the principle planet has no aspects to it use the fixed mileage figure (see Table A, page 296).

4. In most cases aspects *between* Uranus, Neptune or Pluto should NOT be used; they should only be used with the other planets. If you know the travel will be over 4,000 miles, then they can be used. Sometimes using Transpluto has helped make a correct estimate.

5. Don't count a conjunction twice when it involves Uranus, Neptune or Pluto, except in the case when it is the planetary line(s) that you're following. If there is more than one, then use the one with the closest orb. Over 6,000 miles use all conjuncts.

Example 1. A person is traveling from Denver to Nashville on his Sun/Pluto lines. The actual distance is 1,018 miles, but what if the person did not have a set destination but only knew that the Sun/Pluto lines went in a southeasterly direction from Denver?

Aspects to the Sun and Neptune for Example 1

Sun conjunct Mercury, 4 degrees, applying
Sun sextile Jupiter, 5.5 degrees, applying
Sun conjunct Pluto, 6.8 degrees, separating (can't use, see #5).
Sun conjunct Venus, 6 degrees applying
Sun trine Mars, 3.2 degrees, applying
Sun conjunct Neptune, 3 degrees, applying (can't use, see #5).
Sun sextile Uranus, 4.5 degrees, applying

Now refer to Table A for more instructions.

---

*Please keep in mind that the validity of this technique has not been completely proven. Perhaps a computer program will show that estimated mileage distances are consistent.

The fixed mileage for each planet was derived from the distance in astronomical units from the Earth to the other planets, using Bode's law. The distances were then converted into miles using the A.U. distances as various percents. Half the circumference of the Earth was used as a basic unit of measurement. Most distances were measured in highway miles.

Sun conjunct Neptune:	Pluto	5,200
3.0° orb	Sun	+ 110
		5,310

Sun conjunct Mercury:	Sun	110
4.0° orb	Mercury	+ 80
		190

Sun conjunct Venus:	Sun	110
4.0° orb	Venus	+ 40
		150

$$150 \div 1.3 = 115$$

Sun trine Mars:	Sun	110
3.2° orb	Mars	+ 80
		190

$$190 \div 1.3 = 146$$

Sun sextile Jupiter:	Sun	110
5.5° orb	Jupiter	+ 560
		670

$$670 \div 9.0 = 74$$

Sun sextile Uranus:	Sun	110
4.5° orb	Uranus	+ 2,440
		2,510

$$2510 \div 8.5 = 295$$

$$
\begin{aligned}
&5,310 \\
&190 \\
&150 \\
&190 \\
&74 \\
+\ &295 \\
\hline
&6,130
\end{aligned}
$$

$$6,130 \div 6 = 1,021$$

Actual highway distance—1,018 (# of aspects = 6)

Calculated distance—1,021

Table A

Listed below is a table of fixed mileage for each planet. These figures are to be used in the division formulas listed below. For short trips *under* 200 miles use Moon, Venus, Mercury, Mars and Sun *without* the formula.

Moon—1 mile
Venus—40 miles
Mercury—80 miles
Mars—80 miles
Sun—110 miles
Jupiter—560 miles
Saturn—840 miles
Uranus—2,400 miles
Neptune—3,880 miles
Pluto—5,200 miles
Transpluto—10,440
Nodes—?
Planet X—?
Asteroids—?

Oppositions, squares, semi-squares, and sesquiquadrates block travel, so they are not used in the calculations. No difference is made in applying or separating aspects.

Conjunction ONLY: 1 to 6 degrees of orb/no division needed.
    6 to 7° orb, then divide mileage by 1.33
    7 to 8° orb, then divide mileage by 1.59
    8 to 9° orb, then divide mileage by 2.0
    9 to 10° orb, then divide mileage by 4.0

Sextile ONLY: 3 degrees of orb or less, then divide mileage by 4.0
    3 to 4° orb, then divide mileage by 5.0
    4 to 5° orb, then divide mileage by 7.0
    5 to 6° orb, then divide mileage by 9.8

Trine ONLY: 3 degrees of orb or less, no division needed.
    3 to 4° orb, then divide mileage by 1.33
    4 to 5° orb, then divide mileage by 2.0
    5 to 6° orb, then divide mileage by 4.0
    6 to 7° orb, then divide mileage by 9.8

II. The Astrology of Local Space

The following article was first published in 1977 in the 6th number of the COSMECOLOGY BULLETIN as published by Charles A. Jayne. Although astrologers had worked with the Horizon System before, Erlewine was the first to define the concept of Local Space as presented here. In particular, the combining of celestial positions (stars, planets, etc.) with directions on the globe (cities, places, etc.) and the concept of relocating towards a planet first appeared here. This was before the advent of the home computer, and Erlewine had worked out the tedious mathematics of Local Space first on a scientific calculator and later on one of the programmables. Today programs that calculate Local Space charts are available on many of the more popular computers.

There seem to be several distinct levels or dimensions to our life, and depending upon the clarity of the day, our awareness may be centered in a dimension ranging from the very mundane on up through an occasional sharing in some sort of more transpersonal or Cosmic form of Consciousness. It is becoming clear to many astrologers in these times that this multi-dimensionality of our life perhaps may best be represented and examined through a series of astrological charts; and that an attempt to extract all levels of our life—the many quite different dimensions—from the geocentric ecliptic chart alone is bound to be a frustrating experience. In a word it is unnecessary.

Astrologers make constant use of three very different systems of coordinates (whether they are aware of it or not) each time they erect a natal chart: namely (1) the Zodiac or ecliptic, (2) the Equatorial system (right ascension and declination) and (3) the Horizon system of coordinates. The actual distinction between these different systems of coordinates are lost to most of us, and they are jumbled together to form some kind of Zodiac pie. It has become my realization that these basic physical planes of reference—the horizon, equator, ecliptic, and

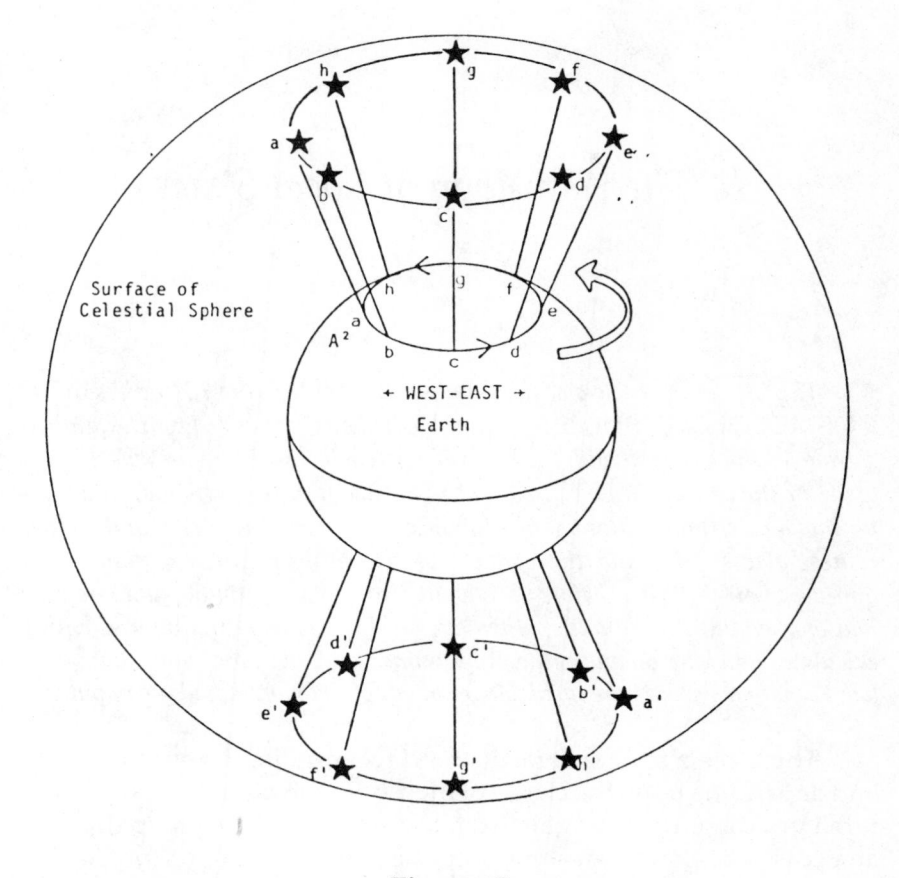

Figure C

Arbor and directly overhead a city at point *c*, (7) Points Z, C, E & S would all be conjunct the Midheaven for this chart.

At this point, it is hoped the reader has some feel for how the geographic sphere fits or matches the equatorial sphere. Perhaps it is clear to you why the equatorial coordinates right ascension (RA) and declination are so important in Mundane (politics, etc.) Astrology. For one, any planetary position can be matched to a spot on the Earth by both longitude and latitude and this is what is done when we trace Eclipse Paths on the globe. There is not space to go into great detail with this subject, but if the reader understands the simple relationship between the geographic and mundane (equatorial) spheres, many interesting ideas may occur.

THE LLEWELLYN ANNUALS

Llewellyn's MOON SIGN BOOK: approximately 400 pages of valuable information on gardening, fishing, weather, stock market forecasts, personal horoscopes, good planting dates, and general instructions for finding the best date to do just about anything! Articles by prominent forecasters and writers in the fields of gardening, astrology, politics, economics and cycles. This special almanac, different from any other, has been published annually since 1906. It's fun, informative and has been a great help to millions in their daily planning.

State year $3.95

Llewellyn's SUN SIGN BOOK: Your personal horoscope for the entire year! All 12 signs are included in one handy book. Also included are political and economic forecasts, special feature articles, and lucky dates for each sign. Monthly horoscopes by a prominent radio and TV astrologer for your personal Sun Sign. Articles on a variety of subjects written by well-known astrologers from around the country. Much more than just a horoscope guide! Entertaining and fun the year round.

State year $3.95

Llewellyn's DAILY PLANETARY GUIDE and ASTROLOGER'S DATEBOOK: Includes all of the major daily aspects plus their exact times in Eastern and Pacific time zones, lunar phases, signs and voids plus their times, planetary motion, a monthly ephemeris, sunrise and sunset tables, special articles on the planets, signs, aspects, a business guide, planetary hours, rulerships, and much more. Large 5¼ × 8 format for more writing space, spiral bound to lay flat, address and phone listings, time zone conversion chart and blank horoscope chart.

State year $6.95

Llewellyn's ASTROLOGICAL CALENDAR: Large wall calendar of 52 pages. Beautiful full color cover and color inside. Includes special feature articles by famous astrologers, introductory information on astrology, Lunar Gardening Guide, celestial phenomena for the year, a blank horoscope chart for your own chart data, and monthly date pages which include aspects, lunar information, planetary motion, ephemeris, personal forecasts, lucky dates, planting and fishing dates, and more. 10 × 13 size. Set in Central time, with conversion table for other time zones worldwide.

State year $6.95

THE GODDESS BOOK OF DAYS
by Diane Stein
Diane Stein has created this wonderful guide to the Goddesses and festivals for every day of the year! This beautifully illustrated perpetual datebook will give you a listing for every day of the special Goddesses associated with that date along with plenty of room for writing in your appointments. It is a hardbound book for longevity, and has over 100 illustrations of Goddesses from around the world and from every culture. This is sure to have a special place on your desk. None other like it!
0-87542-758-8, 300 pgs., hardbound, 5¼ × 8, illus.   **$12.95**

SPIRITUAL, METAPHYSICAL & NEW TRENDS IN MODERN ASTROLOGY
Edited by Joan McEvers
This is the first book in a new series offered by Llewellyn called the *New World Astrology Series*. Edited by well-known astrologer, lecturer and writer Joan McEvers, this book pulls together the latest thoughts by the best astrologers in the field of Spiritual Astrology.

- Gray Keen: Perspective: The Ethereal Conclusion.
- Marion D. March: Some Insights Into Esoteric Astrology.
- Kimberly McSherry: The Feminine Element of Astrology: Reframing the Darkness.
- Kathleen Burt: The Spiritual Rulers and Their Role in the Transformation.
- Shirley Lyons Meier: The Secrets Behind Carl Payne Tobey's Secondary Chart.
- Jeff Jawer: Astrodrama.
- Donna Van Toen: Alice Bailey Revisited.
- Philip Sedgwick: Galactic Studies.
- Myrna Lofthus: The Spiritual Programming Within a Natal Chart.
- Angel Thompson: Transformational Astrology.

0-87542-380-9, 288 pages, 5¼ x 8, softcover   **$9.95**

ARCHETYPES OF THE ZODIAC
by Kathleen Burt
The horoscope is probably the most unique tool for personal growth you can ever have. This book is intended to help you understand how the energies within your horoscope manifest. Once you are aware of how your chart operates on an instinctual level, you can then work consciously with it to remove any obstacles to your growth.

The technique offered in this book is based upon the incorporation of the esoteric rulers of the signs and the integration of their polar opposites. This technique has been very successful in helping the client or reader modify existing negative energies in a horoscope so as to improve the quality of his or her life and the understanding of his or her psyche.

This book has a depth often surprising to the readers of popular astrology books. It has a clarity of expression seldom found in books of the esoteric tradition. It is very easy to understand, even if you know nothing of Jungian philosophy or of mythology. It is intriguing, exciting and very helpful for all levels of astrologers.

0-87542-08805, 592 pages, 6 x 9, 24 illus., softcover   **$14.95**

URANUS: Freedom From the Known
by Jeff Green
This book deals primarily with the archetypal correlations of the planet Uranus to human psychology and behavior to anatomy/physiology and the chakra system, and to metaphysical and cosmic laws. Uranus' relationship to Saturn, from an individual and collective point of view, is also discussed.

In reading *Uranus* you will discover how to naturally liberate yourself from all of your conditioning patterns, patterns that were determined by the "internal" and "external" environment. Every person has a natural way to actualize this liberation. This natural way is examined by use of the natal chart and from a developmental point of view.

The 48-year sociopolitical cycle of Uranus and Saturn is discussed extensively, as is the relationship between Uranus, Saturn and Neptune. With this historical perspective, you can see what lies ahead in 1988, a very important year.

0-87542-297-7, 192 pages, 5¼ x 8, softcover   **$7.95**

STAY IN TOUCH

On the following pages you will find listed, with their current prices, some of the books and tapes now available on related subjects. Your book dealer stocks most of these, and will stock new titles in the Llewellyn series as they become available. We urge your patronage.

However, to obtain our full catalog, to keep informed of new titles as they are released and to benefit from informative articles and helpful news, you are invited to write for our bi-monthly news magazine/catalog. A sample copy is free, and it will continue coming to you at no cost as long as you are an active mail customer. Or you may keep it coming for a full year with a donation of just $2.00 in U.S.A. ($7.00 for Canada & Mexico, $20.00 overseas, first class mail). Many bookstores also have *The Llewellyn New Times* available to their customers. Ask for it.

Stay in touch! In *The Llewellyn New Times'* pages you will find news and reviews of new books, tapes and services, announcements of meetings and seminars, articles helpful to our readers, news of authors, advertising of products and services, special money-making opportunities, and much more.

The Llewellyn New Times
P.O. Box 64383-Dept. 098, St. Paul, MN 55164-0383, U.S.A.

• • •

TO ORDER BOOKS AND TAPES

If your book dealer does not have the books and tapes described on the following pages readily available, you may order them direct from the publisher by sending full price in U.S. funds, plus $1.00 for handling and 50¢ each book or item for postage within the United States; outside USA surface mail add $1.50 per item postage and $1.00 per order for handling. Outside USA air mail add $7.00 per item postage and $1.00 per order for handling. MN residents add 6% sales tax.

FOR GROUP STUDY AND PURCHASE

Because there is a great deal of interest in group discussion and study of the subject matter of this book, we feel that we should encourage the adoption and use of this particular book by such groups by offering a special "quantity" price to group leaders or "agents."

Our Special Quantity Price for a minimum order of five copies of *Planets in Locality* is $38.85 Cash-With-Order. This price includes postage and handling within the United States. Minnesota residents must add 6% sales tax. For additional quantities, please order in multiples of five. For Canadian and foreign orders, add postage and handling charges as above. Credit Card (VISA, MasterCard, American Express, Diners' Club) Orders are accepted. Charge Card Orders only may be phoned free ($15.00 minimum order) within the U.S.A. by dialing 1-800-THE MOON (in Canada call: 1-800-FOR-SELF). Customer Service calls dial 1-612-291-1970. Mail Orders to:

LLEWELLYN PUBLICATIONS
P.O. Box 64383-Dept. 098 / St. Paul, MN 55164-0383, U.S.A.

Inconjunct/Quincunx ONLY:
>   1 degree or less, no division needed.
>   1 to 2° of orb, then divide mileage by 2.0
>   2 to 3° orb, then divide mileage by 4.0

STAY IN TOUCH

On the following pages you will find listed, with their current prices, some of the books and tapes now available on related subjects. Your book dealer stocks most of these, and will stock new titles in the Llewellyn series as they become available. We urge your patronage.

However, to obtain our full catalog, to keep informed of new titles as they are released and to benefit from informative articles and helpful news, you are invited to write for our bi-monthly news magazine/catalog. A sample copy is free, and it will continue coming to you at no cost as long as you are an active mail customer. Or you may keep it coming for a full year with a donation of just $2.00 in U.S.A. ($7.00 for Canada & Mexico, $20.00 overseas, first class mail). Many bookstores also have *The Llewellyn New Times* available to their customers. Ask for it.

Stay in touch! In *The Llewellyn New Times'* pages you will find news and reviews of new books, tapes and services, announcements of meetings and seminars, articles helpful to our readers, news of authors, advertising of products and services, special money-making opportunities, and much more.

The Llewellyn New Times
P.O. Box 64383-Dept. 098, St. Paul, MN 55164-0383, U.S.A.

•   •   •

TO ORDER BOOKS AND TAPES

If your book dealer does not have the books and tapes described on the following pages readily available, you may order them direct from the publisher by sending full price in U.S. funds, plus $1.00 for handling and 50¢ each book or item for postage within the United States; outside USA surface mail add $1.50 per item postage and $1.00 per order for handling. Outside USA air mail add $7.00 per item postage and $1.00 per order for handling. MN residents add 6% sales tax.

FOR GROUP STUDY AND PURCHASE

Because there is a great deal of interest in group discussion and study of the subject matter of this book, we feel that we should encourage the adoption and use of this particular book by such groups by offering a special "quantity" price to group leaders or "agents."

Our Special Quantity Price for a minimum order of five copies of *Planets in Locality* is $38.85 Cash-With-Order. This price includes postage and handling within the United States. Minnesota residents must add 6% sales tax. For additional quantities, please order in multiples of five. For Canadian and foreign orders, add postage and handling charges as above. Credit Card (VISA, MasterCard, American Express, Diners' Club) Orders are accepted. Charge Card Orders only may be phoned free ($15.00 minimum order) within the U.S.A. by dialing 1-800-THE MOON (in Canada call: 1-800-FOR-SELF). Customer Service calls dial 1-612-291-1970. Mail Orders to:

LLEWELLYN PUBLICATIONS
P.O. Box 64383-Dept. 098 / St. Paul, MN 55164-0383, U.S.A.

Inconjunct/Quincunx ONLY:
> 1 degree or less, no division needed.
> 1 to 2° of orb, then divide mileage by 2.0
> 2 to 3° orb, then divide mileage by 4.0

Matrix AstroMap programs from Llewellyn

The technique of relocation astrology is on the leading edge of new astrological research. This technique offers a way to examine which parts of the world, which cities, and which directions are in harmony with your chart.

Perhaps there is an area of the country that feels very inviting. What can you expect if your job or circumstances send you there? What can you expect in terms of prosperity, relationships or luck? Is there someplace special that will bring out the best in you?

If you are thinking of moving to a specific city, or if you have a choice of cities to move to (anywhere in the world), this program can help you make that all-important decision. It can help you determine the good and negative aspects of each choice. And these factors relate directly to *your personal chart*. You can also use this program in your astrological work to help others make the same decisions.

AstroMap is the first relocation package ever to offer you complete interpretations of its findings. Just enter your birth data and the information on the place(s) you want to check out and get a full report on how you relate to that locale.

For the IBM-PC and its clones:

Complete *AstroMap* program with all the on-screen interpretations as well as printed reports. For IBM, clones and compatibles with 256K and 2 disk drives (or a hard disk).

3½ inch disk: 0-925182-18-4, $99.95
5¼ inch disk: 0-925182-19-2, $99.95

The above program is passworded specifically for your personal use and will be sent to you directly from Matrix Software. Please order from Llewellyn Publications.

Screen-only version has all of the screen capabilities of the package above, but no printed reports. Same system requirements as above program.

3½ inch disk: 0-925182-10-9, $49.95
5¼ inch disk: 0-925182-11-7, $49.95

Coming Soon
Geo-Maps

Matrix Software is currently completing development of a **Local Space Map** program to supplement the text of Steve Cozzi's book, *Planets in Locality.*

If you would like to be notified as soon as this program becomes available, please complete the form below, or write similar information on a separate piece of paper, and mail it to:

Llewellyn Publications
P.O. Box 64383-098
St. Paul, MN 55164-0383, USA

Kindly send information on the *Geo-Map* program
as soon as it is available to:

Name_____

Address_____

City, State, Zip_____